1900 LIVERPOOL LIVES - THE THREADS THAT BIND

Hugh Gault

Gretton Books
Cambridge

First published in 2019 by Gretton Books

© Hugh Gault 2019

The moral right of Hugh Gault to be identified as the author of this work has been asserted in accordance with the Copyright, Design and Patents Act 1988

All rights reserved. Apart from any use permitted under UK copyright law no part of this publication may be reproduced, stored in a retrieval system, or transmitted, in any form or by any means without the prior written permission of the publisher, nor be otherwise circulated in any form of binding or cover other than that in which it is published and without a similar condition being imposed on the subsequent purchaser.

A CIP catalogue record for this title is available from the British Library.

ISBN   978-1-9998510-2-6 (paperback)

Set in 9/11 pt Arial

The publisher has no responsibility for the continued existence and/or accuracy of third party websites referred to in this book.

Printed and bound by 4edge in the UK

1900 LIVERPOOL LIVES - THE THREADS THAT BIND

Contents	**Page**
Preface	vii
1. Introduction	1
2. Blackstock Street from 1840	11
3. Crosby from 1850	37
4. Blackstock Street in 1900: Pubs, courts and factories	49
5. The people who lived in Blackstock Street in 1900	79
6. Courtenay Road in 1900 and the people who lived there	105
7. Conclusion: Similarities and differences	129
Notes	136
Bibliography	158
Index	171

Illustrations

Page	Illustration
v	Blackstock Street and its Vauxhall surroundings
vi	Courtenay Road and its Crosby/Waterloo surroundings
7	No. 2 court, Silvester Street, north of Blackstock Street
46	View from Lord Street of junction with North and South John Streets 1908
52	Scotland Road 1908
62	Blackstock Street Gardens
62	Eagle Vaults, Blackstock Street
71	Palatine Engineering water meter advert 1893
72	Advert for Palatine Engineering hot & cold water tap 1893
97	Train crash at Waterloo station 1903
108	Diagram of Courtenay Road and residents in 1901
111	Sandheys Avenue
112	The Hollies, Agnes Road
122	Hydro hotel, West Kirby
128	Waterloo-with-Seaforth Urban District Council 1899

Copyright permissions

Every attempt has been made to secure the permission of copyright-holders to include extracts. Any omissions should be notified to the publisher as soon as possible who will be pleased to rectify them.

BLACKSTOCK STREET, VAUXHALL

Blackstock Street and its Vauxhall surroundings in Liverpool
from Ordnance Survey map Lancashire CVI.10 (25") 1908, Reproduced with the permission of the National Library of Scotland.

COURTENAY ROAD, CROSBY

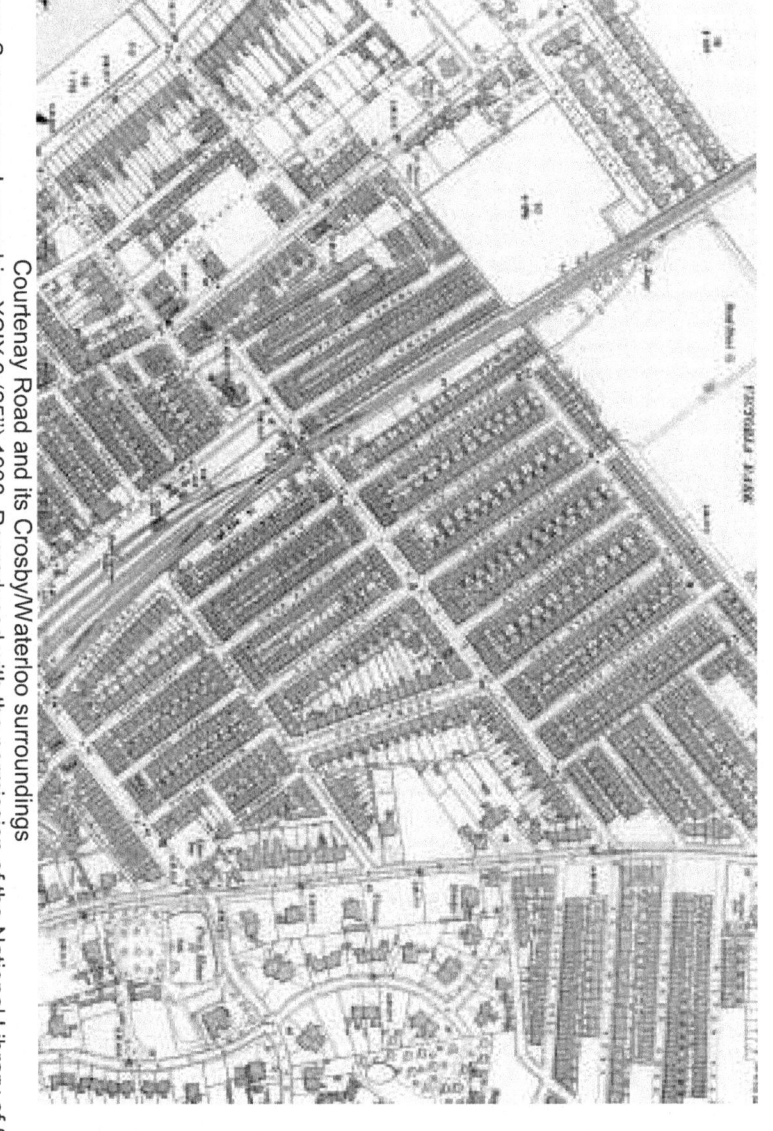

Courtenay Road and its Crosby/Waterloo surroundings from Ordnance Survey map Lancashire XCIX.9 (25") 1908. Reproduced with the permission of the National Library of Scotland.

PREFACE

This book follows the approach of Marilyn Silverman and her colleagues from the University of Toronto in using "a *local-level focus* to build general interpretations of both the past and the present", but has no pretensions to academic anthropology.[1] It differs in not imposing a particular theoretical framework, leaving the reader to supply the analysis and conclusions that best fit their perspective. This is deliberately, therefore, a narrative and descriptive approach from which each reader can take as little or as much as they choose. Some people may perhaps be disappointed, but others will certainly be relieved, that Gramsci is only mentioned once in this book - and you have just read it. Such theoretical frameworks have their place, but the absence of one hopefully makes this a more accessible book as a result.

To that extent it follows the approach of an earlier era, of which a prime example might be the Liverpool docklands history project of the 1980s. One of the publications from that initiative describes the life and work of those living in Athol Street,[2] which lies little more than half a mile north of Blackstock Street, with Athol Street on both sides of Vauxhall Road, whereas the western end of Blackstock Street abuts it. There is a fifteen-minute walk between them. Ayers permits the information she has compiled, and her informants, to speak for themselves. That was my objective too.

Some buildings from 1900 still stand in Blackstock Street 120 years later, though not many and only on the north side of the street. Those that do are mainly used for storage, some having been adopted as they were and some cannibalised to fit today's requirements. But much of the street is now a wasteland and the only building fulfilling the same function as it did then is the Eagle Vaults pub at the western end. Nobody lives elsewhere in the street today as hundreds did in 1900. After dark on a winter's night it is a forbidding place and perhaps that may not have changed hugely since 1900. The difference today is that all the noise and smoke and smell, the human and industrial vibrancy that must have existed then, has gone - for not only would the houses and factories have lit up the street in 1900, the people would have brought vitality as well as, in a few cases, threat. Today the risk is absence, isolation and decay, rather than presence.

Courtenay Road in Crosby on the other hand is virtually identical today to 1900. Four of the houses on the southern side of the street have been replaced but the other twenty-three are exactly as they were then. Even the twenty semi-detached houses are very large by today's standards, for they were built with six bedrooms each. There are also three detached houses, completed last and with eight bedrooms. The contrast with Blackstock Street remains marked.

To explain the title of the book a little more: One meaning of 'bind' is being tied down or trapped, as much by your circumstances as by anything else, even bound and confined as if a prisoner, but it also has positive connotations, the belonging that family, work and community bring; and there are binds or links between different communities too, as there were between Blackstock Street and Courtenay Road. Lives in Liverpool in 1900 were far from insular, let alone monochrome - as the index to this book demonstrates. Cotton is particularly associated with Lancashire and was usually shipped through Liverpool - in as a raw material and out after the mills had processed it - for while the Liverpool cotton exchange was founded at the start of the nineteenth century, the city's cotton connections stretch back to the seventeenth. In addition, just as Gulliver snapped the cords with which he was tied to the ground when wrecked on the shore of Lilliput so did those for whom Liverpool was only a staging-post in their journey. The Lilliputians had used what were ropes to them but to Gulliver were more like cotton threads. For Tim Pat Coogan, who also invoked the Lilliput analogy in his 2016 book on Michael Collins, "Change is effected, and history made, by a combination of will and circumstances".[3] That captures the essence of the stories told in this book and so it is called 'The threads that bind' for a number of reasons.

My thanks for their help to Graeme Milne, Senior Lecturer in Modern History, John Belchem, Emeritus Professor, and Janet Jones, Harold Cohen library, University of Liverpool; Kay Jones, Curator of Urban Community History and colleagues at the Museum of Liverpool; Pauline Scotland and Helena Smart, Team Leaders, Archives, Liverpool City Council and staff at Liverpool Records Office; Gillian Morgan, Information Service Librarian, Alice Ronson and their colleagues at Crosby Library; Fred Forrest and Graham

Preface

Jones, Liverpool History Society; Ruth Loughrey and colleagues at Unilever Collections at Unilever Arts, Archives and Records Management, Port Sunlight; Neil Sayer, Archdiocesan Archivist, Liverpool Metropolitan Cathedral; Lindsey Earner-Byrne, Department of History, University College Dublin; Barrie Lees; Trevor Hildrey, archivist, Merchant Taylors' School, Crosby; Jacquie Adams, Secretary to the Pilling Trust Fund; Joel Hansen, Scottie Press; Anne Taylor, Head of Map Department, as well as Ian Pittock and other staff at Cambridge University Library Map Room.

I am hugely grateful to Graeme Milne and Neil Sayer for assisting further by commenting on a draft. Three others also took on this task: Jan Howarth, David Poole and Michael O'Neill, historian of St Anthony's parish, Scotland Road. All but David have lived and worked in Liverpool for many years and I found their knowledge and experience invaluable, not only and not least because I have moved there only recently. I hope they can all see the impact that their comments have had.

Liverpool Records Office is housed in the refurbished Central Library in William Brown Street next to the Walker Art Gallery and opposite St George's Hall. The Central Library re-opened in 2013, a wonderful feature of the city-scape of central Liverpool and even more exceptional inside, demonstrating not only that libraries remain at the hub of communities but that they can uplift the spirit architecturally as well as feed the mind intellectually. It has been a pleasure to work there, one that I plan to repeat in the future.

Hugh Gault
Liverpool

January 2019

1900 Liverpool Lives - The Threads That Bind

1. INTRODUCTION

In the middle of the eighteenth century Daniel Defoe thought Liverpool "one of the wonders of Britain" and so it is today, famed for its culture, architecture and history, as well as the more obvious attractions of music, football and humour. In the late twentieth century, as the city struggled through docks closures, soaring unemployment and industrial relations mayhem, seeing the funny side was a necessity for sanity and survival, even one of the few positives. It is now very much on the up, with people moving in rather than out, and a magnet for tourists and students. It is one of only twenty-six UNESCO world heritage sites in the UK, for example, but it is unlikely that it is this that appeals to prospective students or new employers. The city has had much to recommend it for hundreds of years though this has been less obvious and better hidden at some times than others.

This book is about Liverpool at the start of the twentieth century, not quite within living memory but not far off it. It compares and contrasts, in terms of their backgrounds, circumstances and the consequences, the people who lived in the two areas shown on the front cover: Blackstock Street, Vauxhall and Courtenay Road, Crosby. The latter area was first administered by the Waterloo-with-Seaforth Local Health Board and Courtenay Road might be said to be in Waterloo, especially as it is also on that side of the railway tracks. However, Waterloo and Crosby became one borough in 1937, the settlements blur into each other, removing any obvious dividing lines between them, and Courtenay Road is as close to the Blundellsands and Crosby railway station as it is to that of Waterloo. Even in the late nineteenth century Waterloo was being referred to as in the township of Great Crosby and as early as 1893 their amalgamation was under consideration as one of the new Urban District Councils (UDCs) to be created the following year.[4]

Many of those in Blackstock Street may have worked there as well. The Vauxhall area of the city was subject to survey and scrutiny from the mid-nineteenth century on, for example by Abraham Hume, a minister there for nearly forty years from 1847, who was so appalled by the living conditions of his parishioners that he set out to find out more to better understand their material as well as spiritual needs. When the area was mapped in greater detail by the Ordnance Survey in 1890, there were two pubs at the western end where Blackstock Street joins Vauxhall Road, the Eagle Vaults on one corner and the Green Flag Vaults opposite. The former is still there in 2019 while the latter has been replaced by a car park. Even Liverpool is not immune to the march of time and much of the area is now a wasteland awaiting redevelopment. Many may have thought it ripe for it in 1900 - not least those who lived there.

Liverpool was the second largest port in Britain in 1900, accounting for a third of the country's exports and a quarter of its imports,[5] the 'gateway of Empire' as Tony Lane called his book,[6] and cementing its place at the heart of Britain's trading and commercial endeavour. The population had increased almost tenfold during the nineteenth century to reach 716,000 by 1901, but it remained split between great wealth and grinding poverty. The journalism of Shimmin and Farrie,[7] for example, had drawn attention to this gulf but it is often one of the first things you read in any book about Liverpool. In 'The Deadly Shame of Liverpool', Richard Acland Armstrong wrote in 1890:

> ... I was appalled by ...[the] contiguity of immense wealth and abysmal poverty ... The hordes of the ragged and the wretched surged up from their native quarters and covered the noblest streets like a flood. Men and women in the cruellest grip of poverty, little children with shoeless feet, bodies pinched and faces in which the pure light of childhood had been quenched, swarmed on the very pavements that fronted the most brilliant shops; and the superb carriages of the rich, with their freights of refined and elegant ladies, threaded their way among sections of the population so miserable and squalid that my heart ached at the sight of them. I had seen wealth. I had seen poverty. But never before had I seen the two so jammed together. Never before had I seen streets, loaded with all that wealth can buy, lined with the haunts of hopeless penury.[8]

While there had been charitable initiatives and corporation developments in the nineteenth century, the chasm had not been closed and in the 1901 Census, for example, domestic service was the single most frequent occupation for either sex, reinforcing this Liverpool class divide. Waller refers to the city's "ulcerated poverty" alongside its "philanthropy and municipal enterprise" and sets out to explain why, after 1841, Liverpool was a Conservative stronghold

Introduction

"given the grim circumstances in which most of the population lived and worked".[9] As John Belchem and Bryan Biggs point out in their introduction to 'City of Radicals', it would be 1955 before a Labour Council was first elected.[10]

From 1832 until 1868 Liverpool returned two MPs and three thereafter, generally two Conservative and one Liberal, until the third Reform Act of 1884.

The two areas chosen are illustrative of the divided Liverpool, though not at the absolute extremes: the recent suburb of Crosby, on the coast to the north, much of which had developed since 1850 and offered better quality housing for those able to escape the city,[11] and Vauxhall ward, the square mile north of the city centre, a combination of "notorious slum housing"[12] and the industry which provided employment for those who were neither dockers nor sailors and kept the city going. As Waller puts it,

> A port predicates traffic in goods, also in peoples. ... Migration shaped [Liverpool's] development, inwards as a conduit of aliens [often Irish], outwards as a sluice for wealth when those with means fled to the suburbs.[13]

The cellars and courts throughout Vauxhall were illustrative of this "conduit", Crosby of the "sluice". Or, to put it another way, Crosby was symptomatic of Liverpool's trading and commercial reputation, Vauxhall of its industrial sector.

The latter "utilised mostly low-paid and unskilled workers"[14] so, for example, Blackstock Street in the heart of Vauxhall was home to among others two carters, a fireman (i.e., a ship's stoker), a blacksmith, a porter and a few small businesses, but much of the street was dominated by rice and flour mills, a tannery and saw mills on one side and a saccharine works and cake company on the other. At one end was a Liverpool Board School and at the other the soap works of Tyson, Richmond and Jones, manufacturers of 'Pure Household Soaps'. Next door to them was another soapworks, part of the leading firm of Wm Gossage and Sons registered in Widnes. By 1900 Tyson, Richmond and Jones was run by James Burnett Briggs for Tyson had long since disappeared and in 1883 Richard Richmond and Joseph Jones had dissolved their partnership.[15] There were several soap and chemical works in Vauxhall in 1900, close to the goods stations of Waterloo and Great Howard Street that would bring in the wide range of minerals and materials which the manufacturing process required and whose proximity would assist the despatch of the finished goods - as would the carters if they needed to be taken to the docks. They would have depended on workers who lived locally but Robert F Jones, later connected with both Gossage's and another soap company Crosfield's, lived in Courtenay Road, Crosby. There were only twenty-seven houses in this residential road, and many of the occupants described themselves as merchants or brokers, the middle men on whom trade depends.[16] Three of the households were headed by those in the cotton industry, two brokers and one salesman, a direct connection to both Lancashire's mills and Liverpool's shipping history. Another was part of a large firm of naval outfitters for whom cotton would have been a key material, but there was also a wool merchant. Another three were shipping agents of one type or another, with a fourth a steam ship accounts clerk. Commerce and trade would depend on clerks to keep a tally, and though the term covered a multitude of grades, it is a fair bet that a clerk living in Courtenay Road would be at the top end, and almost certainly among the 30% above the income tax threshold.[17] There was a bank manager, an estate agent, a private secretary to a brewery, a cashier in an advertising agency and an accountant. There was both a timber broker and a timber merchant as well as a fish salesman, a dried fruit merchant, a hide broker and a jute goods manufacturer. Two houses were empty and another three were headed by women living on their own means, one of whom had been widowed when her ship-owner husband died in the 1890s. The remaining house was headed by a man aged twenty-eight whose father was a city councillor and coal merchant with several depots throughout the Liverpool area. The timber merchant was of a similar age but only one other household was headed by someone still in their thirties.

    Most of the houses would be rented and only the family of the jute goods manufacturer and one other lived in the same houses in both 1891 and 1911. Ten years or less seems to have been the median stay, for only four households who lived there in 1901 had done so in 1891 and similarly another four families were there in both 1901 and 1911. For many of whatever age, provided they continued to prosper, Courtenay Road would be followed by a move nearer the coast, either elsewhere in Crosby or further afield in Blundellsands. This demonstrated publicly that not only had they maintained their status but had enhanced it.

Blackstock Street had been called Canning Street in 1835.[18] Curiously, a Mr Blackstock was a barber and wig maker in the 1780s whose shop was just round the corner from where the cotton traders met,[19] while an Edward Blackstock was one of the original twenty-eight shareholders in the Herculaneum Pottery in 1806.[20] Perhaps when the city grandees came to rename the street in 1839 one or other of these connections was recalled. While some of the houses dated from earlier than 1835, the industry was not as well developed as it was by 1850 (for which another Ordnance Survey map of the street exists). Most of the residential properties remained the same at the turn of the century, though seven courts had been reduced to five[21] and were then numbered (Nos. 1, 3, 5, 11, 13) rather than being labelled with the misleading and over-optimistic names they had been assigned in 1850.[22] Providence Place and Economy Place had been demolished but it seems another had been added (No. 16).[23] In effect not only had the pretence that poverty was the same as economy been removed but hope had disappeared as well. Many of the industries were different with, most notably, the north side of the street dominated by a huge glass factory in 1850, including two massive kilns, which by 1890 had been replaced by a rice and flour mill and a tannery. A drug and mustard mill and a lime works had become an oil mill and a timber yard. Public health considerations may have played some part, particularly in the removal of the lime works, though a nearby road was still called Limekiln Road, so more than a memory remained.

Blackstock Street therefore had a few courts, in other words small back to backs with one window upstairs and one down but no through ventilation, and, if sub-divided, at most two rooms on each of the two floors, but the streets north and south, respectively Ford and Paul Streets, each had many more. There was a mortuary on Ford Street doing brisk business and the courts on both streets faced the rear of the factories whose main entrances were on Blackstock Street. As a report to the Liverpool Domestic Mission Society put it,

> ... I entered a court - the picture of dingy misery. It is a large square block of building: two rows of houses face each other, with two blank walls blocking up the free current of air in the other direction. The court is miserably flagged; here and there are pools of stagnant water and small heaps of refuse rotting around. I enter one of the houses, descending into the kitchen by a step ...[24]

The reports often blamed drink for the dire circumstances in which many court-dwellers lived, but whether this was cause or consequence must have varied from one family to the next. Even those who set out with a determination to live as cleanly as they could must have found their energy sapped as they were dragged down by their surroundings and perhaps by their neighbours. They would be faced continuously by reminders not only of their poverty but of society treating them as expendable, as the dregs. To escape and live a different future would have required extraordinary resilience - or luck. Living in a court was like being in a "barracks", the evocative and appropriate name that Pat O'Mara and many others used for them.[25] To make it bearable, particularly for those who spent most of their time there, might depend on the kindness of neighbours and the friendships that could be struck with them.[26] As Kanya-Forstner puts it, the "crowded streets of Liverpool were fertile ground for the growth of close female friendships".[27]

Blackstock Street is about quarter of a mile long and it is possible to get a sense of what it must have been like in the middle of the nineteenth century from a combination of the Ordnance Survey map, Gore's Directory of 1853 and newspapers of the time. It was unpaved and runs from Vauxhall Road in the west to Bevington Bush in the east, with all the courts and much of the industry concentrated on the north side. Entering at the Vauxhall Road end, the Eagle Vaults on the northern corner was opposite the yard of a coach-builder Joseph Wade who moved there in 1852, "respectfully solicit[ing] a continuance of the favours ... so liberally received during the last nine years" in the nearby Burlington Street, as he put it in an advert in the *Liverpool Mercury*.[28] There was an attempt five years later to sell off a parcel of land that included Wade's yard[29] but he continued to prosper there, still advertising coaches for sale in the late 1870s. The first court was Battersby Place made up of eight houses, most of which were sub-divided. The far end was closed off by the wall of the glass factory, as were the next four

Introduction

No. 2 court, Silvester Street, north of Blackstock Street © Scottie Press

courts too, and all the courts had only the narrowest of openings on to Blackstock Street. There was little ventilation and the same stale vapours from the factories would hang over the courts almost indefinitely, so while a gale might provide some respite it would chill the occupants crowded in to damp and unhealthy buildings. In 1867 the Council's Health Committee recommended £3 be paid to the owners of one Blackstock Street court if they made "the passage at the end of the court" about four feet wider.[30] That such a minor alteration was thought useful demonstrates just how grim they must have been. Next to Wade's on the south side was the office of a soapboiler alongside the soap works then called Tyson and Richmond (before Joseph Jones became the third partner) which in turn was next to Jordan's varnish and colour works. There were three other factories on the south side before Bevington Bush School on the corner with Bevington Bush Road. On the north side was Irving, Son and Jones, mainly a starch manufacturer then but increasingly a rice miller, and Nicholson's tannery with the yard itself let to Smyth Bros. tanners.[31] There were two more courts and a number of houses/shops before the drug and mustard mill and the lime works on the northern corner with Bevington Bush Road.

Three streets north was the ward and parliamentary boundary running down the middle of Arley Street and Summer Seat [sic] continuing, on the other side of Vauxhall Road, along Chisenhall Street.[32] Vauxhall was part of Exchange parliamentary constituency from the Redistribution of Seats Act 1885 to 1918 when part of the ward remained in the Exchange Division and the rest was assigned to the neighbouring Scotland constituency. Three streets south of Blackstock Street, still in Vauxhall ward but nearer the city centre, was Naylor Street. This had not changed at all from its 1835 footprint and by the turn of the century there were some larger employers, such as the Mersey Oakum Works, an oil and tallow manufacturer, bag and sack dealers, a fish curers and hide factors, but most of the properties were occupied by people working for themselves or with a few others. Fish and hides were connections with Courtenay Road, and there were two small scale soap manufacturers and a cotton dealer's office[33] as well. Most, however, would not have required middle men to intercede on their behalf for the two butchers, ship's carpenter, rigger, bootmaker, warehouseman, tarpaulin manufacturer, shopkeeper, engine driver and painter would have found their customers themselves, as would the five carters and two mariners who lived in the street.

There were then public houses on the corner of nearly every street where it joined Vauxhall Road. In 1874 a man was killed in nearby Tithebarn Street because he refused 6d to a group of toughs who demanded it for a quart of ale.[34] After knocking him to the ground, they kicked him across the street while a crowd looked on. When they needed to attract new landlords, pubs were advertised as being in good drinking districts. This was one of them.

It was less than six miles from this part of Vauxhall to Courtenay Road, but they might as well have been in different worlds. Someone in Naylor Street, for example, who was described in Gore's Directory as a manufacturer would be doing the making themselves, up to their armpits as much as the butcher; whereas a manufacturer in Courtenay Road was a factory owner, with others providing the labour.

Another telling contrast was that, while both were similar distances from the Mersey, in the case of Blackstock Street this was

Introduction

a relatively narrow part of the river dominated by the docks, with ships moored as they were loaded and unloaded, while for the residents of Crosby it was in effect the coast. In 1900 their view would have been of ships coming in on the tide or already underway as they carried cargoes across the globe. Prosperity enables those who enjoy it to buy all sorts of things beyond the means of the poorest, including mobility. But money also buys space, mental as much as physical, and the better health and prospects that go with it. The following pages illustrate this differential and the impact not only on quality of life but on life chances.

In order to understand how Blackstock Street, Vauxhall and Courtenay Road, Crosby came to take the form they did in 1900, it may be helpful to examine first the nineteenth century history that led them to this point.

1900 Liverpool Lives - The Threads That Bind

2. BLACKSTOCK STREET FROM 1840

In December 1821 Archibald Mansfield (1796-1839) succeeded his father as manager of the Herculaneum Pottery, opened in 1796 on the site of a former copper works on the edge of the Mersey in Toxteth Park. At first things went well, with a fifty-year lease negotiated with the Earl of Sefton in 1800 at an annual rent equivalent to less than £4000 today, reflecting the Earl's support for development in the area, shares were issued in 1806 when Archibald's father Ralph Mansfield was the manager and in 1807 the company leased a house in Duke Street where the factory's wares could be shown off nearer the city centre in, literally, a 'ware-house'.[35] Trade in the 1820s proved perilous and, whether because of this or disgust at his low starting salary of £100pa, Archibald Mansfield left in 1823 to start his own pottery in Canning Street, the previous name for Blackstock Street, building a factory there in 1824. This prospered initially but did not survive his death. Attempts to sell the premises failed and in 1841 it was auctioned off and used for other purposes.[36] In 1840 the Herculaneum Pottery itself was closed, and the contents sold, to make way for the dock of the same name.

Other companies in Blackstock Street struggled during the 1840s. In 1845, for example, Thomas Stockdale and Sons, a candle and imperial oil factory, with warehouses in Manchester and Birmingham as well, and its products widely available elsewhere, took out a series of adverts that may have reflected an increasing desperation to sell their goods,[37] for though there is no report of bankruptcy the Blackstock Street premises were soon closed. In 1848 and now empty, the premises were rifled during a burglary, including by the person who was supposed to be acting as their caretaker.[38] Thomas Eyre & Co, a paint factory suffered fires in both 1846 and 1849. On the first occasion the damage was kept to under £400 but on the second even insurance of £2000 would not cover it.[39] There were also injuries on this latter occasion and private fire brigades that rushed to the scene were prosecuted for deliberately colliding with each other as they raced to get there first.[40]

Liverpool had one licensed theatre in 1840, the Theatre Royal granted its patent by George III seventy years before, while among the unlicensed theatres were those well-enough regarded, such as the Liver, Queen's Theatre (or Circus) and Sans Pareil, to feature in the guide to Liverpool included in a railway companion of this era.[41] In addition, there were several minor theatres with a reputation for licentious and depraved performances. The nineteenth century journalist Hugh Shimmin had written in the *Liverpool Mercury* that these have "a tendency to promote the growth and foster the evils attendant on juvenile delinquency and public immorality". And no doubt some were close to the "licensed promenade of pros--titutes" that he found elsewhere in Liverpool and particularly railed against.[42] There was a minor theatre on the corner of Blackstock Street and Vauxhall Road until it was dismantled in 1843, the stage flooring, gallery supports, staircases and other fittings sold at auction that May.[43] There is no record of closure having been enforced by the authorities but, as the patent theatre monopoly was dissolved that year, this minor theatre may have recognised that it could no longer compete.

Not surprisingly, some of the residents featured in newspaper reports as well. In early 1845 an illicit still was uncovered in one of the Battersby Place courts by an excise officer with the appropriate name of Mr Sheriffs. The defendants were fined £30 each but, as this would have been way beyond their means, must have accepted the alternative of three months in gaol instead.[44] Another resident, John Hamilton, was tried in both 1845 and 1846 for serving alcohol illegally in one of the other Blackstock Street courts. The first time he tried to claim he was out of town and the party of ten men and two women were friends on their way from Ireland to America, but he was fined 20s nonetheless. On the second occasion he was let off with a caution, the difference being that, although two of the six men on his premises were drunk, they no longer had glasses of ale before them.[45]

There were few other newspaper reports of crimes committed in Blackstock Street during the 1840s and, though a burglar was sent to prison for eighteen months in 1847, this was the exception.[46] Generally, there would be little to steal. People were more likely to witness or experience a fire than a crime.

In 1842, the year in which Liverpool Council first "assumed rudimentary control over public health and house-building",[47] the Liverpool Anti-Monopoly Association commissioned a report on Vauxhall ward from John Finch (1784-1857), who in turn employed six working men to collect the information on the 23,892 people who lived there.[48] Finch's report was reprinted in 1986 with an additional introduction that described the general conditions in the ward:

> To the stench that must have arisen from the thirty and more factories, processing over twenty different products – from iron and lime to soap, vitriol and ale – all cheek-by-jowl with the homes of the Vauxhall inhabitants, there was added [in the 1840s] the ever-present smoke of the railways. To the overcrowded population were added a massive proportion of the hundreds of thousands of starving immigrants who fled the Irish famine and found some sort of refuge ... [300,000 in Liverpool in a single year – of which the Vauxhall and Scotland wards] took the brunt of this influx. Cholera and dysentery ended the forties ...[49]

The rich made sure that industry and other nuisances were not permitted in the areas where they lived, while "Chemical works, oil mills, artificial-manure factories, gas works, and diseased cattle receiving-centres, made living in Vauxhall ward particularly abominable".[50]

There were then 5973 separate families in Vauxhall, of whom 4930 were included in Finch's canvass, with his report identifying, and sometimes providing separate results for, individual streets. 177 (2.96%) of the Vauxhall families lived in Blackstock Street, one of the main thoroughfares in the middle of the ward, comprising 528 people (2.21% of the total).[51]

	Finch information	Blackstock Street		Vauxhall ward	
		N	%	N	%
1. Nature of occupation	Middle class	12	6.78	881	14.75
	Labourer	86	48.59	2628	44.00
	Widows & other women dependent on own means	25	14.12	783	13.11
	Trade or employment	51	28.81	1621	27.14
	Not ascertained	3	1.69	60	1.00

	Finch information	Blackstock Street		Vauxhall ward	
		N	%	N	%
2. Type of trade or employment	Best employed –shipping (Sailors, fishermen, pilots; Sail-makers, riggers block-makers; Shipwrights, ropers)	7	4.32	302	6.00
	Next best employed – machinery and merchandise (Smiths, engineers; Millwrights, wheelwrights; Engravers, watchmakers; Iron boiler-makers; Iron moulders; Sundry other trades)	18	11.11	360	7.15
	Next best employed – articles of domestic use (Coopers, brush-makers; Bakers, millers; Printers, book-binders; Tinmen, braziers)	9	5.56	166	3.30
	Next best employed – General labour	86	53.09	2628	52.23
	Next best employed – building operations (Slaters, plasterers; Painters, plumbers, glaziers; Joiners, cabinet-makers; Brick-layers, stonemasons; Sawyers; Nail-makers)	12	7.41	406	8.07
	Next best employed – in connection with articles of clothing (Shoe, boot-makers; Tailors)	5	3.09	387	7.69
	In least employment – female occupations Widows and other females	25	15.43	783[52]	15.56

Table 1a: Finch 1842 survey results comparing Blackstock Street with Vauxhall overall

Tables 1a above and 1b below compare the people in this street with those in Vauxhall as a whole on some of the basic information in Finch's survey.

On item (1), the nature of their occupation, Blackstock Street was similar to the ward as a whole in the proportion of families comprising women and those in trade or other employment, but had a higher proportion of labourer families and less than half the percentage describing themselves as middle class. Leeds Street had the highest number of professionals, but on Finch's categorisation the middle class predominated along Vauxhall Road, on the main roads to the east and around Great Howard Street to the west. One in two of the Blackstock Street families were headed by a labourer while less than one in fourteen claimed to be middle class. As in the ward as a whole, one in seven households comprised women only, while a little over a quarter were in trade.

Item (2) combines two of Finch's tables on the nature of that trade and the degree to which people were fully employed. It omits both the middle class and those in item (1) for whom the information was not known. The overall totals for item (2) are 162 for Blackstock Street and 5032 across Vauxhall. Labourers were in the middle, neither the most fully nor the least employed, while the women in Finch's study were restricted to female occupations and it seems the least likely to be employed. Blackstock Street was similar to Vauxhall overall in both these categories, but people in Blackstock Street tended to be more fully employed (the top three categories) than were those in the ward, though a lower proportion were connected with shipping, the most fully employed of all. The explanation is not that the street contained proportionately more artisans, but on the whole the residents seem to have avoided the building, shoe-making and tailoring trades, where employment was least certain and, in that sense, most hazardous. The most obvious difference is in the second category where, in percentage terms, many more people in Blackstock Street were employed in machinery and merchandise than was the case across the ward. Looking into this group of trades in more detail, only five of the other thirty-seven streets had more smiths and engineers, and none had more millwrights and wheelwrights. Naturally numbers in each street were small in these individual trades and therefore a difference of one or two would stand out, but equally it is likely that people clustered close to the factories that provided them with work.

In one sense Blackstock Street was a vibrant manufacturing area at this time, as an Ordnance Survey map for 1850, as well as Finch's survey, shows. A huge glass works, its main entrance on Vauxhall Road, ran for two-thirds of the north side of the street, behind five of the courts and the starch factory and stores that opened on to Blackstock Street itself, but many of the industries reflected Liverpool's history rather than its commercial future - indeed they were a throwback rather than a look forward.[53] But how could it be otherwise for this was a period of transition characterised by an increasing but not necessarily developing market, and predominantly by improvements in production. The industrial revolution had long since taken hold, chiefly evident from the processes by which goods were manufactured in factories by mass labour rather than by individuals at home, but the goods themselves had not changed much as yet. Nor would the merchants and traders necessarily have any incentive to develop them. Profits were rising on the back of efficiency and increased output and in any case educating the market to seek alternatives was neither realistic nor an affordable option. Tanning and pottery both served needs for warmth and cooking that had been evident for millennia and remained everyday human requirements.

Item (3) in Table 1b reports the earnings per week of each family of the labouring classes (i.e., omitting the middle class). Not surprisingly, Finch and his collaborators found it more difficult to establish this information in every instance, with the comparator totals for Blackstock Street and Vauxhall ward reduced accordingly. Some of the discrete earnings categories Finch reported are combined to keep Table 1(b) manageable and in order to highlight the key discrepancies between the street and the ward.[54]

It can be seen that, whereas almost a third of the families in the ward were without any apparent income at all, this was the case for about a fifth of those in Blackstock Street. Indeed, less than half (46.76%) of the families living there had to survive on 11s or less per family per week, whereas over 60% of those in Vauxhall as a whole did. Yet, even at the 11s level, the per capita amount per person per day would be under 5d.[55] This was not just to buy food of course, but to provide all the family's basic necessities (including rent, heat and clothing as well). No wonder that footwear was thought a luxury, tailors and bootmakers were only intermittently employed and pawn shops were as visible as pubs. Alcohol provided an escape but earnings would rarely be enough on their own to purchase it. Even for the better off, ill-health might be costly and prolonged sickness or injury could be calamitous for the family.

Finch information		Blackstock Street		Vauxhall ward	
		N	%	N	%
3. Earnings per week of whole family of the labouring classes (i.e., excluding middle class)	0s	30	21.58	1342	30.59
	1s-6s	11	7.91	425	9.92
	6s-11s	24	17.27	906	20.65
	11s-16s	26	18.71	579	13.20
	16s-20s	27	19.42	562	12.81
	20s-30s	20	14.39	512	11.67
	30s-40s	1	0.72	41	0.93
4. "Indigent families" dependent on	Charity, pawning, crime (prostitution)	22	50.00	1052	49.48
	Savings, credit, relations, casual employment	22	50.00	1017	47.84
	Parish relief and other assistance	0	0	57	2.68
5. House and cellar tenants and families in lodgings among the labouring classes	Families in houses as tenants	113	68.48	3028	59.47
	Families in cellars as tenants	33	20.00	828	16.26
	Families lodging in rooms and cellars	19	11.52	1236	24.27

Table 1b: Further 1842 survey results comparing Blackstock Street with Vauxhall overall

A higher proportion of the Blackstock Street families had earnings above the 11s level but only one family earned above 30s per week. Blackstock Street was poor but it was slightly better off than the average for the ward as a whole.

Finch calculates 9s 3d as the average earnings per family across the ward, similar to the average agricultural wage in England and Wales in 1850/51,[56] but notes the huge discrepancy between the 3432 families trying to live on 5s 9d per family per week while the remaining 955 families had 21s 6d each. Even in an area such as Vauxhall, therefore, there was a 4:1 differential in this group between the "better off" and the most impoverished. Blackstock Street families would have been slightly less unequal but even here the differential may have been 3:1.[57] It is important to note though that this refers to relative inequality; in absolute terms nearly every non-middle class family living in Vauxhall would be struggling compared to many areas of Liverpool and especially to those of the non-labouring class living outside the city but working in it.

Finch provides information for 2126 "indigent" families which, as his report explained, are "only a portion of the inhabitants in this condition [of want], but [for whom] all the information under this head ... could be collected".[58] Item (4) covers 36% of the total number of families in the ward but almost half of those for whom the earnings data under Item (3) was available (48.5% of 4387). Of these, almost half (1052 families) depended on "promiscuous charity, pawning and crime", almost as many (1017) on savings, credit, relatives and casual employment, while the remaining 57 (of whom more than 60% were women) relied on parish relief and other assistance. Although in Finch's table the third category on which the largest group depends is characterised as "crime", the report explicitly refers to it as prostitution.[59] By contrast only 44 families (32% of the 139 for whom the earnings data was available) in Blackstock Street were revealed as "indigent", and while it is conceivable that those in the street were less open with this information it is as likely that this was less marked a feature of their existence. None received parish relief, and they were split equally between Finch's other two categorisations. This confirms the picture above of Blackstock Street being slightly better off than the ward average, but by no means well off.

When indigent families headed by, or comprising only, women are considered, and the parish relief category is disregarded, 37.5% of those in the ward relied on charity, pawning or crime and

62.4% on savings, etc. In Blackstock Street the percentages were 27.8% and 72.2% respectively, again adding to the picture of relatively less poverty and behaviours that might be associated with it from necessity, such as the "enforced immoral practices resulting from insufficient earnings" as the Liverpool activist and Birkenhead manufacturer James Samuelson (1829-1918) described prostitution in one of his many books.[60]

The final section of Table 1b considers the basics of housing among the labouring classes. As the figures in Item (5) refer to families, consequently nearly 5000 people in Vauxhall were lodging in rooms and cellars - which, as Finch noted, meant that they did not own any furniture. The significance of this is that they had "pawned or sold all that they possessed for food, and taken lodgings to obtain shelter". The report adds "Their numbers are daily increasing, and they form the most destitute part of the population".[61] One quarter of those in the ward were in this position, while this was the case for one in nine of the Blackstock Street families. One in five of the latter lived in cellars whereas one in six families did across Vauxhall as a whole. This might mean a higher proportion of cellars in Blackstock Street than in the ward, but it could equally mean that more families were crowded into them.

Finch's report provides other data on the quality of people's accommodation and on observed cases of sickness, but as the numbers get increasingly small so does their utility. They do confirm though the overall pattern of Blackstock Street being impoverished, but slightly less so than was Vauxhall as a whole. The report furnishes further qualitative information, however, such as letters from shopkeepers to support and add to the tabulated data,[62] and the number of cases in the borough relieved by the Liverpool Dispensary (54,093 cases in 1841), a branch of which was in Vauxhall, and which was seeking additional donations to meet increasing demand.[63] The report also points to the benefit people in Vauxhall derived from being able to send their children to the local North Corporation School. However, it must be assumed that the cost of 1½d each per week, even though Finch describes it as a "trifling sum", would have proved prohibitive for most families in the neighbourhood. Indeed, there were only 875 pupils in October 1841 before "the whole of the Catholic, and a portion of the Protestant, children [were] withdrawn by their parents" following a vote by the borough Council for conformity to some of the practices of the Church of England, reducing numbers by two-thirds to 301 by January 1842.[64] Even after the 1870 Act, when school boards were introduced, compulsory education was not enforced for many families depended on their children working to make ends meet,[65] though it was mandatory in theory from 1880 for those aged between five and ten. It was still charged for into the 1890s and it was only the removal of fees in 1891 that made compulsory education feasible.

Finch's survey took place before the worst of the Irish famines in 1845-1847 of course. In the 1851 Census (leaving aside for the moment people living in the courts) twenty-two, or 40%, of the fifty-five families listed in Blackstock Street were headed by someone born on the mainland but thirty-one of the other heads of household came from Ireland (with one born in Germany and one in Malta). Their wives and many of their children had often been born in Ireland too, confirming Tarn's observation that

> Not only were [Liverpool and Glasgow] the ports of entry into England and Scotland respectively; they were also frequently the places where flight stopped because the Irish very often had not the means to go further.[66]

Some of the Irish immigrants who had recently moved into Blackstock Street described themselves as shoe-makers. Houses 12 and 13 comprised just such families, who, including six lodgers, numbered nine shoe-makers between them, all born in Ireland and all in their thirties or younger. There were at least three others in the street (at houses 17, 41 and 54).[67] Only two people described themselves as tailors. Yet, as Charles Mackay explained in his series on labour and the poor in Liverpool in the *Morning Chronicle* in 1849,

> Many boys, who afterwards became tailors, learn the first rudiments of the business at shirtmaking. When they grow up, they come over to England in search of employment as tailors, and generally have to resign themselves to work for the sweaters. They are not fit for better work. There are great numbers of Irish tailors of this class in Liverpool.[68]

The Liverpool Sanitary Act 1846 that came into force at the start of 1847 required that the local authority establish a public health service and Dr William Duncan (1805-1863) was the first Medical Officer of Health in the country. His 1847 report identified that Vauxhall ward was the highest in the borough for deaths from fever and diarrhoea, whereas the wealthy Abercromby was at the other extreme. Mortality was even higher among the Irish immigrants who often lived in the poorest and "worst-conditioned" streets. Just over one person in seven in Exchange Division died that year from all causes, whereas even in the neighbouring Scotland area it was shy of one in fourteen. In his 1849 report Duncan listed the streets in which there had been more than ten deaths from cholera that year. Although Blackstock Street did not feature, the two streets to the south were the highest in the city: Paul Street with 71 deaths and Oriel Street with 80. Both streets were sewered and Duncan concluded that it was the Irish crowding in Oriel Street and the insufficient supply of water in Paul Street that were the most likely explanations.[69] As there were also 58 deaths in Ford Street to its immediate north, Blackstock Street was perhaps fortunate not to suffer as severely as the streets around it. While it was wider, and therefore possibly better-ventilated, there must have been other preventive factors in play as well.

The Thirteenth Annual Report of the Poor Law Commissioners in 1847 included a report by Alfred Austin on the relief of the Irish poor in Liverpool.[70] In the first four months of 1847 more than 140,000 immigrants arrived from Ireland and the system was so overwhelmed that at the end of January more than 22,000 people were being issued with bread and being given tickets for soup each day. From February 1847 Liverpool was divided into thirteen districts with 24 relieving officers taking responsibility for particular localities. It was they to whom people had to apply for poor relief, they were visited at home and had to return each day to receive the relief. This reduced the average number of people receiving poor relief each day to about 8000, with a maximum of 10,845. The report claimed that the amount of relief given out had not decreased markedly, but that it was now better targeted on the destitute and otherwise necessitous. A couple of years after this, when the worst of the famine was over, people began to return to Ireland, nearly 35,000 between 1849 and 1853.[71] Since the cost to the public purse was of the order of £8500 (more than £500,000 today), many of these "removals" would have been assisted, in some cases forced, rather than voluntary.

Ramsey Muir's publication marking the 700th anniversary of the City's Charter is among those that have promoted Liverpool's reputation as a pioneer of housing reform, citing the series of Acts between 1842 and 1864 that laid down standards for future house-building.[72] However, this should be treated cautiously for, as Iain Taylor points out,

> Liverpool's reputation for pace-setting action in the field of public health and housing ... needs a more balanced assessment by social historians. The list of Liverpool 'firsts' has diverted too much attention from later, less incontrovertibly beneficial developments.[73]

As evidence of this, Taylor asserts that the opposition of the Liverpool Land and House Owners Association in 1884 put Council plans on hold for fourteen years: little demolition and no municipal house-building took place in the late 1880s once sanitary concerns had disappeared and the last building for six years occurred in 1891 while demolition increased. In other words, slum clearance then continued without sufficient replacement housing being provided for the people who had been displaced.[74] This only changed at the start of the twentieth century when the Council saw it had a wider responsibility than just economic return. For example, 2392 dwellings were built between 1900 and 1914 (compared to 503 in the previous fourteen years).[75]

In a 1955 article Lawton looked in detail at the 1851 Census information from eight areas within the Liverpool borough boundary and nine outside it. Two of the former, areas VI around Great Howard Street and VII including parts of Scotland Road, were not far from Blackstock Street.[76] Lawton drew conclusions about the occupations of the inhabitants and noted the huge number in area VI born in Ireland (59.2%), frequently poor tailors and dressmakers, or often labourers lacking even these rudimentary skills for whom the general nature of Liverpool industry did not require them to have more specific skills.[77] These sample areas were close to Blackstock Street but the following looks at the 1851 composition of the street itself.

The 1850s

Nobody in the street was in their seventies and indeed only seven were in their sixties, with the oldest aged sixty-five. Apart from a few women (and older children still at home) in their twenties, the adults were concentrated into the three decades between thirty and sixty, with all but four of the fifty-five households headed by somebody over 30. Yet what comes across most strongly, and in several ways, is the variety of those in the street. This shows itself, for example, both in the range of employment and in the housing circumstances.

Thirteen of the thirty-seven inhabited houses, or over one-third, were sub-divided. In three instances they were occupied by more than two families each and in the worst case by five families comprising twenty-two people. This would almost certainly mean that at least one room was occupied by more than one family. Another house contained sixteen people in three families and the third fourteen people across five families. Conversely, two families employed a servant: a butcher with three small children and a dog-breeder with a wife and two daughters living two doors down. Only two people lived on their own, both women, one a house-keeper in her sixties and the other a servant in her fifties. Even where there was only one family in a house, this meant as many as nine people in two cases. At no. 65 a forty-five year old corn porter Moses Cullen lived with his second wife Elizabeth aged thirty-two. His three older children aged seventeen to twenty-one were living with them and had been born in Ireland, as had Moses and Elizabeth. But they also had four younger children under nine all born in Liverpool. The three older children worked as a housekeeper, (rubbish) collector and a baker. Next door at no. 66 James and Maria Fitzpatrick had seven children, aged between twenty-one and seven months. Only the oldest son was working, as a labourer like his father, so this family would have been dependent on two less certain incomes compared to the four coming in next door.

In an effort to make ends meet thirteen households accommodated lodgers, thereby making the street more overcrowded and probably squalid as well.[78] Often the lodgers followed the same trade as the head of household so that, in addition to the neighbouring properties of nine shoemakers mentioned above, the boatmaker at no. 14 took in four lodgers who also described themselves as boat-makers, labourers lodged with labourers and one of the tailors had a dressmaker and shop boy among his lodgers.

Only three fourteen year olds were formally employed, one as a dressmaker, one as a servant and one as a fisherman alongside his father. Although some must have been working informally, others were said to be 'at home' unable to find work as yet. The fowl-dealer Thomas Cafferdy had a wife and five children but even the two who might have been working were not and the family was one of those in the most overcrowded circumstances. While many children were in the same trade as their parent, for example the two sons who owned their own carts like their mother Mary Simpson at no. 86 or the lime-burner Thomas Galley at no. 132 who also bore the same name as his father,[79] others had gone their own way. These included Hugh Clyde, the tobacconist son of a mariner at no. 6, the two sons of John Hubell, a starch-maker, who were both book-binders, the plumber son of a wash-woman and another book-binder whose mother was a seamster. These were skilled trades that may have reflected parental aspiration as well as personal ambition and observation of their parent's circumstances.

Thirty-five years later Hugh Clyde was a tobacconist in the Scottish town of Largs on the Ayrshire coast. There were similarities to Liverpool in that Largs was at the start of the Firth of Clyde, but the location was more like Crosby than Vauxhall. Hugh Clyde had clearly improved his circumstances, lifting himself out of Blackstock Street, but ironically his whereabouts at this time are known only because his Largs shop was broken into with a false key and six ounces of tobacco stolen. The burglar was an apprentice blacksmith but his skills in making a key that worked only resulted in a further thirty days on top of the three weeks he had already spent in jail.[80]

The ability to progress was more evident among sons than daughters. The latter were much more likely to have occupations as constrained as their parents. Although the daughter of a tanner had become a French polisher, being a servant, dressmaker or cotton-spinner was more likely. One woman described herself as a shoe-maker's wife, and another as that of a cooper (who had absented himself on the day of the Census if not permanently), but there were no families in which both parents were working outside the home.

Four heads of household described themselves as sailors or mariners, two of whom were born on the mainland, one in Ireland

and one in Malta. All four lived with their wives and one child (perhaps their only one), all but one aged over forty and all living in properties shared with another family. It might be assumed from this that, though they were not well off, they had put down relatively stable roots compared to many sailors.[81] At the other extreme were those who kept the city supplied with the basic necessities, two butchers and four bakers. One of the butchers had been born in Germany but had married a Liverpool woman, while the other at no. 28 (mentioned above) was well enough off to employ a servant to help look after his three young children. One of the bakers was Moses Cullen's seventeen year old son Richard who may have been learning the trade, perhaps doing so with the three Magee bakers, John and his younger brothers William and Thomas Magee who lived with him. There were twenty-two labourers and one stevedore, varying in age from seventeen to fifty-eight, and though only one described himself as a dock labourer several of the others may have worked there given the proximity of Blackstock Street to the docks. The two carters may have got much of their trade from there too, as perhaps did the three cart-owners in the Simpson family.

Many of the other trades have already been mentioned above (for example, shoe-makers, tailors, book binders and boat-makers), but there were in addition four in the building trade (two plasterers, a joiner and a carpenter) and three dealers (one in milk, one fish and one unspecified). Another three men described themselves in professional and managerial terms as the foreman of a tanyard, an engineer and a wheelwright/blacksmith. The foreman may have worked in the street, as might the starch-maker already referred to, for both industries had undertakings in Blackstock Street then, and the engineer may have been employed at one as well. The *Gazette* reported that William Gore, the wheelwright/blacksmith, went bankrupt two years later, with his creditors receiving less than one-fortieth of the money owed to them.[82]

According to Historic England,[83] the glass bottle factory that dominated the north side of Blackstock Street had started as Orford and Fosters before 1818 and in 1850 ownership changed from Foster to John Cannington and Co. The company placed a series of adverts in the *Liverpool Mercury* in 1851 to draw in new customers:

To WINE, SPIRIT, ALE AND PORTER MERCHANTS,

SODA WATER AND GINGER BEER MANUFACTURERS. Messrs John Cannington & Co (successors to Mr Foster) having taken the VAUXHALL GLASS WORKS, for the purposes of manufacturing BOTTLES of all descriptions, are now prepared to supply an article of the best quality and workmanship upon the most reasonable terms. WHOLESALE AND FOR EXPORTATION.[84]

The adverts seem to have had the desired effect for the company prospered, expanding into the Cannington Shaw & Co partnership in St Helens in 1866, and subsequently subsumed into United Glass Bottle Manufacturers from 1913.[85] There is also evidence that Cannington sought to run the company as well as he could and in accordance with his Wesleyan principles. For example, in November 1856 the company was summonsed for the furnaces belching black smoke in contravention of the bye-laws. Rather than just promising that it would not recur, or claiming that nothing could be done as had the owner of a glass works in Kirkdale and the Blackstock Street tanners Smyth Bros previously,[86] Cannington received advice from a number of smoke inspectors and glass works owners on how to prevent it happening again and was able to tell the court that their suggestions had been taken on board. The company was fined £5 with costs then,[87] and the advice must have been appropriate for the issue did not reappear until 1871 when the company received a 10s fine for excessive smoke.[88] As glass manufacture was one of the areas on which Liverpool smoke inspection concentrated after the 1855 Improvement Act, and the Council's Smoke Prevention Sub-Committee began 653 prosecutions between then and 1866, the Vauxhall glass works was far from the worst offender.[89] Indeed, the nearby tanners Smyth Bros would be prosecuted again in 1864 and 1866.[90]

When John Cannington died in 1896 aged 73 it was reported that

> The Wesleyan body in Liverpool has sustained a heavy loss by [his] death ... [for], though crippled for a quarter of a century, owing to an apoplectic stroke, [he] has till quite lately taken an active part in the work of Cannington, Shaw and Co, of St Helens, the well-known bottle manufacturers. His purse was always open to assist any Wesleyan enterprise at Liverpool and St Helens, and some chapels were almost wholly built by him.[91]

This included the chapel at Mersey Road, Crosby opened in 1891 to which he had contributed £2000.[92] Cannington lived nearby in Crosby and the Waterloo-with-Seaforth Local Health Board minutes record one of their 1874 improvements as flagging the "footpath on one side of Cambridge Road at side of house owned by John Cannington".[93] He left £6000 in his Will for Wesleyan organisations, often those benefitting Ministers' daughters and widows,[94] and bequeathing the Vauxhall glass works, valued at £4000 (about £250,000 today), to his son Arthur Kershaw Cannington.[95]

In 1854 the Lancashire and Yorkshire Railway sought to open up the northern docks by adding a branch line that would cross several city streets. When the proposal first came to the Health Committee in December 1852 it was reported to include Blackstock Street,[96] causing alarm among the residents who must have feared the street would be cut in half and homes demolished. In fact it was a misprint for Blackstone Street, though it continued to be recorded as Blackstock Street as the scheme developed. As one newspaper reported,

> This branch line passes over the town streets by means of massive iron bridges, at an average height of 22 feet from the level of the ground, placed respectively at Sandhills Lane, [five other streets] and Blackstock Street. The bridges cross the streets at a considerable angle, necessitating the use of gigantic girders, of an average length of about 100 feet and about 30 tons each in weight.[97]

That the misprint continued unchecked is perhaps indicative that such developments could happen in areas such as this, notwithstanding the Health Committee's aims. What is certain is that such blight would not have been contemplated for a moment, let alone permitted, in more affluent areas of the city whereas the quality of life of Blackstock Street residents was deemed less important.

The Tyson and Richmond soap works featured in two of the biggest stories of the 1850s. In January 1852 one of their travelling collectors was found to have embezzled over £700 (about £50,000 today) by the simple expedient of going to the company's ledger, seeing what was owed and collecting it in the usual way. But rather than handing it over to the company he then kept it for himself. When he was apprehended in Belfast he admitted the offence but nearly all the money had gone.[98] At the end of the decade two youths employed by the company were convicted of trying to poison the font at the Roman Catholic chapel (actually a schoolroom) by adding chromate of potash that they had taken from the soap factory. Worshippers would have marked their foreheads and lips with holy water from the font as they entered the chapel. The youths acknowledged their guilt and were fined £10 each or six months in prison if they could not pay.[99] They may have been prompted not only by the general tension around the re-establishment of the full Catholic hierarchy in England in the 1850s but by the specific initiative started in Blackstock Street in 1856 to build a proper Catholic church for what might be as many as 1400 Catholics "consisting of the poorer class of the Irish population" in this part of Liverpool.[100] Two and a half years later the foundation stone of the new church, 'Our Lady of Reconciliation of La Salette', was laid in Eldon Street by the Roman Catholic Bishop of Liverpool.[101] Like many Catholic churches and schools built in the nineteenth century, it depended on "the pennies of the poor" as well as on rich philanthropists.[102]

In 1886 an article in *Liverpool Review* walked the reader through the Tyson, Richmond and Jones "working soapery" on Blackstock Street. No doubt this remains fascinating to industrial archaeologists of the Victorian age, but is of limited value to the social historian and probably tedious in the extreme for the casual reader. It began with the portentous "you enter through huge gates" before swiftly collapsing into a "pile of buildings devoted mainly to storage purposes". The article did contain one nugget though: the original soap house of this firm, then known as Lombard, Tyson, stood at the bottom of Shaw's Brow, now William Brown Street; in other words, at what is today Liverpool's cultural centre.[103]

There were two spectacular fires: in 1853 at the rice millers Irving, Son and Jones where the damage may have amounted to £10,000 but much of the stock was saved,[104] and in 1858 at the sugar warehouse of James Leitch (or Leech) and Co. where the premises were gutted, with the headline in one newspaper 'The Great Fire of Liverpool'.[105]

Perhaps most striking though was the whale caught upstream in the river Mersey at Ogglett (now Oglet near the airport) and taken to Mr Batty, an oil manufacturer in Blackstock Street. The whale weighed 6½ tons and its tail exceeded 7 feet in width, though the report does not specify (and probably did not know) what type of whale it was. That this was an exceptionally rare event seems to have been missed, concentrating instead on the expectation "that Mr Batty will clear between £40 and £50 by the transaction".[106]

The 1860s

The first half of the 1860s was the time of the American Civil War when Lancashire's cotton imports dried up. Although this did not have a direct effect on Blackstock Street, it did coincide with a relatively quiet period there - perhaps for much the same reason of helplessness, with no riots against the blockade the American North was imposing despite the unemployment and distress it caused in Lancashire.[107] In contrast, there would be riots in 1878, particularly in Preston, when the cotton masters sought to reduce wages. The 15th Earl of Derby compared these with the 1860s, concluding that it was "injustice not privation" that had caused them "whereas in the American war every operative knew that the cause of his suffering lay beyond the reach of English hands to remove".[108] Six months later in November 1878 he anticipated "a winter of insecurity and discontent"[109] and in December Clarke Aspinall, the coroner of Liverpool, proposed a scheme "for giving free breakfasts to the poor … during the hard weather and distress". Although Derby thought it "a doubtful way of helping them … if others take it up I shall do so too".[110]

The second half of the decade was different. In 1866 a forty year old labourer Michael Smith living in one of the Blackstock Street courts came home to find the woman he lived with in "close conversation" (i.e., in bed) with another man. Smith was thrown down the stairs and kicked so violently that he died the following day. Witness accounts varied and the verdict was manslaughter rather than murder,[111] but had the assailants been defended by John Cobb they might have got off completely. His practice, based in Dale Street near the police court, undertook the full range of legal tasks, but Cobb himself spent much of his time in the court as the preferred advocate of many of those charged in this period, defending hundreds of cases between 1857 and 1871. That he could be relied on to stand up to authority was already evident when *Porcupine* appointed him Solicitor-General in the hypothetical June

1861 government they proposed for an independent Lancashire based on that of the Southern confederacy.[112] In 1858 he had secured a dismissal for a man charged with running a brothel of thirty prostitutes and in 1867 for a publican trading on a Sunday.[113] In 1866 the sugar refiners Leech and Sons had dismissed a couple of dozen union men "in consequence of their not attending to their duty", appointed a non-union man as foreman and a campaign of harassment culminated with the dismissed workers breaking a window at the foreman's home. Cobb had a boy claim to have thrown the stone, though not to breaking the window, and this case too was dismissed.[114] In 1868 Cobb defended a fraudster with the Dickensian name of Tully Egan who had obtained 2700 rice bags from the manufacturer without paying for them. He had pretended that he was being paid to take them to the docks but then persuaded the manufacturer that he had sold them to the Blackstock Street rice millers Irving, Son and Jones instead. The bag manufacturer was instructed that the rice miller would pay him but when he went there found that they had already paid Egan.[115] Although there is no record of the outcome, Cobb must have got him off because twelve months later Egan received six months for indecent assault on a seven year old girl[116] and then in 1870 eight years penal servitude for attempted theft of £70,000 by forging an order for a cash deposit box.[117] This may have been the end of Egan's increasingly dangerous criminal career, but it was certainly the last time he appeared in the newspapers.

The 1870s

Five years after the Egan fraud, Irving, Son and Jones experienced an even more devastating fire than the one that had hit them in 1853. On this occasion nearby buildings were threatened and £50,000 worth of damage done with the mill totally destroyed.[118] Indeed, so devastating was it that it became more economic for the firm to sell off its carthorses rather than keep them stabled when there was nothing to deliver. Their horses were included in a sale of fifty working horses, some of which had worked at a Runcorn factory that had also burnt down while the remainder belonged to Liverpool cart-owners who had fallen on hard times.[119]

The lime works (referred to earlier as replaced by 1890) was advertised for sale or to let in September 1873. Although the advert did not require that any buyer had to use it for different purposes, this must have been anticipated for the advert stated that, although it currently comprised limekilns, eight stall stables, dwelling house, offices, etc., the "greater portion of premises are vaulted and fire-proof, suitable for manufacturing purposes of any description".[120]

Other businesses were advertised for sale in the 1870s, one of which had already been under the hammer several times. This was a sugar refinery (though not the Leitch one) that had first been advertised in April 1855 but failed to be sold at auction that summer[121] and was re-advertised the following year.[122] Ten years later, and then occupied by Messrs Crosfield & Co., it was sold for £2000 at an auction ordered by the Court of Chancery.[123] Crosfield may have been the tenant prior to 1866 but he was certainly the owner thereafter for in 1873 he and his partner put it up for sale once more:

> To be sold by private treaty
> A very desirable sugar refinery in a central situation in Liverpool, which has been carried on up to the present time, and is capable of working about 200 tons per week. The plant being of recent construction, is in good working order and excellent condition.
> Intending purchasers please apply to Edwood, Crosfield & Co., 20 Blackstock Street[124]

If it was sold then, the new owners soon thought better of their purchase for less than three years later it was on the market again:

> To be sold by private treaty
> The complete sugar refinery lately occupied by the Blackstock Sugar Refining Co (Ltd), situate in Blackstock Street, Liverpool, with the new warehouse adjoining capable of holding 2000 casks of sugar. The machinery is of the most improved description and capable of refining per week 350 to 400 tons of sugar of the best description.
> … apply to AW Chalmers, No. 5 Fenwick Street, Liverpool.[125]

There is nothing unusual in this pattern since owners would always be weighing the net income being generated against the capital to be accrued from a sale. For the workers, however, there must have been almost continuous anxiety for, even if the use remained the same, would they still be required and, if they were, would their wages remain the same?

This site became part of the Liverpool Saccharine Company which first appeared in an 1878 advert: "TO FARMERS, COW-KEEPERS, and Others - CATTLE FOOD for Sale, made from pure Indian corn only. Apply to the Liverpool Saccharine Co., 20 and 23 Blackstock Street".[126] Fifteen months later the company would keep up the tradition of factory fires when the top two storeys were burnt out and several thousand pounds worth of damage caused.[127]

It had been William Nicholson on whose death the tannery occupied by Smyth Bros. had been sold in 1865. A few years earlier John Tapp Smyth, one of the three Smyth brothers, had been among the largest creditors of John Nicholson (presumably William's father) and as one of two trustees had everything in the older Nicholson's Will assigned to him for the benefit of all the creditors.[128] He must have acted honourably for the tannery to remain in the Nicholson name. John Tapp Smyth died in 1878 and the partnership with his brothers (one of whom also worked at the tannery while the other was a country gentleman in Herefordshire) was thus terminated "by effluxion of time".[129] One of Tapp Smyth's executors was a relative with the colourful name of Worsley Battersby, better known as a coal merchant, pit proprietor and yacht owner who competed at both the Royal Mersey and Royal Thames Yacht Clubs.[130] There is an ironic symmetry between a dank pit and a grimy court, but this Battersby was too young to have given his name to the court off Blackstock Street, though one of his ancestors may well have done. It fell to Battersby to sell Tapp Smyth's house in Cheshire that had been leased from the Earl of Shrewsbury in 1870 for 99 years.[131]

The first newspaper adverts seeking a specific employee began to appear in the mid-1870s. On two occasions these were for skilled workers at Wade's coachworks, who might well not be available locally and for whom a Liverpool-wide trawl was required. In October 1878 Wade advertised for a "good Body or Carriage maker", as well as a lad.[132] It may be that on this occasion he was unable to find the skilled worker he required for two years later his business closed down and everything was sold off at auction:

twelve first class waggonettes, phaetons, gigs, whitechapels, drags, etc; useful bay cob, harness, new handcart, spokes, felloes, benches and vices, 20 pairs of wheels, shafts, bellows and hearth, anvils, axles, springs, scrap iron and sundries.[133]

It is conceivable, though unlikely, that Wade's demise was due to the forthcoming trade recession of the 1880s, but it certainly cannot be laid at the door of the 1889 strikes by dockers and seamen or the rise of the new unionism that took place at that time.[134]

But some adverts were for unskilled, and young, people for whom the requirement was at least "good character" and might also be educational standard. In 1874 The Eagle Vaults "Wanted a young woman as SERVANT and to assist in the bar. Good character required"[135] and in 1877 "Wanted a strong girl for housework. No cooking. Salary 4s per week. Good character required."[136] The following year the soap-maker William Gossage and Sons "WANTED, a respectable youth as ASSISTANT in an office. Apply, by letter …"[137] What is not clear is whether these employers had given up on word of mouth and knew that suitable applicants would not live in the neighbourhood or were deliberately seeking candidates from outside the area who would be unknown to, and perhaps untainted by, any local contacts.

The evidence to explain why this might be part of their thinking is not hard to find. In September 1878 a police officer was stabbed with a cotton hook at a warehouse[138] and

> … the dead body of a female child was found in the cellar of the Corporation Schools, Blackstock Street. The body was sown up in a piece of white flannel, and placed in a mat basket. It was taken to the deadhouse, where it awaits an inquest.[139]

Things would get even more unsavoury a year later when two labourers were alleged to have killed another in number seven court. The first newspaper report was:

> Thomas and James Murphy, brothers, were charged with causing the death of James Campbell, a man employed at a galvanised iron works, Neptune Street … It appeared that the prisoners were fighting a man in a court off Blackstock Street, when the deceased, who was very drunk, called out to know what was the matter. The prisoners

> thereupon, [it] was alleged, commenced an attack on him, and kicked him into a cellar, inflicting injuries about the head and the body, from which he died ... Both prisoners, however, strenuously denied the charge, and said the deceased was a well-known 'corner man' [in other words, a rough who hung around street corners] of violent character, who had frequently been in the hands of the police. The magistrate remanded the case for a week.[140]

While another report two days later added

> A woman named Bridget Cearns was now called, and stated that on the night in question six or seven couples were fighting in the court. Witness told the deceased not to interfere as it was a 'family affair'.

Cearns claimed to have seen Campbell "fall down the cellar steps, but could not say what [had] caused him to fall". Another witness Mary Clesham said Thomas Murphy was in his "stocking feet at the time", a significant point as a coroner had previously returned a verdict of wilful murder against Thomas Murphy only.[141] But could he have given Campbell the fatal kicking in his socks?

When the case came up at the assizes in November there was a different report again. Not surprisingly, the defence argued that the witnesses were untrustworthy and in a fatal fight it would be impossible anyway to say with certainty how the injuries were inflicted. Both Murphy brothers were found not guilty.[142] A violent fight was bad enough, but this had involved several couples, a man had died and witnesses could not be trusted.

Any prospective employer who craved respectability would be bound to recruit elsewhere if they could.

After the 1870s

Even when there was no actual violence the threat remained, hanging over the area and distinguishing those who were trying to get on with their lives as peaceably as they could from those who had succumbed to a "lazy, cowardly and brutal existence". In 1884 the authorities tried to clear up the streets:

> Another batch of Liverpool cornermen were summonsed yesterday for obstructing the footpaths in various parts of the city. Convictions

were not obtained in all the cases, but from the evidence adduced there could be no doubt that the majority of the defendants preferred idleness to industry, and, consequently, had what the police describe as no visible means of subsistence. Moreover, in regard to several of the parties, it was said that they existed on the proceeds of robberies from drunken men. Many of the defendants constantly frequented public houses and street corners, their favourite resorts being the neighbourhood of Scotland Road, Vauxhall Road, ... Blackstock Street ...[143]

By contrast, though perhaps just as deliberate for attempts to counter the prevailing orthodoxy and encourage people to become involved in beautifying an area such as this were not unusual (as in 'Best Kept ...' competitions today), the prizes given out by the Liverpool Window Garden Association that summer included those for two window boxes commended at no. 43 and at house 2 in court 3.[144]

In conclusion, Blackstock Street may not have been the poorest or roughest area in Vauxhall, but it was remarkable enough on both counts. Factories changed hands often[145] and fires were almost as regular an occurrence as fines for smoke nuisance. People's living arrangements were even more hazardous with reports of babies accidentally suffocated in the overcrowded conditions, or dying from exposure,[146] as well as periodic outbreaks of cholera, typhoid and other diseases reflective of the insanitary circumstances. Parents could, and were, summonsed if their children did not attend school. Yet it was easier for those who could afford it to salve their conscience by contributing to charity than by taking action on their doorstep. In 1880, for example, one Blackstock Street firm sent a £50 cheque to the Mansion House Relief Fund set up in Dublin for the relief of distress in Ireland. They might have sent twice that "... but since the receipt of your letter it has been decided to establish a fund in [Liverpool], to which we shall subscribe the one half of our donation."[147] This was the same amount as the 15th Earl of Derby sent, to the Irish Relief Fund administered in Dublin even though he preferred to focus his charity on Lancashire if he could, and even though in this instance he thought the "distress ... wildly exaggerated".[148] Better than nothing at all, of course, but still far from what was required.

Two years earlier Derby had pondered on the future for the area:

> The reflection is often present to my mind - will all this immense material prosperity of Lancashire continue? It has sprung up in less than a century: will another hundred years see the end of it? And, if so, what will remain? The docks certainly: they are built as if for endless duration: a few public buildings here & there; but the hundreds of thousands of cheap ugly brick cottages, built in rows, & all alike, will have crumbled away: a few years of neglect is enough to destroy them and, being on the surface of the ground, not even the foundations will show.[149]

The key questions for Blackstock Street must have been whether it would rise on the Liverpool tide or sink back, or perhaps how long the rising tide would last in Liverpool and the extent to which Blackstock Street would be dependent on it.

3. CROSBY FROM 1850

In 1850 Courtenay Road did not exist and Crosby itself was a small village. Things had begun to change slowly when a local sanitary district was formed after the 1848 Public Health Act and from 1856 when the Waterloo with Seaforth Local Board of Health met for the first time.[150] From July 1848 the Lancashire and Yorkshire Railway opened a single line through Crosby between Waterloo and Southport, with travel between Liverpool and Waterloo by bus until the line was extended to Sandhills to join the existing Liverpool line in August 1851.[151] As Marshall explains in his history of the Railway:

> Suburban traffic between Liverpool and Crosby soon overtaxed the single line, and early in 1851 plans were prepared for doubling between Sandhills and Crosby and for adapting Crosby as a terminus for suburban trains. ...[The] new Crosby station ... was opened on 1 June 1852. Presumably the double line was opened about the same time. The doubling to Southport ... was brought into use at the end of September 1852.[152]

Crosby was no longer just a mark on the map but would increasingly become a significant settlement as the advent of the railway, as it often did, led to housing development.

Indeed one end of Courtenay Road would abut the railway (as the image on the front cover shows) and one of those who would grow up there was the economic historian Charles Ryle Fay.[153] His grandfather

> has a footnote in railway history, having invented the chain rail brake in 1857 (a point which Fay characteristically makes, literally with a footnote ...). In 'Huskisson and His Age' the note reads:
> 'My grandfather, Charles Fay, 1812-1900, was superintendent of the Wagon Department of the Lancashire and Yorkshire ... Railway. ...
> '... [He] became Carriage Superintendent of the Carriage Works, attached to the Locomotive Department before transferring to the Wagon Department. In 1857 he patented his chain brake, which gripped simultaneously all the wheels of the train ... In a competition held on the Oldham incline into Manchester Victoria ... his brake won. ... After a run of some twenty years his brake was ousted by the Westinghouse Air Brake.'[154]

A major thoroughfare, Oxford Road, had to be further developed and extended before any of the later side roads, of which Courtenay Road was one, could be contemplated. In 1867, and again in 1869, a deputation attended the Local Board of Health meetings, firstly to argue for the necessary sewerage and road-making of Oxford Road and, on the later occasion, to question the funds available for completing Oxford Road.[155] It would be 1873 before the Waterloo builders Costain and Kneen secured the necessary funding and 1875 before this part of Oxford Road was adopted.[156] These builders had come to Merseyside in 1865 from the Isle of Man and were Richard Costain, the founder of the Costain company that is one of the largest construction firms today, and his future brother-in-law Richard Kneen. Based initially at Blundellsands and Horwich they dissolved their partnership (as joiners and wheelwrights as well as builders) twenty-three years later in 1888.[157] Subsequently,

> The [Costain] company's first venture outside Merseyside was the construction of workforce accommodation for a steel company at Redcar, north-east England, during the First World War. But it was a move south to build houses in the booming suburbia around 1920s London that really sparked the family firm's expansion. Costain became known both for the construction of large 'gentleman's residences' in leafy Surrey and estates of more modest dwellings, such as that built to house Ford's workforce at Dagenham, Essex.[158]

To complement the Costain and Kneen work on Oxford Road, a year after they had started another tender was accepted from a Liverpool building company (Peter Walkden & Co) to undertake the sewerage and road-making at the north end of Oxford Road.[159] Walkden may have prospered initially but the building company seems not to have lasted as long as Costain, but then few have.

As with any development pushing out into the countryside, there is a pioneer and somewhat haphazard feel to these undertakings, and the first residents must have been prepared to put up with much discomfort as the expansion of Waterloo and Crosby ground on. Two examples illustrate this frontier nature:
- in 1878 William Simcock, a rent and rate collector for the Local Board of Health, disappeared. For a while it was thought he might have absconded with some of the Board's money, though in the

event this seems not to have been the case. However, the Board was right to be alarmed for he had helped himself to some Government tax receipts that he also collected in the area.[160]
- in 1880 plans for three nearby roads were submitted by another Liverpool builder Reginald Radcliffe. These were approved by the Board but the first cottages he put up in one of the roads (Norway Street) were condemned as unfit for human habitation almost immediately they were completed. Local residents subsequently complained to the Board about Radcliffe's building intentions on another plot.[161]
Not quite the Wild West of the same era perhaps, but there were clearly cowboys about!

Building plots in Courtenay Road had been advertised as early as 1863,[162] perhaps optimistically and certainly prematurely, for the first mention in the newspapers of any residents came in the announcement of births, first in 1881 and twice in 1882 at numbers 23, 13 and 9.[163] None of those mentioned (the Goodbody, Karck and Blackwood babies and their families) were among the occupants of the road in 1900. Even young families did not stay that long. The other point to note, needless to say, is that Blackstock Street residents (almost) never advertised their births, deaths or marriages in the newspapers - though the deaths of factory owners might be, such as John Tapp Smyth or William Duckworth, one of the original owners of the lime works.[164] Possibly some people in Blackstock Street might have done so if they could have afforded it but the majority had learned, or thought, such announcements inappropriate and unwarranted given limited life expectancy and expectations. Life was too harsh and brutish to permit of niceties such as this.

By the 1881 Census there were twelve even-numbered houses listed in Courtenay Road (two of which were empty) and four odd-numbered ones (nos. 23-29). This might suggest that the northern side of the street had yet to be completed, an entirely logical supposition given that the building would be progressing outwards from Waterloo in this direction. Two of the households were headed by women, Mary Roberts aged 56 at no. 6 and Theresa D'Arcy aged 61 at no. 22. Both had grown-up children living with them, Mary Roberts' three sons (all cotton brokers) and a daughter (an artist) and Theresa D'Arcy's two sons. Only the D'Arcy family and one other household did not employ at least one servant. The youngest households were the Macks at no. 18 (he was a 26 year old shipping clerk) and the tea merchant Edward Goodbody aged 29 and his eighteen year old wife Elisa, who would announce the birth of their first child the following month. The oldest was at no. 29 where William R Jones, a 72 year old librarian lived with his wife Sophia, two daughters and a grandson. Although the early occupants of the road included a number of brokers and merchants, as it would in 1900, it had more of a maritime flavour in these first days than it would twenty years later. There was a Master mariner, the 50 year old Edward Drenning at no. 10, and a Surveyor of shipping, the 47 year old George Creighton at no. 24, as well as a marine insurance agent and Mack the shipping clerk. None of those living there in 1881 were still there at the turn of the century (and, indeed, only Edward Drenning was still there in 1891). Table 2 at the end of the chapter summarises the residents over the thirty-year period 1881-1911.

In 1880 another local builder, Richard R Morris, from Brighton-le-Sands applied for permission to erect "three detached dwelling houses on the north-west corner of Courtenay Road and Oxford Road" and his plans were approved.[165] Although he too seems not to have founded a building dynasty, he clearly knew how to build houses that lasted.

When Courtenay Road was completed in late 1881/early 1882, there were three larger detached houses (nos. 1, 3 and 5), each comprising eight bedrooms, and twenty-four six-bedroom semi-detached properties (nos. 2, 4, 6-24, 25, 27 and 29), with the even numbers ending at 24. In March and April 1882 there were attempts to both sell and/or let no. 1 on the corner of Courtenay Road and Oxford Road, with the adverts appearing contemporaneously so that the house was advertised for sale at £1400[166] while it was also available to rent at £75 per annum.[167] It seems that there were no takers, for the following month two houses were put up for auction. As these were described as being on the corner, they were probably numbers 1 and 3 (though it is not impossible that they were numbers 3 and 5):

By Order of the Mortgagee
by Messrs Branch & Leett
On Wednesday the 24th inst... [sale by auction] ...

> Two freehold dwelling-houses on the northerly side of Courtenay Road, Waterloo, in the township of Great Crosby, and at the corner of Oxford Road there. ...[168]

The mortgagee may have been the builder Morris or even Astrup Cariss who, if he did not own no.1 previously, must have purchased it at the auction. What is certain though is that a few months later in autumn 1882 Cariss was trying to sell the house, this time for £1450. The house was now described as overlooking the sea with about 800 yards of land. The advert was to be placed from 19th September to 16th October but it last appeared in the newspaper on 4th October,[169] with the jute goods manufacturer Peter Walter Marsh and his family moving in. They already had three daughters and a son living with them and another three daughters and a son would be born in Courtenay Road, starting with Salome in August 1883.[170] Salome is, to say the least, a distinctive and unusual name, but rather than being chosen with the character in the Bible in mind it was the name of her maternal grandmother, Ann Marsh's mother Salome Fowler.[171]

In 1890, when their fifth daughter Mildred was about two, they advertised in February for a nurse, offering a "comfortable home for any one really fond of children," and in May for "a good plain cook".[172] Two years later in October 1892 they sought a housemaid-waitress to start the following week.[173] In each of the adverts they specified the age they wanted: about 25 on the first two occasions and about 27 on the third. In each instance this would make the employee about ten years older than their oldest child, thereby setting them apart by this means as well as with respect to their role and function in the household. The eighth and last Marsh child Annie was born in 1893 and the family still lived at this address in 1911, the longest residents by some distance (the Townshends at no. 27 were the next longest, first appearing in the Waterloo Directory for 1888).

The man who had sold the Marsh family the house, Astrup Cariss, was a chartered accountant and well-known Liverpool figure. He was secretary of the Liverpool Institute in 1859 and had letters published in both the *Journal of the Society of Arts* and *The Athenaeum*.[174] In 1868 he published a book on the accounts of building societies and two others in 1883 on arbitration and double-entry book-keeping. When the latter first appeared, a review in the

Times judged it to have come into an area that was already overcrowded,[175] but it must have done well for a second edition followed a year later which the *Morning Post* commended as rapidly becoming the standard work on the topic.[176] In November 1881 he had been defeated in the Liverpool municipal elections, standing as a Liberal in Abercromby ward, and remained on the Liberal Association Executive Committee as chairman of the Rodney District in early 1883.[177] However, things must have been going badly wrong for him already and, while it is not possible to be certain whether this started with misfortune or malfeasance, ill-luck or ill-will, it rapidly escalated. He was made bankrupt in early 1884,[178] the ultimate indignity for a Fellow of the Institute of Chartered Accountants, and the ultimate irony for someone who had written about accounting standards. He had debts of £6000 and the public examination was set for 25th January 1884 but "as the bankrupt is reported to have absconded, the appointment is a mere matter of form".[179] Yet worse was to come for, in addition to his debts, Cariss had disappeared with £343 belonging to the Lancashire Ladies Arts Society of which he had been both secretary and treasurer.[180]

Cariss' early sale of no. 1 Courtenay Road may have been an attempt to repay some of his debts or, more likely, add to the cash pile that would enable him to do a bunk and flee his creditors and the courts. Astrup Cariss never appears in British newspapers after 1884 (other than an advert for his book in 1887) and it is at least conceivable that he emigrated, perhaps to Norway given the etymology of his name.

In the mid-1880s much of the road was marketed by a Liverpool estate agent Thomas Ellis Priest who, as he was also secretary of the Hercules Permanent Benefit Society,[181] may have been doing it either on their behalf or with their backing. His first involvement seems to have been in 1884 when he offered one of the semi-detached houses for sale at £1000.[182] Six months later he was advertising several of them,[183] but was probably unable to attract sufficient interest for his next advert that May was specific that all twenty-four semi-detached houses were available: "To be sold, in lots to suit purchasers, the Semi-detached DWELLING HOUSES Nos. 2 to 24 and 7 to 29, Courtenay Road, Waterloo. Rents £45 and £50. Tenure freehold."[184] Priest's advert implies, and other information confirms, that in several instances the houses were being sold with sitting tenants. For example, just two days later the tenants at no. 9, possibly still the Blackwoods, were seeking "a well-trained, respectable girl as NURSE in a small family. Foreigner or Scotch Protestant preferred. Wages according to capability."[185]

It is unlikely that they were all sold at this point, and certainly not to individual purchasers, for a number were soon available at reduced rents,[186] figures which became even more explicit from March 1890: "Very pleasant and desirable RESIDENCES (in close proximity to the shore) ... Rents £42 10s and £40 per annum".[187] In other words, the rents had been reduced by as much as 15% in three years while, as further evidence that Priest may have been struggling, this advert was placed jointly with a Richard Seward of Great George's Road, Waterloo. Nos. 2, 14 and 22 were still available for rent at £42 10s in July 1892, by which stage Priest had teamed up with somebody called Halliwell, and they were describing themselves as accountants.[188]

No. 15 was one of those that went through a number of changes in this period. By 1887 it was occupied by the Winshurst family, who may have responded to Priest's 1885 adverts. Clarence Winshurst, a solicitor in the Bateson, Warr and Winshurst practice, was then aged 27, and he and his wife Maria from Rock Ferry on the other side of the Mersey announced the birth of their first daughter in the *Morning Post* in July 1887.[189] Six months later Mrs Winshurst was off-loading her own governess: "A LADY wishes to RECOMMEND her late GOVERNESS; very kind to children; French, German, music, Latin; salary £35".[190] On the face of it this seems an odd decision as her children might soon need a governess themselves, but it may be that money difficulties or other reasons forced this change on the family. Twelve months after this, at the start of 1889, another daughter was born to the Winshursts,[191] and although the family were still living there with their two daughters and two servants at the time of the 1891 Census, the house had become a Ladies' School and Kindergarten by 1894 run by a Miss Rollit with two vacancies for pupils to board.[192] Previously known as Miss Rollet, she had been the Principal for over eleven years at the nearby Maghull Ladies School,[193] which catered for six boarders but often had two vacancies as well, thereby putting a huge dent in her budget. It may have been an inheritance that drew her to the Crosby area for she offered a "pleasantly situated" and furnished house close to the shore at Blundellsands for a few months,[194] perhaps to tide her business over the boarding vacancies. She named her new venture Albany College but it seems to have sunk without trace once she had given up appealing for extra boarders. Indeed, the last advert the following January was slightly different to those that had preceded it in 1894:

> WATERLOO - Albany College, Courtenay Road - HOME SCHOOL for GIRLS. Seven boarders received. Terms moderate, inclusive. References. Visiting Masters. RE-OPENS JAN 22.[195]

Vacancies were not mentioned, possibly because all seven places were available, and it seems unlikely that they would be filled in time for the school to re-open ten days later. By 1901 the house was occupied by a 40 year-old timber broker Charles Hughes and his wife, though they would soon move on to a larger house in Blundellsands.

This was not the only house in Courtenay Road to be touted as a school in the mid-1890s for there was what claimed to be an Anglo-French school run by Madame Hortense Lockie, though the only evidence for this is that three children also called Lockie passed an elementary music exam in 1895 and one, presumably her son, advanced to the next grade the following year.[196] There are no other mentions of Hortense Lockie or her alleged school in the Liverpool newspapers, nor of the three budding musicians.

No. 7 by contrast was first advertised by its owner for letting while she was away during the winter of 1885/86 then, when she had no takers for the winter let, was offered more generally.[197] By 1888[198] it was occupied by James Wilson, the Chief Superintendent at Liverpool Post Office, his wife and their three young sons, but it was empty again soon after the 1891 Census when the rent asked was £40.[199] (It was also empty in 1901.) Wilson had started as a postal clerk in Dumfries in 1865, had been transferred to Liverpool in 1867 and over the next twenty-five years had worked his way up to the post of Chief Superintendent, supervising 126 post offices and more than 1000 "officers of all ranks". He was appointed the Preston postmaster in March 1892,[200] was handpicked to take temporary charge of an office in the west of England in January 1893 and while there was appointed as Derby postmaster in

September 1893. There was speculation that he would next move on to Leeds[201] but in November 1896 the Duke of Norfolk, Postmaster-General, appointed him to take over at Hull.[202] Nevertheless, he may have got to Leeds eventually for in 1907 James Wilson, late Postmaster of Leeds, received the Imperial Service Order in King Edward VII's birthday honours.[203]

A few of those living in Courtenay Road in 1891 were still there in 1901, three of whom have already been referred to: Marsh at no. 1, Fay at no. 20 and Fanny Townshend, the widow of a shipowner at no. 27. But there were four others:

- the great-grandson of the 2nd Earl of Radnor, Laurence Pleydell-Bouverie, a cotton salesman at no. 13. His wife and daughter were living with him in 1891 but by the turn of the century he was alone; even their servant had left.
- John Pilling and his family at no. 19. He may have been an accountant previously, and perhaps still was, but by this stage described himself as living off his own money.
- William Hart, a hide broker with Heyworth, Hart & Co., and his family at no. 23
- the Rayners at no. 16. In the 1891 Census John Rayner described himself modestly as a woollen draper. This might have been how he started out but by this time he was an established naval outfitter and contractor to the government, with a shop at 24 Lord Street in the centre of Liverpool and a large factory at 51-54 Regent Street. He died in May 1894[204] and his son Frank Rayner, already living at Courtenay Road, was there in 1901 now with his wife and young son. He seems not to have succeeded to his father's business though for one of the executors, William Rayner, gave the Lord Street address as his own.[205]

In 1895 no. 9 advertised for a general servant specifying, as their predecessors had done ten years before and as had the Marsh family in 1892, that they were seeking a Protestant.[206] This might have been done to guard against Irish applicants, particularly Irish immigrants who made up the bulk of the Catholic population in Liverpool, as perhaps would the requirement that those interested write initially. While Blackstock Street employers might look outside their immediate area to find respectable candidates, people in Courtenay Road conflated respectability with religion and therefore paraded their prejudices more openly. Both may have come to much the same thing, of course. At the very least a written application would demonstrate literacy, a factor that might weigh as heavily as religion for some prospective employers.[207]

View from Lord Street of junction with North and South John Streets 1908
352 ENG/2/1410 © Liverpool Record Office, Liverpool Central Library

No.	Census 1881*	Waterloo Directory 1888	Census 1891	Census 1901	Waterloo Directory 1906	Waterloo Directory 1909	Census 1911
1	-*	Marsh	Marsh	Marsh	Marsh	Marsh	Marsh
2	Kelly	empty	empty	Horrocks	Horrocks	empty	?
3	-*	Christie	Christie	Roberts	Roberts	Bowman	Bowman
4	Barry	empty	Graham	Arnold	Arnold	empty	?
5	-*	Rylands	Statham	Miller	empty	Arnold	Arnold
6	Mary Roberts	Edwin Roberts	Gill	Mackenzie	Mackenzie	Mackenzie	?
7	-	Wilson	Wilson	empty	Drysdale	empty	?
8	Kirkman	Kirkman	Clapton	McKinstry	empty	empty	?
9	-	Blackwood	empty	Taylor	Taylor	Taylor	Taylor
10	Drenning	Drenning	Drenning	Jones	Acton	Acton	Acton
11	-	Townsend	Townsend	Bathgate	Bathgate	empty	?
12	Gardner	empty	empty	Slatter	CVC Dawbarn	empty	Slater
13	-	Bouverie	Bouverie	Bouverie	empty	empty	?
14	empty	empty	empty	Ashworth	Ashworth	Ashworth	?
15	-	Winshurst	Winshurst	Hughes	Fletcher	empty	?
16	empty	John Rayner	John Rayner	Frank Rayner	Frank Rayner	Frank Rayner	?
17	-	Gilling	Sheridan	Eaton	Tankard	Tankard	Wilkie
18	Mack	empty	Luck	Stewart	Baumgarten	Baumgarten	Baumgarten
19	-	empty	Pilling	Pilling	Prout	Prout	Prout
20	Vokes	empty	Fay	Fay	Fay	empty	?

47

No.	Census 1881*	Waterloo Directory 1888	Census 1891	Census 1901	Waterloo Directory 1906	Waterloo Directory 1909	Census 1911
21	-	Jack Tipple	Frederick Tipple	John Brown	Frances Brown	Frances Brown	Frances Brown
22	D'Arcy	McNeilly	McNeilly	Webster	Dobson	empty	?
23	-	Hart	Hart	Hart	Joseph Dawbarn	Joseph Dawbarn	Joseph Dawbarn
24	Creighton	Bedell	Lancaster	Rougetel	Rougetel	empty	Bradshaw
25	M?	Newson	Newson	Edith Parker	Edith Parker	Edith Parker	Edmund Parker
27	Whiteman	William Townshend	William Townshend	Fanny Townshend	Fanny Townshend	Fanny Townshend	Fanny Townshend
29	Jones	empty	Wilkinson	Hall	Hall	Hall	Hall

Table 2: Residents summary for Courtenay Road, Crosby 1881-1911

Key
* not yet built; building application for nos. 1, 3, 5 was made 2nd August 1880 in 1901 Census and other years
in more than one year but not 1901 Census

4. BLACKSTOCK STREET IN 1900: PUBS, COURTS AND FACTORIES

The bleak situation of people in the Blackstock Street and Vauxhall community was brought into harsh focus by events of the 1890s that tested to the limit the few coping strategies they had available. This was not the "unsavoury incidents such as the Liverpool police scandals of the early 1890s" that Jose Harris refers to,[208] for she provides no detail and when Lancashire newspapers and the *Times* nationally are examined, all that turns up is one case of police assault and false imprisonment of a domestic servant in July 1891.[209] This might be indicative of police attitudes and behaviour more generally but is hardly conclusive on its own. There was, however, a police purge of 'immoral houses' (i.e., brothels) in 1890/91 with 818 people prosecuted for keeping and running 300 disorderly houses.[210] Father James Nugent (1822-1905) was instantly aware of the implications:

> ... great numbers of unfortunate women would in consequence find themselves homeless on the streets; ... a house in Liverpool [similar to the one recently opened by the Poor Servants of the Mother of God in Streatham should] offer shelter to these poor outcasts ...[211]

Nugent would soon turn 'should' into 'could' and 'would'.[212]

In 1894 the *Liverpool Post and Echo* published an inquiry into unemployment, taking evidence from some unemployed people and distinguishing those unable to find work (described as Class A) from those unable or unwilling to work because of ill-health, intemperance, hereditary incapacity, etc. (Class B).[213] In other words, a similar contrast to, but not the same as, the deserving/undeserving dichotomy that has been used to differentiate the poor since Elizabethan times and is still used today by some politicians who prefer individual to systemic explanations of why people are on benefits. The distinction in the Liverpool report was more subtle and further established that the primary reasons for unemployment among Liverpool residents were either the seasonal and fluctuating character of much of the port's trade or the system of casual employment that applied throughout the city. William Grisewood, the Secretary of Liverpool Central Relief and the Charity Organisation Society, claimed that the poor comprised one fifth casual labourers (chiefly in the docks), one in eight cotton and general porters, and a similar proportion bricklayers, plasterers or painters whose work was for a season only and not at all for three months of the year.[214] The widows of labouring men accounted for many of the rest, with the main causes of poverty unavoidable through irregular employment, old age and lack of savings. Much less frequent were "avoidable" causes such as drink or laziness, sheer indolence and the pauper spirit, and improvidence. "Willingness to work" was therefore not the absolute that it is sometimes portrayed as being; opportunity to work was even more critical.

Grisewood asserted that philanthropy should not just be random alms-giving but planned and aware of the consequences, no doubt enabling him to contrast Protestant scientific charity with allegedly profligate Catholic alms-giving. There was some justification for this in the 1891 papal encyclical *Rerum Novarum* in which Pope Leo XIII supposedly upheld the Catholic Church's traditional view of charity, that is to say "the rich would be saved by munificent alms-giving and the poor by patient suffering".[215] Even if Pope Leo did not hold these views himself, arguing that the elimination of poverty was "the most effective weapon against socialism" and that this required permanent re-adjustments not just temporary charity, several senior clerics appear to have done so. Another analyst of papal encyclicals, for example, quoting the Belgian economist Charles Périn refers to "the poverty of the masses [being] necessary so that the rich could have the opportunity to practise the duty of charity".[216] Belchem distinguishes the Liverpool Domestic Mission and St Vincent de Paul Society as characteristic of the two extremes,[217] while Kanya-Forstner draws attention to the anxiety that poor people should not exploit benevolence and relief with the Domestic Mission arguing that "prodigal alms-giving" had worse effects than occasionally denying support to those who deserved it.[218] At the core of these perspectives is the view that giving relief was an end in itself rather than as a means, or in order, to effect change. Father Nugent, however, held a different view, developing many practical initiatives to help the most vulnerable in nineteenth century Liverpool.

Kanya-Forstner notes that an offshoot of the Liverpool Domestic Mission, the North End Domestic Mission, was set up in 1858 on Bond Street (north of Blackstock Street between Vauxhall and Scotland Roads) with the aim of bringing "the spirit of Christianity to the homes of the neglected".[219] By the turn of the twentieth century, Blackstock Street would be surrounded not only by Anglican and Catholic churches that in some cases ministered to the physical, as well as moral and spiritual, needs of their parishioners, but by the relief organisations that based themselves in the vicinity. These included, for example, the Catholic Benevolent Society, the Liverpool Well-Doers in Limekiln Lane (founded in 1893 and still there today)[220] and the Magdalen Home refuge and night shelter for fifty fallen women in Bevington Bush (opened by Father James Nugent in 1891) and run by Mother Magdalen (Fanny) Taylor and the Poor Servants of the Mother of God.[221] According to Devas,

> Mgr. Nugent, aided by generous friends both Catholic and Protestant, had already purchased a big building, formerly used as public baths and wash-houses in Bevington Bush, but time was required before this could be adapted to its new use, and it was not opened till late in the following Autumn [1892]. The old temporary Refuge in Limekiln Lane was then converted into a night shelter for homeless women ...[222]

The "generous friends" included Mrs FD Gossage, Mr W Crosfield and John Cannington for their donations of £100, £25 and £5 respectively were among those listed.[223] These three had connections to Blackstock Street through their factories, while James Samuelson, who often represented workers and trade unions in Liverpool, donated £10.

Although not everyone would be described as 'fallen', there was no need to seek any further explanation for their poverty for most people in Blackstock Street were born into it:

> The generationally poor were explained by the system, their poverty was part of their place and therefore, implicitly, also their identity - hence character could damn them irrespective of their helplessness to change their situation.[224]

Buttressed by, or perhaps hemmed in, by relief organisations, there was a self-fulfilling prophecy at work even if not all accepted it philosophically. There would be little expectation of their prospects either.

The subsequent winter in 1894/95 exacerbated the situation, for the country experienced an extensive and deep freeze that went on for what seemed like months (and may have rivalled, even if it did not surpass, the winters of 1861, 1881, 1947 and 1963).[225] One writer has described it as "of North American proportions".[226] Up to

Scotland Road 1908 © Scottie Press

mid-December 1894 it had been unusually mild, even warm,[227] but just before Christmas a severe gale wreaked havoc with shipping off the north-west of England. A crew of nineteen men were lost when their ship sank and another nine were thought to have drowned when two Hoylake fishing boats capsized.[228] At the end of that week the whole country was affected by "violent gales [with] considerable damage and loss of life". The sea was being whipped into a fury, ships were sheltering at anchor in the Mersey and snow had begun to fall.[229] On new year's day it was reported that areas from Ulster to the north of Scotland and down the east coast as far as Norfolk were severely disrupted. Reports were still coming in of ships that had sunk in the North Sea, with liners struggling in the Bay of Biscay, while Liverpool was cold but snow-free.[230] Severe weather in Scotland in early January then reached Liverpool by the 10th, with six degrees of frost and lakes in the parks thronged with skaters.[231] But this initial burst of enthusiasm from the better off was soon curtailed and by the 12th everybody was doing their best to keep out of the cold:

> Weather of great severity was experienced over the United Kingdom … In Liverpool …, following upon the hard frost of the past week,

came an easterly gale ... accompanied in the early hours [of the 13th] by a heavy fall of snow

that in some places had been whipped into drifts.

This began to thaw later in the day when it rained but had frozen solid again by late afternoon.[232] The following day the local paper reported that

> Yesterday and during the previous night about 1400 men and 220 horses were engaged in ... clearing [the business] streets of the city, 400 extra hands having been put on by the scavenging department. Over 500 tons of salt were used in ... melting the snow.

Predictably, though, "the suburbs were not so fortunate"[233] and there were foreseeable consequences with, for example, one four year-old child enveloped by flames as she stood too close to the fire while her parents were out at the shop. Rolling her in the snow put the flames out but she was taken to hospital in a serious condition.[234] A rapid thaw led to floods across the country, a pattern that was made much worse when heavy snow fell again the following weekend. Having exhausted the use of 'severe' as a heading for its daily bulletins on the weather, the *Liverpool Mercury* resorted to 'remarkable' in describing the snowfall accompanied by "thunder and vivid flashes of lighting, [with] at one point an intense darkness" that afflicted London and elsewhere on Monday 23rd January.[235] The violence of the storm set church bells ringing.

On occasion the heavy snow did provide work for some of the unemployed who made their way to the Corporation depots, with the regular scavenging department taking on another 600 to 700 men on 30th January. But

> ... there are still a large number of men who have failed to get employment, and to them and their children the snow and the biting cold serve but as additional pangs to their suffering.[236]

For a fortnight hundreds had been getting a bowl of soup each afternoon from a van in front of St George's Hall staffed by the Liverpool Unemployed Association. The Food Association in Limekiln Lane had supplied the soup and, while each recipient had to pay a farthing a bowl, some people were giving away free tickets to those who had no money, many of them children. The Corporation's Health Committee had a vigorous debate over whether buying 1500 tons of salt to spread on the streets in the latest snowfall at 10s a ton should not have been spent instead on the unemployed. It was left to individual councillors to put up placards in every district asking for unemployed men to help clear the snow.[237] When the Committee report reached the City Council, the chair of the Health Committee explained that six-inches of snow had fallen on 29th January over 300 miles of Liverpool streets (i.e., 1.3m cubic yards) and even had there been places to dump it, and enough carts to carry it, mechanical and chemical means would always have been required to clear it.[238]

There were then daily reports of the severe weather until near the end of February. House boilers burst and ice formed in the Mersey. On 18th February a letter from Rev. Charles Garrett, superintendent of the Liverpool Mission,[239] outlined the distress in the city and the help his colleagues had received from the employees of companies such as Henry Tate to alleviate it. They had personally provided relief to over 2000 women and children with food parcels.[240] Alongside Garrett's letter it was reported that the distribution of soup outside St George's Hall would now cease since it had been portrayed as an advertisement for the charities involved, and "the powers that be have now authorised help and relief to the suffering poor", including "although late" a relief fund set up by the Lord Mayor.[241]

In 1901 there were nearly 9000 immigrants ('aliens' as they were labelled, i.e., people born outside Britain) amongst the settled Liverpool population, an increase of almost 31% in the twenty years since the 1881 Census.[242] These numbers were swelled by those who were in Liverpool only briefly - for example, by another 5530 foreign cattlemen (principally from Argentina, Canada and the USA) in 1902 who were expected to disperse.[243] Immigrants added to the diversity and vitality of the city but, in the absence of sufficient house-building, one consequence was more overcrowding. The Royal Commission report on Alien Immigration commented both on the necessity for bye-laws to deal with overcrowding and the associated initiative undertaken by Dr EW Hope (the city's Medical Officer of Health at the time) to use female sanitary inspectors "to instruct the poorer classes in the conduct of their houses".[244] It was said that women welcomed this intervention in their lives, and perhaps they did when it related to family health and protection, but some of the inspectors must have come across as out-of-touch nosey-parkers. Entering people's homes in this way, however, would provide an obvious way for bye-laws on overcrowding to be enforced - though how this would result in anything other than putting people on the streets had not been resolved.

That such uninvited intrusions into people's homes were countenanced, let alone permitted, appears remarkable today. However, since the Torrens Act 1868[245] and even into the 1920s, the "night-man" could enter bedrooms to check that those over ten of different sexes were not sleeping in the same room. They often did of course, even in the same bed for warmth or necessity, and their parents bundled them outside if they thought the night-man was expected, as the writer George Garrett recorded in his diary.[246] The motivation was moral policing as much as checking on overcrowding, but clearly could have been used to that end had appropriate action followed it. But with only 14 houses built in the Exchange district during 1900, while 334 had been demolished,[247] overcrowding was an increasing rather than diminishing problem.

Hope's 1900 MOH report reinforced this in detail: the population in Exchange had decreased by 14% from 49,175 in 1890 to 42,405 in 1900, meaning that there were one in seven fewer people to be accommodated - but in even fewer habitable houses. As the latter had decreased by 1566 (19%), overcrowding was worse overall with six people on average per inhabited house in 1891 rising to 6.4 in 1901. Abercromby and Scotland districts also had fewer inhabited houses in 1901 than ten years earlier but their falls were respectively only a third and a quarter that of Exchange. This picture of an area in decline reflected a trend that had been evident since 1881, one that Hope attributed in his report to the removal of insanitary dwellings in Exchange, a gloss that other information does not support. There were still a huge number of court properties in the district and, even though Blackstock Street was far from the worst, the combination of poor quality housing and unsavoury factories must have rendered it notably unpleasant.

Hope's report contained other revealing statistics about the Exchange district, the only area in Liverpool where the death rate exceeded the birth rate:
- at 36.5/1000 the death rate in Exchange was 6% higher than in Scotland ward (34.5/1000) and nearly 60% above the city average (23.1/1000);
- the birth rate at 31.4/1000 was 6% below the city average of 33.4/1000 and far below Scotland ward's 40.8/1000;
- perhaps more positively, though, it had the lowest notification of infectious diseases and nobody in Exchange had died from small-pox in 1900.

All three might suggest an older population in Exchange. It is assumed of course that notifiable diseases and threats to public health were no more likely to be concealed from the medical authorities there than anywhere else, and given that there were no instances of typhus in Blackstock Street in 1900 and fewer than three people in the street died from diarrhoea, this seems a reasonable supposition. Diarrhoea was a significant killer elsewhere with a large number of streets with three or more deaths from that cause listed by Hope in his report.

Housing

In writing about Athol Street, half a mile north of Blackstock Street up the Vauxhall Road, Ayers underlines some of the points already made about the Vauxhall area and Blackstock Street in the previous century.

> By the turn of the century housing had become very run down. Very few of the dwellings ... had only one family living in them [as they had when first built]. In some streets, people occupied cellars right up until the blitz. The area was also a centre of industrial activity. Noise, foul smells and pollution added to the misery of those who lived there. Poorly clad, verminous, vulnerable to disease and, for the most part hungry, the men, women and children ... scratched out a bare existence less than two miles away from the centre of one of the most prosperous cities in the world.
> Nevertheless, welded together by bonds of common misfortune and interdependence, the people of the area established their own

sense of identity and worked out the best possible strategies for survival.[248]

… irregular income and low wages had … forced women to develop strategies to ensure the survival of their families. Born of generations of trying to manage, these survival strategies had become part and parcel of daily life.[249]

Many of these strategies were the same for poor people everywhere, as uncovered for example by Silverman and Earner-Byrne in Ireland, including letters of appeal to the wealthy and the churches, confiscating the earnings of young children to help with the family budget before education became compulsory, and a reliance on mothers who worked outside the home (as well as inside).[250] Short-term credit was largely closed off to people who had no collateral against which to borrow unless they pawned their few possessions (perhaps Sunday best clothes during the week or a labourer's tools at the weekend when they would not be needed), or took out a loan from the local moneylender. Although moneylenders (and indeed pawnbrokers to a lesser extent) were judged harshly for taking advantage and exploiting those with no other option, they clearly served a demand that was not met in any other way. A small sum to tide people over was a necessity, though paying it back without repeating the process the following week was more problematical. As Melanie Tebbutt has pointed out, moneylenders infuriated philanthropists and others who did not require them, but equally they often "aroused … the uncertain gratitude of their own community".[251]

Liverpool was widely thought a black spot for moneylending, and it may well have been, but as Sidney Payne, a member of the Cheshire and Lancashire Moneylenders Association who himself had a shop in Liverpool, explained to a 1925 Select Committee, this was largely because, as well as 1380 moneylenders overall, 1100 of them were women of whom he knew little but believed were mainly small operators providing a service in their local area. He thought they had been given an undue prominence, in part because of the dubious evidence provided to the Select Committee the week before by Dorothy Keeling, Secretary of the Liverpool Personal Service Society and Chairwoman of the Moneylending Committee of Liverpool Women's Citizen Association.[252]

In 1908 the Board of Trade published an enquiry they had carried out in 1905 into the cost of living for the working classes, particularly housing rents, an exercise that they would repeat in 1912 (published in 1913).[253] Rather than a generalised national report, this compared and contrasted rents and prices in different areas with, in addition, detailed sections on particular areas (such as Liverpool and Bootle pp274-283). Their description of a typical Liverpool court, in which many of the working-class lived, applies to those in Blackstock Street:

> [It] consists of a strip of land with a frontage of 30 feet to a narrow street, and a depth of 60 feet abutting at the far end the high walls of warehouses or factories, or upon the windowless backs of other houses of what is known as the 'straight-up-and-down' type, i.e., having a depth of one room only. Under the floor of one of the rooms of the front house is a tunnel or passage 3 feet wide and 5 or 6 feet high giving access to the land in the rear. On this strip of back land, only 30 feet wide, are placed two rows of three-storey houses facing each other with their backs against other houses, each with a frontage of 11 feet and the same in depth including the thickness of the walls. This leaves barely 9 feet from window to window. Two conveniences are provided, one at each end of the court. In some of the courts of more modern construction, while the tunnel entrance is done away with, one end of each alternate court has been blocked up by houses, which prevent a circulation of air through each court. The rent usually charged for this class of house is from 3s. to 4s. per week; where the occupier lets a room (as frequently happens) he usually charges 1s 6d a week for this accommodation.[254]

Many of the court houses in the street in 1901 were occupied by carters and their families, highlighting the proximity of the docks. The most heavily occupied court house by a single family according to the Census was that of the coal carter Edward Knott, his wife and six children, eight people in all, while four houses were shared by two unrelated groups. Often a man (or sometimes a woman) was lodging with a family.

Political Representation

The mix of factories and residential dwellings in Blackstock Street, not to mention the fact that many of the latter were little more than shelters, indicated that this was a poor area. Yet it was precisely this that made the street and the Vauxhall area generally a target for the Conservative caucus that AB Forwood, the leading Conservative in Liverpool in the late nineteenth century, espoused. As he put it,

> Liverpool is a very remarkable illustration - if any justification is needed - of the necessity of public control, to ensure health and save the toiling thousands from the evil consequences which the avarice and greed of individuals might inflict.[255]

Forwood's status in the national as well as local party

> ... derived from [being the] political manager of the country's most successful Conservative organisation. Forwood, by virtue of speaking for Liverpool, and Liverpool, by virtue of Forwood's purposefulness, were commanding the attention of Westminster and seeking a share in decision-making.[256]

But Forwood did not intend mainly, and certainly not purely, to provide a voice for the dispossessed. Indeed, Waller says that the attraction to Forwood of single-member constituencies after the 1884 Reform Act (and the associated Redistribution of Seats Act the following year) was that the illusion of enfranchisement might appear to be attained in areas such as this while in reality the interests of the many continued to be submerged by those of the "propertied influences".[257] Dual voting by the factory owners and their managers who lived elsewhere could ensure this, as might their placemen on ward committees. Waller asserts that "perhaps one-quarter of the electorate in Exchange Division was non-resident" and reports that in the 1885 election "200 merchants with plural votes" had to justify this to the registration court.[258] From a high point of 8000 electors in 1885 the Exchange electorate steadily declined to less than 6000 by 1906, and Forwood's aspirations were to be largely frustrated for only in 1885 and December 1910 was a Conservative elected. The seat was held by the Liberals from 1886 to 1895 and then by the Liberal Unionists until the Liberal landslide of 1906. From 1897 to 1906 the MP was the free trader Charles McArthur[259] who, after his defeat in 1906, became Conservative MP for the neighbouring Kirkdale constituency from 1907 to his death in 1910.[260]

At the municipal level, meanwhile, JG Taggart, a labourer in Tate's sugar refinery, won Vauxhall ward in 1888 as Liverpool's first working-class (and Irish Nationalist) Councillor.[261] He was unopposed in the 1892 council election that resulted in a Liberal administration from 1892 to 1895,[262] which Brady describes as a brief interlude in a century of Conservative domination.[263] In 1895 six additional wards were created and most of the additional seats went Conservative. The Council then comprised 64 Conservatives, 32 Liberals (including aldermen in both cases)[264] and eleven others, of whom nine were Irish Nationalists with Taggart and one other in Vauxhall. Taggart was again unopposed in 1898, with the Conservatives strengthening their control with 74 seats and the Liberals reducing to 26. There were then ten Irish Nationalists.

Pubs

The 1830 Sale of Beer Act was brought in to break the monopoly of publicans and brewers, enabling any ratepayer to acquire a beer licence for two guineas, and by the 1840s there were 900 beerhouses and 1500 public houses in Liverpool, hence the title of Freddy O'Connor's exhaustive survey 'A Pub on Every Corner'.[265] However, there never seem to have been more than two licensed premises in Blackstock Street, which in 1850 were The Grapes and the Eagle Vaults (though there would have been several drinking dens and other unlicensed premises). By 1900 the two pubs were the Eagle and the Green Flag, on the corners opposite each other at the junction of Blackstock Street and Vauxhall Road.

Blackstock Street was far from being unusual for most roads that adjoined the east side of Vauxhall Road had pubs on both corners: Naylor Street, Oriel Street and Paul Street to the south; Arley Street and Eldon Street to the north, for example. With one exception, the other roads that ran parallel to Blackstock Street south of the major east-west thoroughfare of Burlington Street had a pub on one corner with Vauxhall Road (Maguire Street, Eldon Place and Bond Street). Ford Street was the only one that had none at all. Of the eight roads that joined the west side of Vauxhall Road in this area four had one corner pub and the other four none, so, in total,

Blackstock Street in 1900: Pubs, courts, factories

there were nineteen pubs in less than eight hundred yards along this stretch of Vauxhall Road. This should not be surprising for women, particularly Irish women, had a "reputation ... for enjoying a drink as much, if not more, than their menfolk".[266]

The Eagle had been owned in the nineteenth century by Joplins Brewery and the licensees at the end of the century were Robert Borrowman until November 1895 and then David Borrowman (no doubt a relative and possibly his son).[267] By this stage the owners were the executors of Henry Joplin but by 1900 there was a protracted dispute over Joplin's estate between the successor company Joplins Brewery Ltd and the Law Guarantee and Trust Society Ltd.[268] Indeed, so finely balanced and protracted was the legal wrangling that it has found its way into the footnotes of Halsbury's Laws of England, not just once but twice.[269] Suffice it to say that the tenant from 1st March 1902 was John Hughes of 2 Clement Street, who paid quarterly in advance a rent of £60 to his landlord Joplins Brewery Ltd. It was then described as "No. 1 Blackstock Street, Fully licensed corner public house with dwelling house attached". In 1906 it was sold, as were all the Joplins Brewery properties, in its case for £1500 to Robert Cain and Son.[270]

The Green Flag opposite was part of the Walkers Warrington Ales estate until in 1921 Walkers merged with Robert Cain to become Walker Cain Ltd. The Eagle continued to be listed but the Green Flag was not[271] and perhaps had already closed, either as part of the rationalisation accompanying the merger or in anticipation of the 1920s municipal housing scheme Blackstock Street Gardens that was built on the site. The Eagle still exists in 2019 and according to some is the oldest pub in Liverpool.[272]

O'Connor includes photographs of both pubs, with that of the Eagle particularly well-defined - even to the extent of the sign for Blackstock Street just to the right of the clock.[273] It seems to have been an exceptionally well-managed pub, only figuring in a newspaper report once during the nineteenth century and then only tangentially. In March 1874 John Mills of the Eagle Vaults and his friend Christopher Meadows, a Vauxhall Road pawnbroker, were out shooting on land for which, they claimed, Meadows had been granted permission to shoot for the last nine years. On this occasion, however, the Waterloo hare-coursing event was taking place on neighbouring land and as the beaters drove hares towards the course, one escaped and was shot by Mills and Meadows. Both had game certificates but they were nevertheless fined 40s and costs.[274]

Blackstock Street Gardens © Scottie Press

Eagle Vaults before the First World War[275]

Pawnbrokers

A key strategy for household survival would be pawning items on a Monday that would not be needed until the next weekend and could be redeemed after pay-day at the end of the week. "Friday night was pay night - debt night, getting your suit out of the pawn shop or paying the moneylender."[276] In 1870 Liverpool had the third highest number of pawn shop licences outside London and industrialised Lancashire as a whole the highest density of licences of any county.[277] This was an expensive form of credit, of course, usually involving both up-front costs and an interest payment on redemption, but needs must and there was no alternative for most people given that they had no security other than the few possessions that could be pledged in this way. It was the equivalent of a pay-day loan today, with costs almost as excessive, though pawning was much more highly regulated.[278]

The moral argument against this cycle of pawning would be, as with alcohol and abstinence, that total avoidance was ultimately easier than trying to give it up: once in it, breaking out was virtually impossible and certainly very painful. However, adhering to such moral principles implies choice, a luxury that few who lived in this part of Vauxhall had. It was an adaptive strategy to put food on the table, less uncertain than gambling, though nevertheless illustrative of short-term thinking, immediate reward but longer-term cost:

> Poor housewives faced the increasing work and responsibility of a growing family with whom income always failed to keep pace, so that not looking ahead frequently became the only ... way of coping with a situation where to look ahead [was] to look forward to a week, a month, or even a lifetime of suffering.[279]

For the poor household, expensive credit was just one aspect of a generally high cost of living based on low income, casual labour and lack of security. Heavy manual work required the frequent purchase of shoddy clothing which in turn wore out very quickly. Poor quality food was bought in small quantities for immediate consumption. A greater risk of default meant the poor frequently paid rents which were quite out of proportion to their income.[280]

No wonder that gambling and alcohol provided an escape, however momentary from the grim tedium of the daily struggle, not to mention the grinding boredom of everyday life.[281] This resulted in "... neighbourhood support networks [particularly for women that] were dependent on shared needs and common values, but were in turn riven with jealousy and mistrust".[282]

Prostitution

Despite the crackdown on houses of ill-repute at the start of the 1890s, this would not have eradicated the "oldest profession", especially not in a port city such as Liverpool. Milne's work on Liverpool's Sailortown is just one illustration of service resilience where, compared to the alternatives, the rewards for the women as well as the needs of the clients ensured its continuation.[283] As John Benson puts it, "Whatever the difficulties, they seem to have been more than offset by the financial opportunities which brothel-keeping offered".[284]

Although prostitution was no more evident in Blackstock Street in 1841 (at the time of Finch's survey) than it was in Vauxhall as a whole, this does not mean that it did not exist or was negligible. Indeed, it would have varied in line with other economic alternatives and social considerations, and the fact that there were factories in the street and busy thoroughfares nearby, as well as the docks, would have meant that there was both a passing trade and a potential, even likely, clientele. It can have been no accident that Father Nugent was looking in this area for premises for his refuge for fallen women and that it would be the converted public baths on the corner of Paul Street and Bevington Bush that became St Saviour's. As it backed on to the school at one end of Blackstock Street, parental concerns may have been aroused and Furnival claims Nugent "had chosen a location that polite society inhabited ... and was not entirely popular ... among the people who lived and worked there".[285] However, when Furnival adds that "Paul Street was a respectable area", it must have improved considerably, given the information above about courts and cholera only a few years earlier.

Paula Bartley makes two points that may be thought relevant. Firstly, new machinery was installed in the Liverpool Magdalen

Home (St Saviour's) allowing laundry to be taken in from ships, factories, etc. as well as from individuals. This was the model of a commercial laundry that the Sisters had pioneered elsewhere to secure adequate financial support.[286] Secondly, the Liverpool Vigilance Committee reversed its crackdown in the late 1890s as it argued this had driven prostitutes and brothels into areas where it was harder to find them.[287] Therefore, even if contact with the "fallen women" themselves did not automatically increase, the location of St Saviour's must have become more widely known, perhaps drawing people to the vicinity if not to the refuge itself, with the necessity of prostitution acknowledged and to some extent tolerated on the basis of "better the devil you know".

In 1901 the head of the Magdalen Home Mary Sills was in her fifties like another two nuns, while six were aged from 23 to 37. Sills' deputy had been born in Liverpool in the 1840s, but the other eight nuns came from Ireland originally. Not all the women being looked after in the Home worked in the laundry, though forty did as laundry workers, two as packers, one as a shirt machinist, another as a lacemaker and one as a needleworker. A resident cook and five domestics (housemaids) looked after the Home. There was also a flower seller Ellen McDonald who seems to have been allowed to continue hawking on her own account, perhaps because she had entered the Home along with another Ellen McDonald aged 15, probably her daughter and presumably the one at risk. In contrast to the nuns, the majority of the fifty-two inmates came from Liverpool, with a smattering from Ireland, Scotland, the Isle of Man and as far afield as Somerset. They ranged in age from 14 to 52, with eighteen under 20 and eight over 40. All but two of the latter were widows. So almost half the women were either in their teens or widowed, demonstrating the heightened vulnerability of those most likely to have become disconnected from, or abandoned by, their family.

There is no evidence that any of the women at St Saviour's were related to those living in Blackstock Street in either 1891 or 1901 (though this assumes that it was their real names that were recorded in the Census). The shirt machinist was an Annie Kerr from Sheffield, but doubtful that she was related to the tailoress Catherine Kerr who lived in Blackstock Street throughout this decade, was sixteen years older at 54 and, while she may have ended up in Liverpool after moving from Ireland where she was born to Sheffield, this is improbable. Kerr is not that uncommon a name, and even though they were both in the clothes trade, they were unlikely to be related. Similarly, a seventeen year old laundry worker Susan Wales might have been from the same family as Albert Wales, a labourer living in one of the courts with his wife and two young children. But, as she had been born in the Isle of Man and he came from Goole, this is also improbable. Indeed, it might be supposed that there were enough Liverpool women requiring a refuge for such links to be most unlikely, even had such proximity not been actively discouraged.

In addition to the mother and daughter McDonalds in St Saviour's, there were also Emily and Margaret Byrne, seventeen and nineteen respectively, who may have been sisters as both were born in Liverpool. Yet, as Byrne is as common a name as Kerr, this may have been no more than chance. It would appear that no other residents were related, either to each other or to those in Blackstock Street.

Factories

As well as the people who lived in Blackstock Street (considered in more detail in Chapter 5 below), many others will have spent most of their waking hours there in one of the nine factories. Indeed, some of them may well have spent more time in Blackstock Street, often working twelve hours each day between Monday and Saturday, than did residents who were employed elsewhere. The factories dominated the street and, in manufacturing goods rather than just trading them, were if not exceptional for Liverpool at least unusual, belying the city's reputation as almost exclusively a port that relied on commerce rather than industry. This marked Blackstock Street out, for there would have been a different but equally distinctive atmosphere by day to that at night, an atmosphere that would have been amplified by raw materials being carted into the factories and finished products taken out - to the railway stations, and in some instances the local markets, as well as the docks. The traffic would have been continuous, providing further employment for those who lived nearby, as would the link the street offered between the main north-south thoroughfares of Vauxhall Road to the west and Scotland Road to the east. Blackstock Street, therefore, was for some the destination while for other workers it was just the convenient cut that shortened the trip.

Consequently, it would have been impossible for Blackstock Street to have the anonymity in 1900 that it does today. Even if people had not been there themselves, they would have smelt it, not least because of the two soap factories that would become part of Lever Bros in later years: Tyson, Richmond and Jones in 1906 and Gossages in 1919.

The further information found for six of the nine factories in the street is set out below.

Tyson, Richmond and Jones
In 1900 the owner of Tyson, Richmond and Jones was James Burnett Briggs (d.1936) who lived on the other side of the Mersey in Birkenhead.[288] Like the glass manufacturer John Cannington, Briggs was a Wesleyan Methodist and may have had more local connections, to Bootle if not Liverpool, for in October 1880 he had married Mary Bromfield, the eldest daughter of Edward Edwards of Merton Road, Bootle at the Balliol Road Wesleyan Chapel there.[289] He may even have been related to Thomas Briggs, the manager of the Eagle Vaults in 1891.

James and Mary Briggs' oldest son Ernest (1881-1947) was born the year after their marriage and went on to win the DSO in World War I, while a much younger son Raymond (1895-1985) fought in both world wars and was awarded the DSO in World War II. The former commanded the Royal Engineers 48th Division and was breveted a Lieutenant-Colonel while the latter was ultimately a Major-General in the Royal Tank Corps. Both have entries in 'Who Was Who?', Ernest listing his school as Merchant Taylors', Crosby, the same as that attended by CR Fay of Courtenay Road between 1895 and 1902. Although not exact contemporaries, Ernest Briggs and Fay overlapped for three years. Another brother Wilfred Briggs (1883-1944) also attended Merchant Taylors', Crosby but the much younger Raymond did not. Intriguingly, when Ernest was admitted to the school in 1891 he gave his address as that of the soap factory in Blackstock Street, perhaps because the family had not yet found a permanent home in the area. His school record also shows that he would be chairman of Lever Bros between 1939 and 1946[290] though this is not mentioned in his 'Who Was Who?' entry, the latter only referring to a company in Dagenham.

As a leading soapmaker in the north of England, Tyson, Richmond and Jones were represented by Briggs on the Northern Soapmakers Association that met every couple of months, with Gossages, Joseph Watson, Crosfield's and Lever Bros among the other companies that attended, more than a dozen in all. Many of the discussions were about sharing and aligning prices - exchanges that would be forbidden today if they represented a manufacturers' ring or cartel that reduced competition. As striking, though, is the seniority of the representatives for it was Lever himself who attended, as did three directors and a manager from Gossages, and AH Crosfield and Robert F Jones, both Directors of Crosfield's and at this time joint Honorary Secretaries of the Association as well.[291] Crosfield would become chairman of the company on his father's death, while Robert Jones, the man who lived in Courtenay Road, had joined the Board at the beginning of 1900 as the director responsible for exports. Jones had previously been manager of another Liverpool soap firm (DC Keeling) and had been retained in that position after Crosfield bought them in March 1897.[292] By 1911 he was also a director of Gossages.[293]

As one of the most aggressive, as well as the most successful and far-sighted, businessmen of his day, and perhaps prompted by the combinations being formed in other industries at the end of the nineteenth century,[294] William Hesketh Lever (1851-1925) may have been thinking of the rationale for a soap combine as early as 1901 and the additional market strength it would be able to offer. Lever Bros was already a very wealthy company, having built on the Sunlight soap brand to expand the firm and give it a remarkable base at Port Sunlight. The next challenge would be to bring other manufacturers under the same management. As the official History of Unilever puts it,

> Several smaller firms ... indicated their desire to join the combine [in 1906], among them Tyson, Richmond and Jones of Liverpool ... Lever welcomed them as proof of his contention that the combine was not merely a strategy for major powers.[295]

There is some dispute, however, as to whether Tyson's was acquired in 1906, as the *Times* reported that October, or not until 1910 as was asserted in a book 'Competition and Monopoly in the British Soap Industry' published more than fifty years later.[296] The latter dates the acquisitions of Barrington's of Dublin and Cook's to the same year and Hazlehurst's to 1911, whereas a Unilever pamphlet on the formation of the company agrees on Cook's being 1910 but pushes Barrington's and Hazlehurst's back to 1911 and 1912 respectively.[297] The latter does not mention Tyson's at all and although it ought to be the more definitive source, one of the difficulties is that the soap combine had an uneasy birth, with the 1906 attempt being abandoned after several firms were scared off by Northcliffe's *Daily Mail* that feared the loss of advertising revenue. Lever Bros sued Northcliffe's papers for libel in 1907 and received £141,000 damages (more than £11m today).[298] There was another legal dispute in 1908 over the use of a brand name by Gossages that applied to Hudson's Soap, taken over by Lever Bros in 1908. The latter were again successful but one by-product was an April 1910 letter from several soap companies refuting one from Lever the previous month referring back to a November 1906 meeting agreeing to dissolve the combine.[299]

Some soap companies were acquired by Lever Bros in 1906 and it appears from other evidence that one of these was indeed Tyson, Richmond and Jones.[300] On the face of it, Briggs was a successful businessman himself, and certainly seemed to be so having subscribed the substantial sum of £50 to the Liverpool appeal for Queen Victoria's Diamond Jubilee in 1897,[301] but was clearly not averse to the overtures made to him by Joseph Watson, the middle man for Lever. Being taken over by Lever Bros would have offered security as well as financial reward, but as the negotiations developed it became clear that it would also offer Briggs a reprieve from the financial obligations incurred in keeping the Tyson company going. By mid-September 1906 Briggs had agreed

> Subject to the verification of figures given, and an agreement to be made, I on behalf of Messrs Tyson, Richmond & Jones, agree to amalgamate our Business with the new Combination, and to take for the purchase of same ...[302]

A week later Briggs provided the company balance sheet Watson had requested and Lever was now directly involved himself, meeting with Briggs initially on 26th September. However, Watson was taken aback by a loan from the Bank to Tyson's of £15,000 (almost £1.2m today), writing the following day "What is this for; you did not mention to me that you were owing anything like this. Have [the Bank] any security for same?" Briggs claimed that this was no different to information he had provided previously and, although the Bank "hold title deeds of land, etc. as security for money advanced, ... what difference this can make I cannot see as it will be part of the purchase money". Nevertheless, the company's overall liabilities exceeded £34,000 and Briggs must have decided it was in his interests to talk directly to Lever for he quickly arranged to see him on 29th September when he hoped "to be able to explain [the] Bank's advance to his satisfaction". Whether he did convince Lever is uncertain, and in any case Lever may have judged it a risk worth taking in the pursuit of his overall strategic aims, but whichever explanation is more accurate Tyson, Richmond and Jones became one of the first soap companies acquired by Lever Bros.

Palatine Engineering
Originally called the Waste Water Meter Co., Palatine Engineering focussed at first on inventions by George Deacon (1843-1909), joint borough and water engineer for Liverpool from 1871 until he concentrated on water from 1880.[303] In 1891 the company advertised in both Birmingham and Sheffield newspapers for "a man accustomed to making metal patterns for [stop]cocks; [and] none but first class men" were to apply to the Blackstock Street address with references and wages required.[304] That it was worth the company's while to advertise as far afield as this indicates the specialist nature of some of the manufacturing skills required, and in 1892 the *Sheffield and Rotherham Independent* was used again on three occasions to seek appropriate staff for their "Brass Cock Trade": in May for both "a Female COREMAKER, to take charge of Coreroom" and "BUFFER MOULDER and COREMAKER (female preferred), accustomed to the trade", and in December for "a few BRASS FINISHERS and IMPROVERS, accustomed to the screw down work, at once".[305]

Southampton Town Council were one of many authorities that had used their products previously and soon agreed a tender for the supply of four waste water meters at £153.[306]

Water metering remained at the heart of their business, and in 1893 they were able to refer to their work for 146 towns, and for government departments, that had saved huge amounts of water by helping to detect leaks and obviate the need for alternative sources. Not only were they very active as both manufacturer and consultant, but they must also have been one of the earliest adopters of advertising to promote their overall expertise as well as individual products.

> **THE SCARCITY OF WATER IN DUBLIN.**
>
> **THE DEACON METER SYSTEM,**
> The invention of
> **MR. G. F. DEACON, C.E.,**
> the Water Engineer of Liverpool, for detecting hidden and underground leaks, is at work in 146 towns in Great Britain and Ireland, and is adopted by the War Office and the Admiralty.
>
> The average saving, without restriction to the inhabitants, exceeds 10 gallons per head per day, and by its means constant service of water is rapidly restored. This has been effected in the case of upwards of a million and a half of people in London alone.
>
> This system can be applied to any water supplies without difficulty, the capital outlay being very small, and infinitely less than that required for a new water supply, which in many cases has been thereby rendered unnecessary.
>
> For full particulars apply to
>
> **PALATINE ENGINEERING CO.**
> (LIMITED),
> **10 BLACKSTOCK STREET,**
> **LIVERPOOL.**
>
> p7787

Freeman's Journal and Daily Commercial Advertiser
4th and 9th November 1893

Adverts for "Sir William Thomson's patent indestructible water taps", for which the company was the sole maker, appeared in *The Graphic* at least monthly and often fortnightly, as well as in other newspapers (e.g., the *Standard* which did not include illustrations).[307] The appeal was two-fold, Thomson having been President of the Royal Society (as well as a friend of Deacon and becoming Lord Kelvin from 1892) and the taps supposedly indestructible, having been used thirty times a day for fifty years under water pressure without deterioration. The adverts included a cutaway diagram of the tap to emphasise its solidity and reliability.

William Thomson (1824-1907) had become Professor of Natural Philosophy at Glasgow University in 1847 aged 22, and he remained closely identified with Glasgow as Baron Kelvin, but he also had Liverpool connections. Over Christmas 1884, for example, he stayed at Knowsley and on Christmas Day his walk with the 15th Earl of Derby was noted in the latter's diary.[308] He was Derby's guest again the following Christmas when they "discussed the origins of the solar system".[309]

Meanwhile, Palatine Engineering's gas engines were first advertised in the *Liverpool Mercury* in 1891, the attraction for the purchaser being that the engines comprised "many new improvements of high speed, great economy and power, giving off between three to six available horsepower".[310] This differentiated advertising strategy underlines that straightforward products (such as taps) were available on a national basis while the trial gas engines were confined to Liverpool initially. As further evidence of this, the company had sent out two consignments of water taps to a London address that were intercepted by a swindler and sold on. He appeared in the Liverpool police court in January 1892 and was sent to prison for three months at the next City sessions.[311]

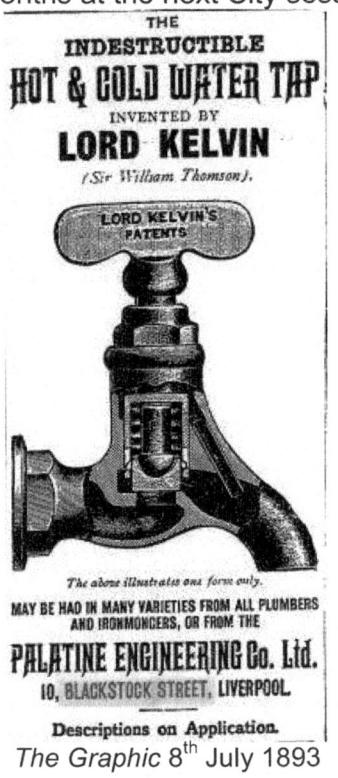

The Graphic 8th July 1893

The managing director of Palatine Engineering, sharing his name with Liverpool's then Medical Officer of Health, was William Hope. In 1894, when Deacon's patents for water meters had long since expired, Hope became aware that the Acme Engineering Co of Liverpool run by a former Palatine foreman were offering to make them for public authorities. He fired off a letter to one such, the Londonderry Corporation, warning them that Palatine had paid several thousand pounds for the Deacon patents and they should beware of "formerly somewhat unsatisfactory employees, [who] have not hitherto made a single meter". Acme's owners took him to court for libel and even before they finished presenting their case Hope settled, apologising if his letter had been interpreted as questioning his former employee's competence. He undertook not to write anything like it again.[312]

By 1897 the company had branched out into making bicycles as well, displaying some of them at the St George's Hall cycle show that January.[313] The *Liverpool Mercury* judged these "ingenious novelties which merit notice";[314] so ingenious that their London agent was sentenced to twenty months hard labour for illegally pawning one.[315] Also in 1897 Palatine employees raised two guineas for the Indian Famine Fund[316] and later Hope and Palatine's Superintending Engineer were both cited along with Lord Kelvin in a 1906 US patent for a liquid meter.[317]

There were 85 newspaper reports about the company in the first decade of the twentieth century, often about Irish authorities that had employed Palatine's meters to curb their losses on water that was literally running away. The company survived to 1980, latterly in Bootle.

Irving, Son and Jones
In contrast to the innovative and diversified strategies of Palatine Engineering, the millers Irving, Son & Jones continued the chequered existence that had been evident since the earliest reports in the 1850s. That they were in a much more traditional and less creative industry may explain, even if it does not justify, their hide-bound approach, and it is perhaps instructive that Irving, Son & Jones seem never to have advertised their products. However, this might mean only that their markets were assured, a supposition supported by the fact that Thomas Robinson Irving, who had run the company for fifty years, left £124,864 (the equivalent of £10m today) when he died in 1895. A few of the staff may have been skilled, but the vast majority were not and so local recruitment would usually suffice.

Energised by the 1889 dock strikes, and the resulting drive to set up unions,[318] the Millers National Union was one of those formed that year.[319] Two years later the company's millers were on strike:

> MILLERS! MILLERS!! MILLERS!!! – Wanted, MILLERS and MILLHANDS to KEEP AWAY from BLACKSTOCK STREET MILLS – All hands on STRIKE. Signed on behalf of the Committee, No. 4 Branch, J BRAZIER, General Secretary, Millers National Union, Oddfellows Hall, Liverpool[320]

That this referred to the Irving, Son & Jones mill was confirmed by a further report less than two weeks later:

> ... the work people of Messrs Irving, Son & Jones, rice millers, Blackstock Street, are still out on strike, that firm not having made the concession of two hours per week asked. The branch was visited by ... the [Union] general secretary ..., who exhorted the men to conduct the strike in a peaceable and orderly manner, and considered their claim so just and righteous that he had no doubt in the end success would crown their efforts, and that financial assistance would cheerfully be granted to the men on strike.[321]

It is not known whether the Union did provide any strike pay but it can be assumed that the workers' demands were not met. The following April a Permanent Board of Reconciliation was set up in Liverpool with the Mayor's agreement in an attempt to resolve employment disputes before they became strikes.[322]

Irving, Son and Jones continued to be dogged by events. In 1892 their stables were put up for sale[323] and in 1894 there was another fire, though on this occasion one easily put out.[324] The firm carried on through Irving's death, his partner William H Jones announcing that

> My late partner, Mr Thomas Robinson Irving, having recently died I beg to inform you that I have taken into partnership my two sons, Mr Arthur Percy Jones and Mr Frederick William Jones, who for the past 13 years have been in business here on their own account as Jones Bros., rice brokers, and with their assistance I shall continue the business with which I have been connected for the past 50 years under the style as heretofore of Irving, Son and Jones.[325]

They were acquired by the Manhu Food Company in 1900.[326]

E&W Pearson

Seed crushing to extract oil is one of the oldest industries and there were many oil mills in Liverpool in the late nineteenth century.[327] Pearson Brothers of Gainsborough in Lincolnshire sent one of the partners William Pearson to set up in Liverpool in 1872, renting the Egyptian Mill on Vauxhall Road initially and buying it himself in 1880. In between Pearson Brothers built a mill in Blackstock Street in 1876. William Pearson died in 1895 but the East India Mill, as Brace calls it,[328] had been enlarged that year and his brother Edward Pearson retained it. Pearson Brothers was one of the seventeen firms that combined to form British Oil and Cake Mills (BOCM) in 1899 and Edward Pearson one of their eleven Directors.[329] The mill itself was burnt to the ground in 1916 and not replaced.

Combinations were increasingly popular at the end of the nineteenth century as a way of reducing competition between firms, increasing their profits, assuring supplies and dominating the market. GKN (Guest, Keen and Nettlefold), Brunner-Mond and Imperial Tobacco remain among the best known today,[330] while BOCM, with twenty-eight mills and twelve refineries across the seventeen firms, accounted for 60% of the seed crushing market.[331] In an industry dependent on the vagaries of supply, and ultimately the weather, combinations could also provide a smoothing effect, not least through increased diversification that it would be difficult for smaller companies to achieve on their own. A 1908 analysis demonstrates the fluctuating nature of the business with net profits ranging from £33,000 in 1905 when raw material prices were high to £91,000 in 1900, with no dividends being paid in 1901 (when the Russian linseed crop failed) and 1905.[332] Ultimately BOCM was taken over by Lever Bros in 1925 for not only did they produce oil for margarine manufacture, but had begun soap-making themselves after the 1920 slump with their 'New Pin' brand a direct challenge to Lever's.[333]

Liverpool Vesta Cake Company

As the BOCM name suggests, one by-product of seed crushing, first stumbled on by accident but increasingly profitable, is the production of cattle cake.[334] According to Brace, the Liverpool Vesta Cake Co. was established in 1895 on Blackstock Street,[335] but it was already one of the leading exhibitors of stock food at the Royal Agricultural Show that June[336] and was awarding prizes at a Cheshire agricultural show in December for the best pair of beasts fed on their cake.[337] The company did advertise in the newspapers very occasionally, but clearly thought exhibiting their products at agricultural shows and donating prizes for stock fed on their cake were the best ways of reaching their market. At the Birmingham show in December 1900, for example, they showed samples of cake, meal and lamb food.[338]

Although the company may have secured some of its supplies from Pearson's, this is not known for certain and in any case this arrangement was unlikely to be exclusive or last throughout the life of the mill for in 1909 the Liverpool Vesta Cake

Co. acquired the International Seed Crushing Co based just off Vauxhall Road, selling the plant fifteen years later.[339]

Liverpool Saccharine Company
Alexander Manbré followed his father into the sugar trade starting the Liverpool Saccharine Company in 1870, subsequently bringing in his brother Alfred and Francis Darbyshire as partners. In 1919 the London factory of Manbré père was bought by Albert Berry to form Manbré Sugar and Malt Ltd. which in turn added the Liverpool Saccharine Company in 1921. With three other acquisitions (two in Liverpool and one in Greenock), this then joined with another company to form Manbré and Garton Ltd in 1926.[340]

Although they started more modestly (see the 1878 adverts referred to earlier), the Liverpool Saccharine Company was to specialise in producing sugars for the brewing industry, one of only four Liverpool firms to do so.[341] In 1908 they produced 20,000 quarters of flaked maize and rice for brewing purposes (over 5% of the total nationwide), the same year they entered into an agreement with seven other companies to determine minimum prices and production quotas.[342] The agreement was initially for three years but was subsequently extended for another three in order to avoid the "disastrous competition" that had been evident previously.

In addition to the 1880 fire already referred to, the company was fined for smoke nuisance in June and August 1882[343] and in 1885 an explosion in the warehouse blew the roof off and badly burned one of the workers who had to be taken to hospital.[344] It took more than an hour to bring the fire under control. One of the few positives at this time, the annual works outing to Chester, had been reported in 1884,[345] but most of the other nineteenth century newspaper reports refer to a clerk who, dismissed by the company after fifteen years' service, altered a cheque for a little over £4 to £5000 and was detained when he tried to present it at the bank. He had been drinking heavily for some weeks before, could not remember anything and was detained at Her Majesty's pleasure.[346] Later that year the Liverpool coroner recorded a verdict of accidental death on an employee who had tried to oil machinery driving charcoal elevators while it was in operation. His clothes had become entangled in the flywheel and he received fatal injuries when his head struck the ceiling.[347]

In 1900 there was an epidemic of arsenical poisoning affecting more than 3000 people (largely in Manchester and Salford) that had resulted from drinking beer contaminated by sugars supplied by a company called Bostock's. This was due to the use of impure sulphuric acid in their manufacture and all the beer using their sugars was destroyed. The expert committee set up by the Manchester Brewers' Central Association concluded in December 1900 that "All the other brewing sugars on the English market have been analysed, and have been found to be quite free from arsenic".[348] Manbré had given evidence to the coroner about one death in Liverpool, pointing out that sulphuric acid was necessary to the manufacture of saccharine but it would be free of arsenic unless made from pyrites. He concluded that this must have been what happened with the Bostock's sugars but only once had he suspected it in the case of the Liverpool Saccharine Company and that had been in 1890.[349] Concerned that it might not only be beer that was affected, the Government set up a Royal Commission under Lord Kelvin which took evidence between 1901 and 1903 and reported finally at the end of that year.[350] They too gave the company a clean bill of health for, as one newspaper reported of their hearing in April 1902, their "invert sugar ... could not have been contaminated with arsenic".[351]

The other three factories in Blackstock Street (the soap factory Gossages, the wood importers RG Tickle & Son and the Smyth Bros tannery) are not covered further here because:
- The main office of Gossages was in Widnes and the factory at no. 8 Blackstock Street did not operate independently of it. It was the overall Gossages company of which Robert F Jones had become a Director.
- RG Tickle & Son had moved to Blackstock Street premises in 1882 and it has not proved possible to find further information about the company.
- Smyth Bros have been referred to in Chapter 2 above. They were confined to four leather trades at the end of the nineteenth century: as leather factors buying and selling on behalf of others, as well as leather merchants in their own right; tanning both cattle hides and sheep skins, and dressing and colouring leather after tanning (curriers) to produce strap butts (suitable for making belts and straps).[352] There is no further information about them.

5. THE PEOPLE WHO LIVED IN BLACKSTOCK STREET IN 1900

A contemporary observer James Samuelson used almost exactly the same words in at least two of his books to describe the miserable slums that existed at the start of the twentieth century just north of Liverpool city centre.[353] This was in an area half a mile north-east of Blackstock Street where Great Homer Street, running parallel to Scotland Road to the east of Blackstock Street, met Virgil Street. As Samuelson put it, "the squalor is not redeemed by [the streets] having been honoured with the names of some of the world's greatest poets". Dryden Street and Iliad Street, both of which still exist, were just as bad, though others have been pulled down as roads were widened and housing renewed. Samuelson continued:

> When we have sufficiently studied the aspects of modern life in the street, we visit one of the dwellings. We go not up but down the steps of one and enter a cellar dwelling, of which there are still vast numbers to be found in some of our large towns, notwithstanding the reforming activities of the local authorities ... Here we find ourselves once more in the midst of social wreckage. ... one is repelled by the foul atmosphere, nor is this to be wondered at when the contents are considered. The cellar is about ten feet by fourteen ... and is lighted by a small window looking on to the area. Against that stands a sewing machine, with some unfinished work; in this instance a coarse, holland apron. Besides this, there is a couple of chairs and against the wall on the far side of the hearth is a dilapidated bedstead, with poor, disarranged coverings. The foot of the bed touches the table, so that there is hardly room to pass between them. A few tiny pictures, in discoloured frames, and a crucifix, serve as ornaments over the mantelpiece ... In this single apartment there lives (if it can be called living) a family of five ...

Perhaps in an attempt to bring some colour to these dismal surroundings, to ameliorate them even if they could not counter them entirely, window garden organisations developed in several large towns during the nineteenth century to support people who were trying to make the best of it. Liverpool was no exception and in both 1890 and 1892, for example, the local newspaper printed lengthy lists of those who had won prizes or been commended in the Liverpool Window Garden Association's annual competitions. On both occasions Mrs Martha Oldham in court 1 of Blackstock

Street was a prizewinner for her window of plants, and on the second a Mrs Aldams (almost certainly the same person) won a prize for a single plant as well.[354] If these were all grown in situ, this was some achievement.

Maps of Blackstock Street at the start of the twentieth century show five or six courts, but only two of them were included in the 1901 and 1911 Censuses. These were the four houses in court 1, and the eight in court 3, both between houses 7 and 9 on the north side of the street. House no. 9 had itself been empty in 1891,[355] but the house was then enumerated as such whereas the later Censuses do not mention the other courts at all. Perhaps they did not exist or perhaps the enumerator missed them? The Liber Status Animarum, or annual Lenten Returns, compiled by every Roman Catholic parish might have clarified this, except that while the summaries still exist in the Liverpool Metropolitan Cathedral Archdiocesan archives the detailed records for areas covered by St Anthony's parish no longer do.[356] The register of parliamentary and municipal electors 1899-1900 identifies people in courts 1 and 3, as did the Census, but not in any others. It can be assumed, therefore, that even though maps show other courts they were empty by this time.

Carters

There were 5000 carters in Liverpool in 1890[357] and one of the striking features of Blackstock Street is that nine carters lived there in 1901. Five of them in the twelve court houses counted in the Census: Arthur Mayne, Albert Rusling (or Rustling in the register of parliamentary and municipal electors 1899-1900) and Edward Knott in three of the four houses in court 1, Thomas Buckhurst and Samuel Hartley in court 3. Four others lived in houses 5, 7 and 13: William Oldham and his son, also called William, at no. 5, James Brannon at no. 7, and the younger Thomas Culshaw at no. 13. Three of them had been born in Epworth, Lincolnshire (Rusling and the two Oldhams) and the other six in Lancashire. At least six of them, and possibly all, worked for Liverpool Corporation, which had stables nearby in Gascoyne Street on the other side of Vauxhall Road and a City Engineer's depot in Oriel Street, two streets south of Blackstock Street and virtually opposite the Corporation stables.[358] Living near to the stables at which you were based would be a necessity given the long hours of work. As late as 1913 the Union was demanding that 6am should be the starting time at the stable (rather than 5.15am twenty years before), "in gears" from 7am to 6pm Monday to Friday and back in the stable by 7pm. They were also seeking specified overtime rates outside these hours with a 2pm finish on Saturdays.[359]

Nor was the pay very good. In 1890 the Union had sought 29s per week for those who drove teams (26s per week for those driving a single horse) and, while they reported that thirty employers soon paid these rates, the majority of carriers did not.[360] In 1900 235 carters appealed for relief, more than 1 in 20 of the total who did so.[361]

In 1881 and 1891 Martha Oldham the Liverpool Garden Association prizewinner lived in house 2 in court 1 with her husband John, another carter born in Epworth (so almost certainly an Oldham relative), but by 1901 the family had moved to 132 Vauxhall Road to be replaced by the Mayne family.

If it might be thought obvious why Blackstock Street was a handy location for a Corporation carter, only bettered by Paul Street in which the William Oldhams had lived in 1891, it is less apparent why four of them should have migrated across the country from Lincolnshire. John Oldham, the oldest by three years, had been born in 1840/1 and at some point in his twenties had moved to Liverpool; William Oldham, born in 1843/4, first figures in a Census return in 1891, by which time he was already in Liverpool; Albert Rusling, then only twenty-one, was still living with his mother, father and siblings in Epworth. His father Henry, like many others in Epworth, farmed a small-holding which would eventually be handed on to Albert's older brother, so Albert himself had to find another way of making a living and carting might be an obvious alternative for a farmer's son. But why Liverpool, a move that he most probably made before meeting his wife Sarah and having their children there? While it might have had something to do with William Pearson's move from Gainsborough near Epworth, this had happened at least twenty years earlier in the 1870s. Perhaps for this reason though, and because of the moves there by John Oldham in the 1860s, and by William Oldham more recently, he was aware of Liverpool and the likelihood of work there, better than in many urban areas and a decided improvement on seasonal work in the countryside.

Which in turn raises the question of what had attracted the Oldhams to Liverpool for John had moved there even before William Pearson left Gainsborough to start his oil mills in the city.

Table 3 on the following pages sets out a summary of the Blackstock Street residents in the three Censuses between 1891 and 1911 and those listed in the 1899-1900 register of voters.

Several conclusions are immediately apparent. That court 3 appears to be empty in 1891 is due solely to clarifying which of the four courts enumerated in that Census (1, 11, 13 and 15) is this one - if any. This task is made more difficult by properties being listed in a different order and contemporary maps indicating there should be at least five anyway. Excluded from Table 3 are the courts enumerated in 1891 but not subsequently. Furthermore, only heads of household are included in the register of voters (therefore excluding partners, children who might be thought old enough to vote and lodgers) and nobody is registered at seven of the eight houses between nos. 15 and 53. In addition, people may have remained in the same street but they often moved between properties: for example, Charles Dell was registered to vote at house 7 in court 3 but by the time of the 1901 Census lodged with David Tait in house 3; Catherine Kerr started in house 5 in 1891 but was in house 13 at the time of both the register of voters and the 1901 Census. In some cases properties appear to have been occupied by relatives: Andrew Quigley registered at house 1 in court 3, but James Quigley in house 51 in the 1901 Census.

The seven households considered in more detail below are those of Harriet Caldwell, Ambrose and Mary True, Catherine Kerr, Samuel and Sarah Hartley, James and Mary Carroll, John and Elizabeth Goulburn, and the McDonalds. They have been chosen to reflect a mix of circumstances: not every household was headed by a woman but every household comprised adult women; Catherine Kerr had lodgers in both 1891 and 1901 (as did several others), but she was the only one who otherwise lived alone; all the other households included families; the Caldwell, True and Hartley families lived in courts at some point; the McDonalds lived in a house that went with his employment.

	House No.	1891	Census 1901	1911	Register of parliamentary and municipal voters 1899-1900
Court 1	1	Briggs	Radford	Toale	Hughes
	3	Scott	Tait/Dell	Bebb	Knott
	5	Kerr/Price	W Oldham/Caldwell	Ward	W Oldham
	7	Hogan	Dobson/Brannon	Hughes	Dobson
	1	Pecro	Brown	Caldwell	Mayne
	2	J Oldham	Mayne	Collins	J Oldham
	3	Fairbrother	Rusling	Corbitt	Rustling [sic]
	4	Hayes	Knott	Smith	Jordan
Court 3	1		Wales	Brookes	Quigley
	2		Kenny/Black	Sinnott	Kenny
	3		Young/Donnelly	True	Chambers
	4		True/Smith	Melia	Garrity
	5		Culshaw/Buckhurst	Fitzpatrick	Culshaw
	6		Young	Tracy	Holohan
	7		empty	empty	Dell
	8		Hartley	Hartley	Hartley
	9	empty	Carroll	Carroll	Carroll
	11	Sweetman	Goulburn	Goulburn	Goulburn
	13	Jones	Kerr/Culshaw	Rodwell	Kerr

House No.	Census 1891	Census 1901	Census 1911	Register of parliamentary and municipal voters 1899-1900
15	Goodwin	empty		
17		empty		
29*		Lanyon	Wilson	
35**	Roberts/ Reynolds/ Corrigan	Roberts	Beggs	
45***	Parkinson	McDonald	McDonald	
49	Hendrick	Bulger	empty	
51	Feeney	Quigley	Hesketh	Bulger
53	empty	Deegan	empty	

Table 3: Residents summary for Blackstock Street 1891-1911

The register of voters would have been compiled earlier than 1899/1900 and also included business people in Blackstock Street who had votes both in this constituency and that covering their home address. The latter are not listed in the table.

Key
* linked to tannery; ** linked to timber yard; *** linked to oil mill
in 1901 Census and other years

Blackstock Street in 1900: The people who lived there

Harriet Caldwell

In 1891 William Oldham and his wife Alice lived at 20 Paul Street with their fourteen year old daughter Harriet, their two sons William and Thomas (then aged eleven and four respectively) and three lodgers, William Glinn a dock labourer, his wife Ann and their son. Both Ann Glinn and Harriet described themselves as charwomen, though Harriet then cleaned offices as well.

By 1901 William Oldham and family had moved to 5 Blackstock Street, with son William, now 21 and also a carter like his father, fourteen year old Thomas a labourer, and another daughter Mary aged seven. Also sharing the house was their oldest child Harriet, now Harriet Caldwell aged 24, and her three children under five (William, Alice and Joseph), though not her husband who may have been elsewhere on Census day or perhaps Harriet had left him to move back in with her parents. In either case she was no longer working so must have been dependent on someone else, perhaps her father.

Already aged 57 in 1901, by 1911 William Oldham was in the Liverpool workhouse with more than 2000 other inmates. He may have been admitted because of age or infirmity, or perhaps because he had fallen on hard times, but prior to entering the workhouse he had already ceased to be a carter, becoming a labourer for the Corporation instead. It is conceivable that this was a compassionate move by the Corporation to keep him in work for as long as possible once he was no longer capable of carting.

His daughter Harriet Caldwell was the only member of the family still in Blackstock Street in 1911, now living at house 1 in court 1 with four children, a son Peter as well as the three from ten years earlier. To Harriet's credit all four were in school, even though the oldest boy William at fourteen could have been sent out to work as Harriet herself had been at the same age. The house was shared with two married boarders, John and Jane Young, both in their sixties and he at 69 older than Harriet's father. John Young described himself as a disabled carter, so may have worked alongside the Oldhams previously and must have had more resources than Harriet's father to keep him out of the workhouse. Harriet was clearly unable to offer her father a place, perhaps because she could not afford to do so, chose not to or both. Still only thirty-four, Harriet had gone back to working as a charwoman and it was her income from this and from the boarders that was sustaining the family for Mr Caldwell had now completely disappeared, leaving Harriet to describe herself as a "deserted wife". This desertion may have happened relatively recently as Harriet said the marriage had lasted fourteen years (the age of her oldest child then), though she may have been putting the best gloss on her husband's absence.

It would be interesting to know how many people Harriet charred for and where. It can be assumed, however, that the tasks involved more than cleaning; indeed, as the daily help she would have undertaken whatever jobs were required of her. These would often be the heavier duties that an employer might not wish a live-in servant to perform or in order to economise.[362] Some broad information is available from the autobiography of Betty Dobbs,[363] a charwoman in London at much the same time, but she had been abandoned by her parents and started working as a char on her twelfth birthday. The bleakness of her situation may well have exceeded even Harriet's.

Little is known of the four Caldwell children, which is positive in the sense that they avoided the scrutiny they would have received from the newspapers if the circumstances of their lives or deaths had been sufficiently scurrilous. The only exception to this absence from the public record is the middle son Joseph who was a fireman (stoker) in a series of short-term assignments for the Royal Naval Volunteer Reserve (RNVR) for a year from April 1919 to February 1920. Born in June 1900 he was old enough to have been conscripted during the tail-end of WWI but, like his older brother William, seems to have escaped this. Harriet's children have slipped from public notice, therefore, which may mean that even if their lives were not always peaceful or fulfilled they were at least averagely blameless.

Ambrose and Mary True

Ambrose True sounds as if he might be a solid and dependable agricultural labourer in a Thomas Hardy novel, or at a pinch a rustic character in a book by George Eliot or Wilkie Collins, but this Ambrose had grown up in Brook Street, half a mile south-west of Blackstock Street on the other side of Exchange station and joining the dock road. Immediately opposite this end of Brook Street was Prince's Dock and in later years the overhead railway that ran from one end of the dock estate to the other. Ambrose's father was a seaman and never seems to have been at home on Census night, indeed perhaps rarely was. In 1881 aged five Ambrose lived in house 13 in court 3 with his mother Amelia, two sisters and a

Blackstock Street in 1900: The people who lived there

brother. Two doors down in Brook Street's court 17 lived his maternal grandmother Marie Hunter, an office cleaner, her son Arthur Smith from a previous marriage and two sons and a daughter from her second marriage to Andrew Hunter. Ten years earlier Andrew and Marie Hunter had been at no. 11 Brook Street with her four Smith children, aged between eighteen and ten, and their first two children aged three and one. (They went on to have another two.) The oldest of the Smith children was Ambrose's mother Amelia who, even if she had not always lived in Brook Street, must have done so for much of her life. It may be supposed that she met her husband, the seaman Edmund Bishop True, virtually on her own doorstep or at least within a few yards of where she lived. They married on 1st January 1872 and their oldest child, Ambrose's sister Susannah, was born two years before him in 1873. Amelia's brother Arthur Smith and her step-father Andrew Hunter were both carters and they may have obtained much of their work at the docks too, with Brook Street an ideal location between this and the stations.

In 1891 Ambrose and his surviving four siblings were living with their Smith/Hunter grandmother, still in Brook Street though at a different house. Their uncle Arthur Smith lived there too, as did her three Hunter children who were their step-uncles and step-aunt. The three men were carters, while Ambrose's grandmother, step-aunt and sister Susannah were charwomen, and he was in his first job as an office boy. Neither Andrew Hunter nor his mother Amelia, let alone his father, were there.

Ambrose's early years were therefore characterised by a number of moves from house to house, all within Brook Street, but perhaps more significantly by a number of household changes as the family formed and re-formed across the generations. It is difficult to judge more than a hundred years later what the impact of this would be for it might be argued that, while the surface impression was of change and chaos, there was also a degree of stability that may have been the key factor for Ambrose, the ballast to which he could cling as other events swirled around him. It is easy to conclude from a twenty-first century western and middle-class perspective that the fracturing was unlikely to be beneficial, but in reality many lives were and are like this without any negative effects being automatic. At the time circumstances may have made it more of a norm.

By 1901 Ambrose lived with his wife Mary, both in their early twenties, at house 4 in court 3 in Blackstock Street with their two small children Edmund Bishop True aged two and their baby daughter Mary. All had been born in Liverpool, as had Susan Smith aged 67 a widow and charwoman who lived with them. Ambrose had become a labourer in an oil refinery, possibly Pearson's, though his entry in the 1911 Census describes him working in a palm oil refinery. By then the family had moved to house 3 next door, so moving house remained a feature of his adult years too, but perhaps to counter the paternal absence and household changes he had experienced as a child, he remained present for his own children. He and Mary now had another three boys and a girl, so with six children overall and still occupying three rooms, there was no longer space for a lodger.

Ambrose and Mary True's oldest son, named after Ambrose's father Edmund Bishop True, was a Royal Navy stoker in the cruiser HMS Hampshire when it sank off Orkney on 5th June 1916. This was unrelated to the Battle of Jutland fought the week before, when HMS Hampshire had come through unscathed, ramming and sinking a German submarine, for on 5th June the cruiser was taking the Secretary of State for War, Field Marshal Lord Kitchener,[364] to Russia. Asked to postpone the trip for twenty-four hours so that the route could be swept for mines, Kitchener refused, and the abysmal weather meant that HMS Hampshire soon outpaced its escort of two destroyers that, unable to keep up, turned back to Scapa Flow.[365] HMS Hampshire was therefore entirely alone when at about 7.45pm it hit a mine or mines.

> Down in the engine room men were trapped. Some of the stokers on duty on the port side were badly burned and the fumes of high explosive penetrated into the stokers' mess deck. A few struggled unavailingly to escape from the suffocating, acrid smoke, but in the darkness they had little hope of finding an exit from the charnel house which the forepart of the engine room had become.[366]

Recent estimates calculate that more than 700 men died,[367] most drowning in the rough seas, though surprisingly at least two stokers survived (Alfred Read and Walter Farnden), both of whom testified at the Admiralty inquiry.[368] Edmund True was not so fortunate.

On the first anniversary of the tragedy the True family placed the following notice in the 'Roll of Honour' section of the *Liverpool Daily Post*:

> True - In sad but loving memory of our dear son, Edmund B True (1st class stoker), who lost his life on HMS Hampshire, aged 17

years. (Gone, but not forgotten. Sadly missed by Mother, Father, Brothers and Sisters.)[369]

This is an exception to the conclusion above that people in Blackstock Street did not make pronouncements about their lives in the press. It naturally reflects the depth of the family's anguish, but they would hardly be alone in that in these years. What it might demonstrate is that families could be disrupted for all sorts of reasons that, as part of everyday life, were understandable and over time became accepted (if not acceptable). However, some events, even in war, were so unusual and unexpected that they could only be handled by exceptional means. 'Closure' is a much over-used word today, but the notice in the paper may have provided Ambrose and Mary with some comfort given how their oldest son had been torn from them.

Already struggling to come to terms with Edmund's death, but perhaps trying to look ahead for their children's sake, the family was struck by tragedy again when two months later their twelve year old son Thomas drowned in the Mersey while trying to retrieve a ball from the river near Egremont Ferry. His older brother (also called Ambrose) was prevented by onlookers from trying to rescue him and it was over an hour before his body was recovered.[370] Although as a seaman's son who grew up in the dockside community, the dangers and power of the sea must have been well known to Ambrose True, and probably to his wife Mary too, it is one thing appreciating this intellectually, even emotionally when it affects your friends and neighbours, but quite another dealing with it when it claims two of your sons, especially in these circumstances. A third of their family had been wiped out in little more than a year.

Catherine Kerr

There were about 2500 tailoresses working in Liverpool in 1890 and the year before about 300 of them had been persuaded to form the new Liverpool Tailoresses and Coatmakers Union.[371] Cowman thought the initial membership to have been about 400,[372] but whichever figure is more accurate the number was small and particularly "negligible in terms of the total number of [about 13,000] women in the clothing industry".[373] Nevertheless, joining a Union at all was a courageous act given that they would be dependent for work on masters who might be antagonised by this step. Some of the women would be employed in workshops as pieceworkers earning as little as 6s per week, "and rarely more than 10s" when 15s was considered the minimum for survival, while out-workers were paid even less, perhaps 1s 3d to 2s for a dozen shirts according to Grant.[374] Both groups were sweated labour in need of a Union to represent them and fight their corner, the out-workers more so but due to their isolation the more difficult to organise and even more easily exploited.

Coinciding with the dock strike, and following the long recession of the 1880s, many Unions had been formed in 1889.[375] It is indicative of the tailoresses' deep grievances that the following June the small membership were prepared to risk their livelihoods further, coming out on strike to demand a two-hour reduction in the working day without loss of pay, and the abolition of piecework. Grant says that the strike only won major victories by the end of the third week when it became clear to the masters that tailors in the region were supporting the women on strike and could not be persuaded to blackleg in their place.[376] But success (though not in the ending of piecework) already seemed assured after the first week of the strike and by 24th June all but forty of the masters had conceded the Union's case.[377]

Catherine Kerr was one such tailoress, then living at 5 Blackstock Street according to the 1891 Census. Born in Ireland in 1846 and claiming to be widowed, she shared this house with a labourer Joseph Price (at 41 only four years younger than herself), his 36 year old wife May and their five children, ranging in age from nineteen to three. The oldest girl was a cotton worker and the oldest son a general labourer like his father, two children were at school and the other too young to attend. The Price family were listed as a separate household so it is not clear whether they paid their rent via Catherine Kerr or simply happened to live in the same building and paid their rent separately. If the former, the rent paid by the Price family for their three rooms must have been at least as important to Catherine Kerr's budget as her earnings from work. If the latter, her two rooms suggest that she was not yet on her uppers given that many families could not afford more than one room for them all.

Curiously, however, the electoral registers for Liverpool identify her at 13 Blackstock Street as early as 1889-1890, as do those for 1894-1895 and 1899-1900. It is conceivable that she had moved to no. 5 briefly in 1891 before returning to no. 13, that she owned both houses but preferred to be registered at the latter, or alternatively that the electoral registers are incorrect. What is certain is that ten years later in 1901 the Census records her in two rooms at no. 13, with Thomas Culshaw also widowed and his three sons occupying the other two. No. 13 was therefore a smaller house, comprising four rooms rather than five, and it might be assumed that her budget remained dependent on rent as much as, or perhaps more than, tailoring. But like the Price family the Culshaws were recorded as a separate household so the same questions arise about how the rent was paid. In this instance, however, it is more likely that the rent was paid through Catherine Kerr as she continued to be on the register of electors and Culshaw never was, either at this or any other property in Liverpool. At any rate the Culshaws must have been contributing at least half the rent with the burden on Catherine Kerr correspondingly reduced.

It may be that Catherine's reasons for moving (back) to no. 13 were entirely economic, perhaps down-sizing in effect, or she may have been forced to do so if she fell behind with the rent and/or the landlord viewed the Oldham and Caldwell family as a better bet at no. 5. Equally, it may be that her relations with the Price family had become strained, whether over the rent or other matters, and a move away was the easiest solution for her. What seems not to have happened is that she took up with Thomas Culshaw, eighteen years her junior, for they were both recorded in the Census as heads of household and this would not have happened had the enumerator been aware that they formed one household between them. They may of course have misled him but there is no reason to assume so.

Like the Price family, the Culshaws had all been born in Liverpool and all but the youngest boy were working: the father as a marine stoker, his seventeen year old son also called Thomas as a carter and fifteen year old John as a message boy. Possibly Catherine minded the youngest Culshaw, ten year old William, when his father was away at sea and this may have supplemented her budget further.

What makes matters more complicated, or clearer depending on your point of view, is that the marine stoker Thomas Culshaw had himself grown up in Blackstock Street. In 1871 aged six he lived with his parents and a younger sister Ann in one of the courts (house 7 in court 5). His father was a labourer, his mother described herself as a "labourer's wife", and there were three others on Census day: their lodger David Leslie Martin, a 50 year old master mariner, an eighteen year old visitor Ann Moore a general servant, and an eight month old baby who was there "for to be buried". The dead baby was named as Andrew Shacklady, a curious surname though one that does have Lancashire roots as well as bawdy connotations, and presumably Ann Moore was his mother, though quite why she had chosen to visit the Culshaws then is not known. Ten years later in 1881 Thomas Culshaw, a labourer in an iron works, was living with his mother, his sister Ann now 13 and two much younger brothers (aged six and one). As his mother was now a charwoman, it may be that his father had died or disappeared and the family now depended on her and Thomas' earnings. It may not be too far-fetched to speculate that "charwoman" was a euphemism in her case and that her two younger boys had a different father or fathers. If this speculation has any merit, it throws an entirely different light on matters for the house they lived at was 13 Blackstock Street, the one which twenty years later in 1901 the widowed Thomas and his three sons occupied alongside Catherine Kerr.

In other words, in 1881 Thomas Culshaw aged sixteen lived at this address with his mother and siblings. By the late 1880s according to the electoral registers Catherine Kerr was there and she was still the primary occupant into the twentieth century, though by then the widowed Thomas Culshaw had returned with his three children. It is possible to say "returned" for in 1891, Thomas Culshaw aged 26 and still a labourer lived with his wife Mary Ellen and their three sons (then aged seven, five and three) in house 4, court 30 Bond Street (half a dozen streets north of Blackstock Street).

In some of these scenarios Catherine was acting on her own initiative, in others making the best of the situation she found herself in. Whether she is viewed as an independent actor or a passive responder may depend on the circumstances that led her to Blackstock Street in the first place, whether she was already, or indeed ever was, a widow, and how her situation changed thereafter.

She does not appear in the 1911 Census nor in any England ones before 1891. There is a Catherine Kerr born in 1846 in Ireland in the 1871 and 1881 Scotland returns but it cannot be established with certainty that this is her. Similarly, there is someone of the same name and age in the 1868 and 1870 records of St Pancras workhouse. However, if these were all the same people her journey would have been from Ireland to Camden by the time she was 22, to Scotland as a servant by age 25, living as a lodger elsewhere in Scotland ten years later with her husband and two sons, before pitching up on her own in Liverpool in the late 1880s. This is not impossible, but it is unlikely.

By 1911 Thomas Culshaw was boarding with another widow Mary Birch and her four children at West Derby Street in Liverpool.

Blackstock Street in 1900: The people who lived there

Mary Birch was four years younger than Culshaw at 42 and he may have deliberately co-habited with widows, though there is no evidence for this. What is not in doubt though is that the 1911 Census identifies another boarder Robert Culshaw aged 6 months. He must have been Thomas Culshaw's son, but who was the mother? The widow Birch might be the most likely, but her two unmarried daughters, Ann aged 23 and nineteen year old Louise, are also possible. Baby Robert is first described as "son" in the return before this is over-written as "boarder". This is particularly illuminating as the 1911 Census returns, unlike earlier ones, were compiled by the occupants themselves in the first instance; the enumerator would check them but only write them for the family when necessary. Intriguingly, Robert Culshaw's name follows that of the younger daughter Louise, so it may be likely that she was the mother. Probably the family compiled the return factually to begin with but then had second thoughts and substituted "boarder" instead.

Comparison of the 1901 and 1911 Census returns also throws light on the flexibility the Culshaws showed in their employment and perhaps in order to remain employed. The older Thomas (who had first worked as a labourer) had ceased to be a stoker by 1911, becoming a dock porter in the cotton trade instead. His son Thomas was still a carter in 1907 for in that year he found himself embroiled in a court case in which a Wigan butcher was seeking damages from the London and North-Western railway company for twelve frozen sheep that had been delivered "damaged, wet and dirty" that July.[378] It had been Culshaw's job to cart them from the wholesaler to the local Liverpool station but his cart had been in a collision with a dock engine and the sheep carcasses thrown to the ground. He re-loaded them and with the help of railwaymen cleaned the dirt off the wrappers. Although Culshaw had a receipt to show he had delivered them to the railway in good condition, and a Wigan railway employee confirmed that they were the same as usual when they arrived there, the carcasses were in transit for at least fifteen hours so must have been thawing at that time of year. The butcher received both damages and a contribution from the railway company towards costs. By 1911, though, and perhaps as a result of this experience and/or the opportunity to replace his father, it was the younger Thomas who had become a marine stoker. He was living elsewhere in Liverpool with his wife and two year old step-son, and would later serve in the merchant marine during the First World War.[379]

John Culshaw had moved on from his juvenile employment as a message boy to become a mason's labourer. Aged 25 in 1911, he was living with his wife and young son at Juvenal Buildings, one of the first municipal blocks built to replace court housing. In WWI he joined the Liverpool Regiment in June 1916 and the following year, either wounded or because of his previous employment, was transferred to the Labour Corps.[380] Only William Culshaw remained in Blackstock Street. Aged twenty and now a carter himself he was boarding with the Sinnott family in one of the houses in court 3.

Perhaps as well as flexibility, the Culshaws were demonstrating initiative for it may be that William took on the cart that had previously been his brother's when that brother became a stoker. In other words, the father found more stable, and possibly more regular, employment on shore and his sons Thomas and William took advantage of the openings this created sequentially for them.

Samuel and Sarah Hartley

In contrast to the frequent moves of Ambrose True in his childhood and Thomas Culshaw throughout his life, Samuel Hartley and his family demonstrate comparative stability.

Samuel Hartley, a Corporation carter born in Liverpool halfway through the nineteenth century, was on the 1899-1900 register of electors at house 8 in court 3. His wife Sarah was ten years younger than him and in the 1901 Census they lived there with their four young children Joseph (eight), Margaret (five), Thomas (three) and Sarah (one). As the oldest had been born in 1892 when the return suggests Samuel was already into his forties, it may be that this was a second marriage for both of them. He and Sarah had married the year before in 1891 and by 1911 nine children had been born, six of whom were still alive. These were the four from 1901, a third daughter Hannah (seven) and a third son William (four). One in three of their children had died during their twenty years of marriage, much of which (if not all) had been spent in the same four rooms of a Blackstock Street court.

According to these Census returns, Sarah Hartley never worked outside the home but even with nine births and six surviving children this does not mean that she did not, only that it was not recorded. In 1901 their family depended on the money that Samuel brought in and on what Sarah's father Thomas Potter who lived with them earned as a cotton porter. The two incomes combined might be enough for a meagre life in a court, but given seven mouths to feed was never going to enable them to better their accommodation. Thomas Potter was 57, only a few years older than Samuel and would have been no more than seventeen himself when his daughter Sarah was born. By 1911 it may be assumed that he had died for he no longer lived with them and it was nineteen year old Joseph who was supplementing his father's income as a cooper's labourer at an oil refinery (perhaps Pearson's).

Samuel Hartley was now a labourer himself in the manure industry. Since this cannot have been an agricultural job in the middle of Liverpool, it may mean either that he worked in the Corporation stables or perhaps was a night soil man. Indeed, either role might be an inevitable step on from his carting task in 1901. Sewerage was in its infancy and the one or two privies in each court used by all the occupants (28 people in the seven occupied houses in court 3 in 1901) would require frequent manual emptying. This occurred from time to time but not as often as required, one of the fundamental tasks of Liverpool Corporation, and indeed any local authority, for reasons of public health as much as individual decency. Even in the recently built Courtenay Road, the collection of ashpit refuse by the UDC took place each week. This was not the 1900 equivalent of today's bin collection, but of domestic sewage.[381] For example, Charles Fay wrote to the Health Committee in August 1900 suggesting the ashpit refuse be removed on Thursday nights rather than Fridays (when the road was scavenged by Council staff) so as to prevent waste paper, etc. being blown about. Fay did not have to be more explicit for "waste paper" carried both meanings and the Health Committee was alert to the implications. The UDC surveyor instructed the Contractor accordingly.[382]

Nobody else in the Hartley family was recorded as working outside the home and the four youngest children were at school.

Two curious features of the 1911 Census return that Samuel and Sarah Hartley compiled in their shaky handwriting are that Samuel's age was given as 55 and Sarah's as 43. Perhaps ten years before they had looked 50 and 40 respectively to the 1901 enumerator but were in reality only 45 and 33; alternatively, perhaps they both knocked a few years off when making the return themselves or had simply lost count. However, the 1871 and 1881 Census returns, when Sarah's age was ten and nineteen respectively, suggest that she would be 50 or thereabouts in 1911. It would appear, therefore, that the ages given in the 1901 return are more accurate than those they supplied themselves in 1911 and it is not immediately apparent why they should be so reduced. The prospect of the workhouse would be coming closer whatever age they claimed, for this could only be put off for as long as their health held up and they could earn enough to live outside it.

In addition, Samuel listed his name and signed as "Samual" in 1911 so this was how he thought of himself whether the spelling was correct or not.

It is not certain whether either of them had been married previously partly because Samuel Hartley is absent from previous Censuses, even that of 1861 when he might be expected to be living with his family in Liverpool. Sarah Hartley, or Sarah Potter as she then was, is in the 1871 and 1881 Census returns, but not the 1891 one under either name. In 1871 she and her father Thomas Potter lived with his sister, a housekeeper, in her Everton home. Thomas was already a cotton porter and Sarah, though only ten, was said to be a servant who, given her age, may have been working alongside her aunt the housekeeper or perhaps in the Everton household itself. In 1881 Sarah was a general servant living in a widowed commission agent's household in West Derby, looking after him and his three children under ten.

Neither Samuel (in either spelling) nor Sarah featured in the newspapers between 1890 and 1919, though someone with the same name as their oldest son did. In 1917, for example, a Joseph Hartley was sentenced at Liverpool City Police Court to twenty-one days prison for army desertion.[383] The National Archives hold 71 medal cards for men of this name, several of whom served in regiments such as the East Lancashire Regiment or Seaforth Highlanders as this Joseph Hartley might have done. Several of them went on to join the Machine Gun Corps, as had Charles Ryle Fay on its formation in October 1915. Two people called Joseph Hartley served with the Liverpool Regiment in the First World War: private JA Hartley and private J Hartley.[384] Neither is necessarily the Blackstock Street one, but the latter is more likely on the basis that only one of the Hartley family (the daughter Margaret E) is ascribed a second initial or name in either the 1901 or 1911 Census returns. This private J Hartley was transferred from the Liverpool Regiment to the Labour Corps,[385] his Labour Corps number corresponding to 68 Company (3rd ILC King's) formed in May 1917 and stationed in France.[386] Subsequently, this was one of the first companies to "volunteer" for exhumation and re-burial work after the war. They were based at Ypres for this gruesome task which would have entailed finding remains in the Flanders killing fields and interring them at Hooge Cemetery.[387]

Blackstock Street in 1900: The people who lived there

Waterloo 1903 train crash
© Sefton Library Service[388]

Another Joseph Hartley namesake was a Crosby photographer who recorded the railway disaster in July 1903 near Waterloo that Charles Ryle Fay, who saw it shortly after it happened, described as "a grisly sight" for six people had been killed and the platform torn up. Another train had been stopped just in time to prevent it "running into the back of the wrecked one".[389]

James and Mary Carroll

As Table 3 above shows, the Carrolls, the Goulburns and Catherine Kerr lived next door to each other in houses 9 to 13 at the end of the nineteenth century and into the twentieth. The Carrolls and the Goulburns were neighbours at nos. 9 and 11 for twenty years or more. All three houses comprised four rooms, but the numbers living in each were very different and the Carroll family never occupied more than two rooms themselves.

James Carroll, his wife Mary Ann and their four children lived there in 1901, and as only he was on the 1899-1900 register of electors it is probable that he was both the main householder and that the family had been there for some time - conceivably since not long after the May 1892 advert in the *Liverpool Mercury* offering it for sale or rent. This does not imply that they had responded to the advert themselves for they may have sub-let from the person who did (whether freeholder or lessee). The four Carroll children were Mary (20), James (15), Peter (10) and William (2) and, though there may have been others, Mary Ann Carroll did not respond to this part of the 1911 Census ten years later. None of the children worked and the family would have been dependent entirely on James Carroll's wages as a stationary stoker except that the other two rooms accommodated four boarders: John McQuade (23) a worker in a flour and rice mill (perhaps Irving, Son and Jones), Mary Hogan (31) and her two small children. Since Mary Hogan was married and McQuade single it may be that they formed two separate households, he in one room and the three Hogans in another. Overall, the house held at least ten people (eleven if Mary Hogan's husband was usually there), only two of whom were working.

Ten (or eleven) people in four rooms is overcrowded by any definition, but when the Carrolls had earlier lived in Toxteth Park in 1891, as well as the oldest five in their family there were three other households. The house they shared was no larger so conceivably the Carrolls thought 9 Blackstock Street comparatively spacious - in other words, the difference between how people conceptualise their own circumstances and how they may look to others from the outside - though neither diminishes the grim reality of the Carrolls' experience.

In 1911 Mary Ann Carroll still lived in the same two rooms at 9 Blackstock Street with her three oldest children, but her husband James had either died or disappeared for she first wrote 'married twenty-eight years' on the return only to cross both out and substitute 'widowed' instead. He may have died, though the Census reveals a James Carroll of the right age, but claiming to be single, a shipscraper living with tens of others in McGinn's lodgings in Soho Street. He may have said he was single in order to fit in with the other lodgers, leaving Mary Ann to all intents and purposes a widow. Her youngest son William was not there either. Mary Ann was not working outside the home, leaving no doubt about this for she recorded 'at home', while her daughter was a mill girl at an oil cake mill (probably Pearson's) and her two sons were both labourers. All three were single and it is tempting to think that they worked at the same factory, perhaps the same one at which their father had kept the kilns burning previously. As with the Hartleys, the ages the Carrolls recorded themselves in 1911 were rarely what might be expected on the basis of the 1901 return: Mary Ann 48 rather than

50, her daughter Mary 25 rather than 30, and James 23 rather than 25. Only Peter seemed ten years older than the age given him in 1901.

The boarders in the other two rooms were James and Mary Mulholland, both in their late thirties and never having had children in their thirteen years of marriage. He was a fireman (a ship's stoker) and she a hawker and must have been comparatively well off among their neighbours with two incomes and no children.

John and Elizabeth Goulburn

The Goulburns at no. 11 were one of the most affluent families in the street. In 1901 John Goulburn (43) was a general labourer and two of the three children were working: James (21) as a "telephone wireman" and Robert (19) as a cotton porter. The youngest son John (15) was not at work and his mother Elizabeth (50) did not report that she worked outside the home. Nevertheless, three incomes for five people far exceeded the situation for any other family. Furthermore, James was in at the beginning of the telephone industry and, while he may have been thought to be taking a risk at the time, it would continue to grow thereafter. The 1901/02 directory for the National Telephone Company (NTC) shows that all nine companies in Blackstock Street already had telephones, one line each, but no individual houses were as yet connected.[390] Even in Courtenay Road only the Marsh family had a telephone at home. Others probably did at their business addresses, for example a Tripe Dresser in Naylor Street was connected, but there was clearly scope for growth, expansion that would soon be limited only by the speed with which connections could be made. There were complaints about this aspect of the telephone service in the 1930s but these were resolved as part of Kingsley Wood's initiatives to develop the Post Office.[391]

By 1911 Elizabeth Goulburn had been widowed, and her son Robert had moved out, but James was still single, living with her at no. 9 and continuing to work as a telephone linesman for the National Telephone Company. This had originally been established as a provincial subsidiary of the United Telephone Company Ltd, but from 1889 it became the retained name as provincial amalgamations were put in place. From 1911 the National Telephone Company became part of the Post Office and, though it was liquidated that year when the Post Office became virtually the only, and certainly the main, provider of a telephone service,[392] James would have continued to prosper. He was clearly doing well enough in any case for his earnings supported his mother and brother John as well. John was still not working, perhaps because his physical or mental health prevented him from doing so, in which case his mother remained his carer. The three of them were the only occupants of the four-roomed house and may well have been envied by others in the street.

None of the Goulburns figured in the newspapers between 1890 and 1919. James would probably be too busy fitting telephone wires, but none of the others did either.

Thomas McDonald

Although not necessarily better off than the Goulburn family, Thomas McDonald was a foreman at Pearson's oil mill and in the early years of the twentieth century (1901 and 1911) he and his family lived in the five-roomed house at 45 Blackstock Street that went with the Pearson's job. His wage was clearly enough to support all the family for it was the only one in both years, perhaps because there was little or no rent to pay on the tied accommodation or Pearson's deducted a small sum from his wages to allow for a subsidised rent. In 1899 Pearson's had combined with sixteen other companies to form British Oil and Cake Mills, first being listed as Mersey Oil and Cake Mills in the 1901/02 NTC telephone directory.[393] Perhaps Thomas McDonald had become foreman around the time of the amalgamation, but he was certainly there as the combination's fortunes fluctuated in the first decade of the new century. As foreman, it may have been his role to lay off and take on workers on the basis of Edward Pearson's assessment of the market. They clearly forged a working relationship that survived the shocks of those years, but given that McDonald was thirty-five in 1901 and Pearson much older, it is unlikely that it went beyond the factory into their personal relations. No matter how enlightened an employer Pearson might have been, he and McDonald inhabited different worlds.

In 1891 the house had been occupied by one of McDonald's predecessors as Pearson's foreman, John Parkinson, his wife Elizabeth and their ten children ranging in age from seventeen to four months. John and Elizabeth Parkinson had been twenty-four and nineteen respectively when their first child was born and had produced another mouth to feed in most years thereafter. None of their offspring were twins and they may have had others who did

Blackstock Street in 1900: The people who lived there

not survive. Perhaps to help with this huge family John Parkinson's parents, both aged 66 in 1891, lived with them, though as he was a labourer in a church cemetery (possibly but not necessarily a grave-digger), their assistance must have been tempered by the extra overcrowding, fourteen people in all, and perhaps limited to minimal additional income for the household. The oldest boy aged fifteen was the one child working, but as an errand boy in the port his contribution would have been tiny.

What is most worrying though is the Parkinson family prospects? John Parkinson's parents could not live much longer and how would, or could, the family cope if the main breadwinner fell ill or lost his job at Pearson's? In the event the family was sundered by Elizabeth's death and in 1901 John Parkinson was living in Everton with five children, four of the six youngest from 1891 and a new addition aged five. It may be that it was the birth of this eleventh child that had ended Elizabeth's life at the age of 41. John Parkinson still worked in an oil cake mill, but now as a labourer and although Abbey Street, Everton was within walking distance of Pearson's, other factors may have prevented or deterred him from continuing as a labourer there. In 1911 he had moved again and now aged sixty was a general labourer, as was his youngest George, now fifteen and the only one still at home.

Construing McDonald family history

Born in Hull, Thomas McDonald was a strawboard liner living there in 1891 with his oldest child Edith R (then aged 2), his wife Emma Louisa (nee Fleming) and her sister Edith F Fleming. Both Emma and her sister had been born in Rothwell, Yorkshire, over 50 miles due west inland from Hull and close to Leeds, but in 1881 had been living sixteen miles north-east of Hull at Hornsea near the east Yorkshire coast.

According to the Oxford English Dictionary, strawboard is a "coarse yellow millboard made from straw pulp, used for making boxes, book-covers, etc.", even shoes, though it is not clear what object(s) Thomas may have been lining. However, less than ten years later, he had progressed from this occupation in Hull to an oil mill foreman in Liverpool. In all probability there would have been an intermediate step, perhaps as a proficient labourer in the oil mill or in Liverpool generally, but what had propelled the McDonalds to move across the country in the first place?

In 1901 Thomas McDonald and his wife, then calling herself Emily, had four young children (two boys and two girls). As recorded on the Census form, these were Edith R (then 12), Dorothy E (9), Frederick C (4) and Thomas N (2). Attention has already been drawn to the age discrepancies between the 1901 and 1911 returns for the Hartley and Carroll families, and the McDonald parents seem to have succumbed to something similar for Thomas recorded himself as 43 (rather than 45, or 46 on the basis of the 1891 return) and his wife as 42 (rather than 44 or 45). The age difference between them remained the same but both had "lost" at least two years. Their oldest child Edith was not recorded as living with them in 1911 but, as the ages for the other three children accorded with those enumerated ten years earlier, the search for youth, if that is what it was, is more likely to have been deliberate in the case of the parents.[394]

What is even more striking though is the different forenames they went by. Thomas remained Thomas but his wife of 23 years was now Louisa instead of Emily [L], Dorothy E was Dorothy Edbur, while the boys were listed as Charles Frederick and Norman. It is probable that the youngest was called Norman to avoid confusion over the use of Thomas, his father's name, but what accounted for the other changes? They seem real enough for the return was completed by Thomas McDonald, with his wife's name mis-spelled as 'Lousia' [sic], hardly a mistake she would have made herself. Given that in 1881 she had been Emma L Fleming, her transformation to Louisa via Emily indicates not only that even the Census is not a straightforward historical record but also in this instance may demonstrate the changing presentation of self as circumstances warranted.

In 1911 the McDonald family at 45 Blackstock Street included Louisa's (Emily's / Emma's) father James Fleming, who at 81 would have been the oldest resident in the street. He had previously been a jobbing gardener (and his wife a laundress) when his family in Hornsea included two sons as well as his daughters Emma and Edith. At that point Scotland was recorded as his birthplace and his age as 46. By the time of the 1911 Census his birthplace was supposedly Dawlish in Devon and he had aged beyond the chronological age of 76 that might have been expected. Had his age been understated in 1881 or was it over-stated in 1911? And, if the latter, why would Thomas and Louisa McDonald do this? The qualifying age for the old age pension introduced in 1908 was seventy so, whatever his claimed age, James Fleming exceeded that threshold though his resources may have precluded him from passing the means test in either event. It may have been an error or, to be most uncharitable, there may have been social rewards for depicting an elderly parent as older than was in fact the case; in other words, Louisa may have been manipulating the presentation of this, as well as the name she went by, to her supposed advantage.

1900 Liverpool Lives - The Threads That Bind

6. COURTENAY ROAD IN 1900 AND THE PEOPLE WHO LIVED THERE

All twenty-seven houses in Courtenay Road had been completed by early 1882, but the surroundings were still primitive and, while a number of the houses had been let on a short-term basis from 1881, they were proving hard to sell. In June 1883 the Board asked their surveyor to submit plans and costings for the road to be sewered and repaired.[395] By the latter they meant levelling, paving, flagging, channelling and making good or, in other words, transforming the area from its appearance as a building site. The following month the surveyor complied but the Board deferred their consideration of his proposals to their next meeting - or at any rate so the minute read[396] though, for whatever reason, it would take nearly three years before the plans received any further consideration. Quite what could have been the explanation for such an extraordinary delay is hard to fathom unless it were for organisational or budget reasons, neither of which is apparent from the minutes. Eventually, the 1883 estimates were approved in April 1886 when it was also resolved that "notices be served on owners of premises fronting the street to do the work required within ... 28 days".[397] Given that it had taken the Board three years to get to this point, they cannot have had any expectation that this would happen and must simply have been observing the legal requirements. If this was the case, they were certainly correct and at the July meeting it was agreed that, as the owners had not responded, the work should be undertaken by the Board.[398] It was completed by the following May, enabling the road to be formally adopted and making the Board responsible for its future maintenance.[399]

With the surroundings at last as attractive as the houses, indeed an Ordnance Survey map in 1893 shows the road then to have been tree-lined,[400] other residents who would still be there in 1901 moved into the road to join the Marsh family. They included the Pleydell-Bouverie family at no. 13, the Rayners at no. 16, the Harts at no. 23 and the Townshends at no. 27. All five families feature in the 1888 Waterloo Directory. Eight houses were still empty then, but with the Pilling and Fay families (at nos. 19 and 20 respectively) arriving before 1891, the road increasingly took on a settled look. For some it would be a stopping place on their way upmarket, but it was no longer just a transit camp for those renting and perhaps without roots in the area.

Waterloo and Crosby were part of the Southport parliamentary constituency from 1885 to 1918 which alternated between Liberal and Conservative control, though successful Conservative candidates enjoyed many more years as MPs than did those who triumphed in the Liberal cause: twenty-six years in parliament over this period against seven years for the short-lived Liberals. Although women householders had the right to vote in municipal elections, parliamentary suffrage would not be achieved until 1918 for women and not until 1928 at the same age as men. Nevertheless, women did play a part in parliamentary politics in the nineteenth century since voting was only one way in which influence could be exercised. For example, there was a branch of the Women's Liberal Association in Waterloo by 1893, one of six in the Liverpool area, and the branch of the Waterloo Primrose League[401] was exceptional in having "parallel positions of Dame President and Lady Secretary ensuring some female input into its executive".[402]

Following on from the summary of Courtenay Road residents in Table 2, the diagram on p108 illustrates how the road looked in 1901, both in terms of the arrangement of the residents and their detached or semi-detached homes. The railway line is immediately adjacent to the eastern end and runs north-south past the Hall and Rougetel properties. The residents considered in more detail, as explained above, are shown in bold.

Charles and Emily Fay

At the end of a list of sentences handed down at the Liverpool County sessions on 10th June 1890 the *Liverpool Mercury* reported that a nineteen year old sign-writer and his older female accomplice had been imprisoned for six months for breaking into the house of Charles Fay at 20 Courtenay Road and stealing a number of silver and electro-plated items worth £50.[403] Nothing particularly remarkable in that for large houses everywhere might be viewed opportunistically as a chance to steal and get some ready cash, and nothing particularly remarkable either that the perpetrators were named as Robert Noonan and Frances Wilson, an unemployed 25 year old. What is more noteworthy is that Robert Noonan is much better known as Robert Tressell (1870-1911) the author of 'The Ragged Trousered Philanthropists', first published in 1914 three years after his death and still in print today as one of the most influential books about inequalities, workers' rights and socialism. Noonan emigrated to Cape Town later in 1890, returning to live in Hastings, the setting for the book, in 1901.

According to some websites Noonan was the brother of one of Fay's "servants",[404] though by the time of the 1891 Census a year later these were Mary Leonard (22) and Hannah Hawkins (13), neither of whom were related to Robert Noonan and may have replaced Noonan's sister when her link to, if not necessarily complicity in, the theft was uncovered. At that stage Charles Fay and his wife Emily lived there with their surviving son and daughter, Charles Ryle (aged 7) and Gladys (aged 4). By 1901 only one domestic servant was listed, 26 year old Elizabeth Price who was responsible for doing everything around the house.

Charles Fay had been born in Manchester in 1841/2 and in 1881 was working there in the shipping department of George Fraser, Son and Company, a cotton business he had joined as an apprentice in 1860. According to his son, he would remain with the company for over sixty years until he retired at the age of nearly 80 in 1921.[405]

His wife Emily was born in nearby Rusholme fifteen years after him. Although a gap of fifteen years between a wife and her husband was not out of the ordinary at the time, Charles was almost forty before Emily's first child was born and nearer forty-two by the time of Charles Ryle's own birth. Emily was the fifth of ten children, whose father Richard Lawton started out as a land agent and surveyor but then became a civil engineer along with her oldest brother John Henry.[406]

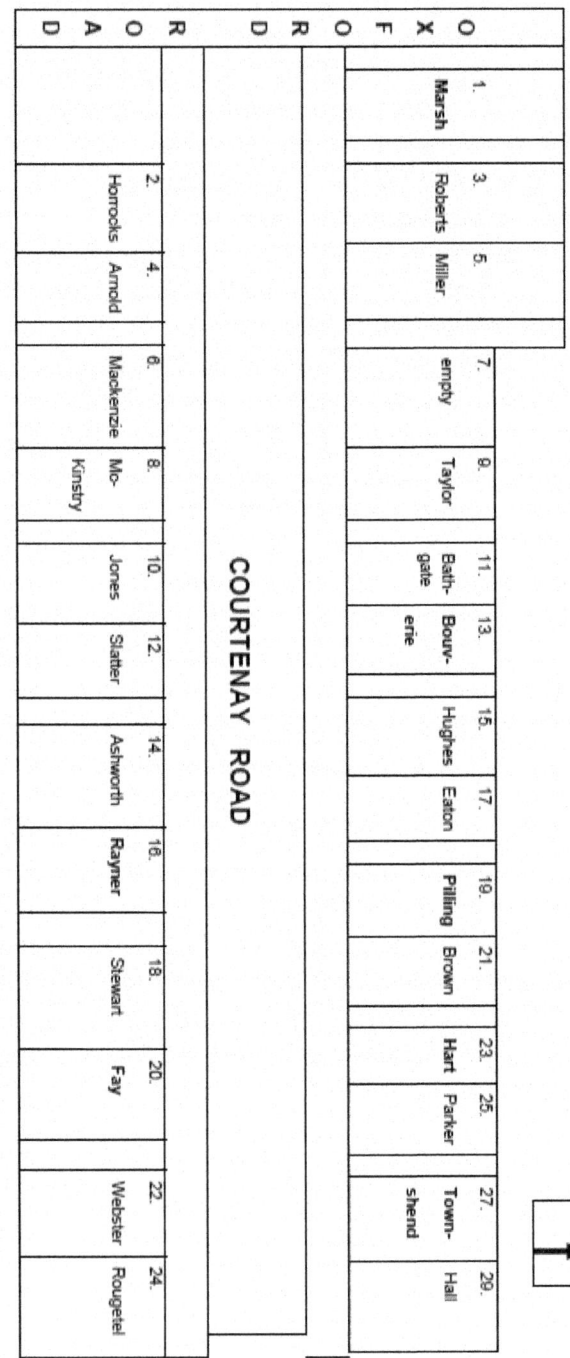

Diagrammatic Representation of Courtenay Road and Residents in 1901

108

Although the Manchester Ship Canal linking 'cottonopolis' (as Manchester was called) to the Mersey was not opened until 1894, it began to be seriously promoted in 1882 when Manchester businesses started to put their money forward to underwrite, and in effect indemnify, the constructors of thirty-six miles of waterway against excessive costs. In September that year the Guarantee Fund as it was known had reached £11,450 (about £1m today), with only eight contributions greater than George Fraser, Son and Company's £100. In 1884 a petition was sent to the Local Government Board requesting Manchester City Council's financial support in building the canal, a request that was agreed by the Home Secretary in December 1884 adding 2d in the £ to the rates.[407] Almost inevitably, Liverpool's worry was competition from cheaper imports for twenty-eight out of the thirty-three towns that would be most affected were closer to Manchester than Liverpool. As the 15th Earl of Derby noted in his diary,

> Received further details as to the scheme for making a deep navigable canal up to Manchester, which seems practicable and may pay, but it is so much against the interests of Liverpool and so unpopular there that I think I had better leave it alone.[408]

Concluding that timber imports might be 4s per ton cheaper through Manchester, for example, the committee Liverpool Council had set up to suggest solutions proposed reductions in the dock and town dues and attempted to bring down the railway charges for onward carriage by reducing their rates.[409]

Unsurprisingly, George Fraser, Son and Company viewed the prospects more positively and Charles Fay became manager of their Liverpool office in 1883, his promotion the primary reason for the family's move out of Manchester. Although Courtenay Road was not their first home in Liverpool, for the family is absent from the 1888 Waterloo Directory when 20 Courtenay Road was empty, they must have moved there shortly after and before the Noonan/ Tressell theft. In the 1891 Census Charles Fay described himself as a shipping agent and in 1901 as a forwarding agent, in both cases employing others in his office. Before the Manchester Ship Canal was open, therefore, he may have concentrated on the more customary, though no less complex, tasks, building up his connections with importers, exporters and shipping companies in the process, whereas after 1894 it might have been the connections on to Manchester on which he focussed. Keeping ships full and turning them round quickly were not only major logistical challenges for the ship-owners, but "also required an efficiently organised system of agents on the spot, capable of securing forward cargoes at agreed rates".[410] As Milne puts it, the task of the shipping agent was to "bridge gaps" and "oil wheels", with an extensive list of contacts and an encyclopaedic knowledge ranging from cargoes to ships' captains to customs being critical.[411] This would have been ideal training for onward shipment to and from Manchester subsequently.

The 1900 Gore Directory for Liverpool gives Fay's office address as Britannia Buildings, 20 Fenwick Street West, categorising him as a forwarding and commission agent.[412] This entry in the Alphabetical Directory is under Fay's name and includes his address in Courtenay Road, whereas there is no mention of George Fraser, Son and Company in either this or the Street Directory.[413] This is somewhat surprising given his son's certainty that Charles Fay remained with the company throughout his career. It might mean that he undertook work on his own behalf as well as for them, that the company had decided to downplay the Manchester connection given Liverpool concerns, or that it was the name 'Charles Fay' that attracted potential contacts, or at least they associated with their needs, rather than necessarily the company he worked for. In 1904 George Fraser, Son & Company became a private limited company, partly to reward "old servants",[414] with the company's total share capital of £160,000 (about £13m today) shared between the existing three partners and four others who were invited to join the board.[415] Charles Fay was not among them, possibly because he was now "semi-detached" from the company. What is clear though is that his separate identification in Liverpool pre-dated the re-allocation of company shares rather than vice versa.

In February 1896 the son Charles Ryle Fay, then a twelve year old pupil at Merchant Taylors' School, Crosby wrote to the UDC to complain about the lack of a lamp in the passage through which he walked to and from school.[416] The Council did eventually lay a gas main so that the public lamp could be provided, but Fay then complained to them that the job had not been completed adequately for the asphalt remained broken.[417] Never one to suffer fools gladly in his later academic career as an economic historian, and not known for his tact or for being cowed by authority, he was clearly speaking his mind even then.

Both Charles Fay and his son were politically active to a degree, but had different party allegiances, and their local Southport constituency oscillated between Conservative and Liberal MPs between 1885 and 1918.[418] Lord Curzon, someone whom Charles Fay knew well,[419] was the Conservative MP from 1886 until 1898 (when he became Viceroy of India). At the hard-fought 1906 general election the younger Fay wrote "Politics is the order of the day here. My father went to hear the Conservative candidate last night. I'm going to hear the Liberal tonight. It will be a very tight fight."[420] It was the Liberal JM Astbury who took the seat from the Conservative incumbent Marshall-Hall, holding it until the January 1910 election when it was regained by the Conservatives.

Sandheys Avenue (opposite Courtenay Road)
© Sefton Library Service

By 1908 the Fays had moved across the road to the even more recently developed Sandheys Terrace, the nearest row of houses to the Mersey, as later did the family of Charles Miller who had been at 5 Courtenay Road in 1901. Miller's wholesale fish business in Liverpool must have been prospering, as Fay's certainly was for he also owned a house in the Lake District, the Rosery at Windermere.[421] Whether the Fays remained long in Sandheys Terrace is not clear for in July 1911 their address from which Charles Ryle Fay was married was The Hollies, Blundellsands, the address of Charles and Emily Fay in the 1911 Census, though Charles Ryle Fay was boarding with his future best man Harold Temperley at Cooper's Hill House, Brockworth, Gloucestershire, a small farm on the edge of the Cotswolds a short distance from the home of his fiancée Alice Hartland in Gloucester.

The Hollies, Agnes Road, Blundellsands
© Sefton Library Service

Three other families had gravitated from Courtenay Road to Blundellsands by 1911, those of Robert F Jones the Blackstock Street soap manufacturer from no. 10 to a house called Lynwood, Charles Hughes a timber broker from no. 15 to one called Wimborne, and J Stanley Webster another timber broker who had lived next door to the Fays at no. 22 to Tacoma, Blundellsands. All three houses can be identified on the relevant Ordnance Survey map, whereas The Hollies cannot.[422] However, there was a house of this name at 1 Agnes Road, Blundellsands in 1916,[423] though this does not necessarily mean the two were the same.

Laurence and Annie Pleydell-Bouverie

Pleydell-Bouverie is of Huguenot derivation and the family name of the Earls of Radnor, but as with all large families, especially in an age of primogeniture, only the direct line of descent through the oldest sons would confer status and landed estate. Younger sons, let alone daughters, would have to fend for themselves and therefore with each succeeding generation minor branches of a family might increasingly disappear into obscurity, well away from public view.

Laurence Pleydell-Bouverie of 13 Courtenay Road was the great-grandson of the 2nd Earl of Radnor but far from the direct line of descent for, according to the family history and Burke's Peerage, he was the grandson of the Earl's fourth son Frederick who earned his living in the church as Canon of Salisbury.[424] The armed forces and the church were preferences for many younger sons in the nineteenth century and both Frederick Pleydell-Bouverie (1785-1857) and one of his older brothers, the 2nd Earl's second son Duncombe (1780-1850), who eventually retired as a navy Admiral before becoming an MP, might be thought typical.

Being a Canon at Salisbury Cathedral was nevertheless a post of power and influence, and though not of the same social standing as an Earl, far from negligible. However, the Canon and his wife had six sons and seven daughters, further dissipating their resources, and Laurence's father, their second son and also called Laurence (1817-1877), was a Lieutenant-Colonel in the 78th Regiment of Foot (before it amalgamated with the 72nd Regiment in 1881 as the Seaforth Highlanders). Pleydell-Bouverie had originally been posted to the 78th as an Adjutant in October 1850 and was promoted to Brevet-Major in December 1854 but continued to be paid as an Adjutant.[425] Although not actively involved in the siege of Lucknow in 1858, the 78th was in support and set upon by the enemy, with Brevet-Major Pleydell-Bouverie one of the few mentioned in despatches and the brevet rank of Lieutenant-Colonel conferred on him as a result.[426] It must be assumed, therefore, that despite being two ranks higher he remained on an Adjutant's pay.

He and Harriet Rivers (d.1893) had married in 1847, and had five boys and one girl (also called Harriet) in rapid succession and all before Lucknow.[427]

Their oldest child was Laurence Pleydell-Bouverie (1848-1920) of Courtenay Road, born in Southampton and supposedly a cotton salesman, who married Annie Hume Gibson/Edwards (1857/8-1904)[428] in 1877 - perhaps coincidentally the year his father died. There are three other things to note about this: Annie was nearly ten years younger than Laurence and, at most, twenty when they married; certainly she was under twenty-one at any rate and yet already a widow; and it may be that her first husband J Edwards also sold cotton and that he and Pleydell-Bouverie were colleagues. Laurence and Annie had one (surviving) child, a daughter called Annie Marian born the same year her parents married and perhaps the reason for it. Like her mother, she was born in Liverpool. Annie Marian was with her parents in Courtenay Road in 1891 but, according to Burke's Peerage, married Harold Whitehead in 1898 at the age of twenty-one, and in 1901 she and her husband had moved to the idyllically-named Rose Cottage in Rawtenstall, Lancashire, living there with one servant. Thomas Whitehead as her husband sometimes called himself was a wool buyer and salesman so he and his father-in-law, even if they were competitors only intellectually, may have had some discussions over the merits of wool and the virtues of cotton. However, Pleydell-Bouverie is listed in the 1900 Gore Directory solely as a "gentleman" of 13 Courtenay Road, not a cotton salesman, which leads to questions about the extent to which he pursued the occupation after marriage or whether it was maintained mainly for appearances.[429]

In the 1901 Census the "cotton salesman" Laurence was on his own, with neither his wife Annie nor a servant being recorded at Courtenay Road, and Annie not being enumerated anywhere else in that Census either. This may mean only that she was out of the country but in 1904 her death was reported at 10 Carlisle Road, Birkdale.[430] As far as is known, none of the immediate family lived there and the house had been empty in 1901, though by 1911 Harold/Thomas and Annie Marian Whitehead lived about a mile away at 14 York Road, near Birkdale Town Hall. York Road is just north of Birkdale Station and had a tramway running down it then, whereas Carlisle Road is south of the station.[431] The Whitehead house had ten rooms, so far from the Rawtenstall cottage of ten years earlier and large enough not only to accommodate their two young sons but also her father Laurence, now retired and living on his own means. They had three servants to look after them, a cook, nurse and housemaid. Interestingly, although Harold Whitehead was designated the head of the household in the Census return, it was Laurence who submitted it. Harold was still a wool buyer and salesman, working for a felt manufacturer, perhaps the same employer as when he lived forty miles away in Rawtenstall, for the Rossendale valley nearby was one of the areas known for felt manufacture at this time.

Although there were very occasional mentions of Charles Fay in the newspapers as late as 1918 when in his seventies he spoke at the Magdalen House annual meeting (and may have been on the committee since he sat on the platform though not a named office-holder),[432] by contrast Laurence Pleydell-Bouverie was never referred to, probably reflecting a quiet and even reclusive life. If it was this that drove away his wife, the more ebullient Annie who was only in her mid-forties when she died, it did not prevent his reconciliation with his daughter, living out at least the last decade of his life with her.

William and Fanny Townshend

In 1853 Henry James Cook (b.1818/9) and John Townshend (1818-1869) were partners in Cook and Townshend drapers at 19-21 Byrom Street (with a bonnet warehouse at no. 29).[433] Their partnership flourished, entirely on the basis of word of mouth recommendations it would seem for they never advertised overtly, and ten years later in 1864 the *Liverpool Mercury* reported on their new building which ran from nos.19-29 Byrom Street. This report, the only mention in the newspapers before 1900, commented

> Within the last few weeks the new and extensive premises erected for Messrs. Cook and Townshend, general drapers, silk mercers, etc in Byrom Street, have attracted attention, no less on account of their size than their appropriateness of design. The business having of late years largely increased ...[434]

The shop was four storeys high and the expansion had only become possible after the properties between 21 and 29 Byrom Street were purchased by Cook and Townshend, a development they must have planned for some time. The newspaper described the premises in detail, even down to the patent Minton floor tiles, and the shop re-opened for business the same day, with the newspaper anticipating that it would receive considerable patronage and would represent the start of "increased success" for the business. Both Cook and Townshend were then in their mid-forties.

In the 1861 Census Henry James Cook and Fanny White Cook (b.1822/3), his wife, lived in Wavertree with their eight children aged between one and fifteen, two servants, a nurse and a governess. The only income was that of Cook the draper himself, which gives some idea of how he must have been prospering. One of the children, called Fanny White Cook after her mother, was then aged seven. Ten years later the two youngest children (Arthur and Bertha) had died but two more had been born, and the eight surviving children lived with their parents in a larger house in Blundellsands. They now had three servants, as well as an unmarried sister of their mother living with them and, as in 1861, three visitors on Census night. The oldest son Charles H Cook was a shipbroker but the next two brothers had become drapers like their father. The daughter Fanny White Cook (1853-1939) and her sister Emily, two years older at nineteen, had left school but were not employed. They were thus an archetypal Victorian family with the men going out to work and the women at home, with servants to look after the house until they themselves left to get married or, more rarely, for other employment.

Meanwhile in 1851, the only Census in which he appears, John Townshend and his wife Eliza (1818-1908) lived over the shop at 19 Byrom Street (as then did the Cooks and their three oldest children at no. 21).[435] John Townshend had been born in Shropshire and Eliza in Suffolk, probably coincidentally the same county from which Henry James Cook came originally. As Fanny White Cook had been born in Derbyshire, the Cook and Townshend partners and their spouses had moved some distance to set up in business together in Liverpool. They may have learned the draper's trade elsewhere first before joining together, but even if they left school at fourteen they must have been very driven from the start for they were just into their thirties and already well-established in 1851. Both Henry James Cook and John Townshend ensured that the Census enumerator added the following explanation for each of them: "(1 of the firm of 2) Employing 10 Shopmen, 4 Saleswomen and 25 Milliners and Straw Bonnet Makers". There may be similarly detailed information provided in the 1911 Census when people completed their own returns for the first time, but this is the most detailed seen in 1851. It might indicate the enumerator's diligence, but possibly Cook's and Townshend's pride that they had come so far in such a short space of time.

Interestingly, it seems that the hub of the operation lay at no. 19 with the Townshends, for while the Cooks and their three sons had both a nurse and "house servant" living with them (seven people in all), the Townshend household accommodated a nurse, cook, "house servant", three draper's assistants and a milliner, ten people in all. This might mean that no. 19 was larger, and/or that more of no. 21 was used as shop premises, but it is hard not to escape the conclusion that John Townshend was even more of a driving force than his partner. Another conclusion that can be drawn is that, of the firm's employees, at least three shopmen, all four saleswomen and all but one of the twenty-five milliners lived elsewhere. It is probable that many, if not all, of the latter worked from home, providing the sort of sweated labour on which entrepreneurs often built their fortunes.

William Townshend (b.1850), aged seven months at the time of the Census in 1851, was the only Townshend child at that stage and may well have remained so. He and the Cook's daughter Fanny must have married as soon as Fanny turned twenty-one for in the 1881 Census, when he was thirty and she twenty-seven, they already had four children aged six and under. They seemed to be doing well for they also had a cook, housemaid and a nurse at their home at 17 Adelaide Terrace, Great Crosby. It may be that it was entirely William's employment as a merchant and ship-owner that enabled the young family to prosper, but it seems at least as likely that the Cook parents had contributed and/or the death of his father John Townshend in 1869 had left William well provided for. The business Cook and Townshend, linen and woollen drapers as the 1894 Directory called them, had continued to expand so that they occupied all of Byrom Street between nos. 5 and 29 and were at

161 Dale Street as well.[436] William Townshend by contrast had over-extended himself for in 1880 his partnership with John George Briscoe as Liverpool merchants was dissolved[437] and in 1882 he started liquidation proceedings himself.[438]

It may be that this was a temporary setback that William survived, perhaps because his father-in-law bailed him out or he still had some of his inheritance left, and indeed in May 1885 he was a guest at the Mayoral 'At Home', one of the prime civic events of the Liverpool social scene.[439] In the 1894 Directory William was listed, but only at his Courtenay Road address for there was no mention of a ship-owner of that name.[440]

William and Fanny White Townshend had moved to no. 27 Courtenay Road in the 1880s and Fanny, supposedly widowed in the 1890s, was still living there in 1911, as were four of her seven adult children. These were her oldest and youngest sons (Henry and Arthur) and her two younger daughters (Bertha and Dora). The children had been born over the fourteen years 1875 to 1889: Henry (1875-1952), William (1876-1954), Alice (1878-1923), Bertha (1879-1962), Dora (1883-1959), Percy (1886-1965) and Arthur (1889-1952), with Bertha and Arthur probably named after the two Cook children who had died in the 1860s.[441] Assuming the accuracy of the family tree on which these dates are based, only one of these Townshend children reached their eightieth birthday (Bertha), though several others came close. Only the youngest had been born while the family lived in Courtenay Road, but with Fanny and William both local to Liverpool, all the children had been born in and around Waterloo and Crosby.

In 1901 the three oldest, including Alice, were listed as shipping clerks while Bertha was a teacher of domestic science. No occupation was listed for Dora, Percy and Arthur and while both boys were probably still at school (aged fourteen and eleven respectively), it would be surprising if seventeen year old Dora was. That Alice was a shipping clerk, and that this was not an error by the Census enumerator, seems a very singular occupation for a twenty-three year old woman in 1901. It suggests either that she was very independent and determined and/or that she and her two older brothers worked for the same shipping firm and that their employment was in some way related to their father's connections.

Courtenay Road in 1900: The people who lived there

John and Eliza Pilling

At no. 19, a few doors down from the Townshends and across the road from the Fay family, lived John Pilling, his wife Eliza, both in their 50s in 1901, their children John Francis 14 and Mary Alice 12, and one general domestic servant Elizabeth Dawson. The Pillings had moved into the house not much more than ten years earlier, and not long before the 1891 Census, having bought what was then either a rented, or more likely, empty property (see Table 2). At first they had two young girls living with them as servants but as their children got older must have decided that, provided she was willing and able, one would be sufficient. John Pilling was a native of Liverpool while Eliza had started life in the Lambeth part of London. They had married late in life and both their children had been born across the Mersey in Birkenhead. Only after Mary Alice's birth, probably in 1889, did they move across the river to Crosby.

In both the 1891 and 1901 Censuses John Pilling is described as living on his own means and, since Eliza had no occupation outside the home, his means must have been sufficient to meet all the household's expenses. Yet this does not seem solely to have been inherited wealth as he is described as an accountant in the 1900 Gore Directory.[442] John Pilling, however, seems to have been an essentially private man and the details of his life remain opaque. There were two John Pilling companies, one incorporated in 1891 and dissolved before 1916, another started in 1897 that lasted into the post-WWI period,[443] but it has not proved possible to establish that either was his. One or other, or both, might be linked to him, as they might to the accountant of the same name who was prominent in the Haslingden and Ramsbottom areas between Blackburn and Rochdale at this time. There was also a well-known loom maker called John Pilling, as there was a convict who eventually ended up in Broadmoor and appeared in civil service reports from the Home Office almost as often as he did before the police and courts.

There is a Pilling Trust that works with other heritage bodies to restore churches in particular and is one of the prime supporters of the current Liverpool Cathedral 2024 fund, but this too has no connection with John Pilling of Courtenay Road.[444] It is tempting to speculate that it was this John Pilling who, living in the Savoy Hotel in 1903, accused two women of entering his room surreptitiously in order to steal from him, but again there is no concrete evidence.[445]

Eliza Pilling is equally enigmatic, never appearing in any newspaper report, but what is known is that the family had moved away from Courtenay Road by 1906 (as can be seen in Table 2). Probably this was because John Pilling had died, for in the 1911 Census a widowed Eliza had moved back across the Mersey to West Kirby with her two children. The 24 year old son John Francis was now a bank clerk at the Bank of Liverpool while his sister Mary Alice, now 22, remained both unmarried and unemployed outside the family home. Eliza recorded that she was living on private means, presumably the same ones that had already sustained the family for twenty years or more, and was well enough off to retain one servant, Margaret Richards who, at 29, would have been experienced and, as servants go, relatively expensive. But since Eliza's house was called 'Coniston' in Princes Avenue, West Kirby, stinting was neither necessary nor an option if 'appearances were to be maintained' (as they say). Ten years earlier the house had not existed.[446]

John Francis Pilling was commissioned Lieutenant in The King's (Liverpool Regiment) in the First World War,[447] but this is the last mention of any of the family in the public record.

William and Louisa Hart

William and Louisa Hart lived two doors down at no. 23 with their one daughter and three sons, all aged between fourteen and nineteen. Both Louisa and her husband had been born in Cheshire, three of their four children in Waterloo and even the oldest, their daughter Gladys, nearby in Litherland so they may have moved to Courtenay Road not long after their marriage about twenty years earlier when Louisa was 22 and William twelve years older at 34.[448] They are notable for the age of their one resident servant Elizabeth Stevenson who, said to be 60 in 1901, may have come with one or other of her employers from their previous home - a family retainer in effect. Certainly, she had been with them at Courtenay Road in 1891, though the Census that year gave her age as 40 (rather than 50 as the 1901 one would suggest should have been the case). The family also employed a second servant in those early years before feeling like other families, including the Pillings, that only one was required once the children were older.

William Hart was a hide broker and his oldest son Roderick at 17 a clerk in his office at Heyworth, Hart & Co., hide, tallow and general brokers of 16 Hamilton Buildings, 24 Chapel Street in Liverpool (which joined Tithebarn Street to the docks and ran past the Royal Exchange).[449] The company had been founded by the previous generation of Heyworths and Harts, and quick on their feet, moved office several times as they and Liverpool grew, and seemed prepared to sell almost anything. Originally at Rumford Place in the 1880s,[450] they were at Exchange Chambers in Bixteth Street ten years later when they advertised the sale of "8000 salted ox hides (all faulty)"[451] and a few years later 1600 bags of "genuine Patagonian raw guano", ex-SS Darwin and ex-Liverpool Quay. Tested for ammonia and phosphate content, not only were catalogues available but samples too.[452] Clearly profit came first; reputation would follow.

The guano sale was perhaps indicative that Heyworth, Hart & Co. were increasingly developing as South American brokers (as the firm would be described later), and their flexibility ensured the company prospered, with William Hart's partner George Heyworth joining the Board of Royal Insurance in 1910.[453] The partnership employed other people as well, but Roderick Hart was the next generation there to learn the ropes as a potential successor to his father who, at 54, may have been looking towards the future. The Heyworth side of the partnership was also plannng a smooth succession for, as the *London Gazette* would report subsequently, George Heyworth withdrew as a partner at the end of 1920 with the firm continuing under the steer of his son Harold P Heyworth, Hart's son Roderick Anwell Hart, Frederick G Jarrett and WS Smyth. It would not be surprising if the last named was part of the Smyth tannery dynasty from Blackstock Street, given the mutual interest in hides and leather. The Heyworth, Hart and Jarrett partnership was eventually dissolved in January 1924.

However, William Hart would die even sooner than he may have expected for in 1911 (and probably before 1906) his widow Louisa, along with daughter Gladys and son Roderick, was among the dozen or so permanent residents at the Hydro Hotel, Alexandra

Road, West Kirby. These were augmented by as many as twenty visiting guests and a large number of hotel staff who lived in.

In a 1900 guide to Britain the picture below was sandwiched between entries for a hotel in Warwick and the Hydro in West Kirby.[454] The picture may have been of either, or perhaps neither, hotel but it gives some idea of how the public rooms in such hotels would have been furnished at the turn of the twentieth century.[455] The cane chairs no doubt subliminally communicated both British seaside, and India and the far east, to those ex-pats who often retired from their postings abroad back to such hotels in Britain, in many cases constituting the majority of residents and thereby keeping the proprietors afloat when few people could afford holidays of any description, even at home. The 1900 guide described the West Kirby hotel as

from 'The British Isles: A Guide for Overseas Visitors' 1900

Comfortable and Homelike [with] A first-class chef and best of food. The en pension terms include all meals, hot baths ... badminton, dances, putting, tennis, etc. Bathing opposite [and an] R.A.C. appointment.

For a widow in her late fifties, as Louisa then was, the attractions of being looked after in such a setting were obvious. Gladys and Roderick, on the other hand, still in their late twenties may have had nowhere else to go or concluded that their duty lay with their mother for the time being. However, the two younger boys had left. Perhaps Roderick had scaled back his active involvement in the hide brokers for he now described himself as a produce merchant. Alternatively, the company could have extended its interests beyond guano and into new areas, purchasing agricultural products alongside animal hides. Liverpool and Merseyside were ideally placed for such expansion, both geographically and financially: in other words, logic and location combined with opportunity, the entrepreneur's ideal.

In 1941 the following notice appeared in the *Liverpool Echo*:

Roderick Hart, Vernon Hart and Edmund Hart sons of William Anwell Hart by his wife Louisa Young are entitled to a share of an estate. Communicate with the Public Trustee, Manchester.[456]

Possibly this signalled the death of Louisa, who would have been heading towards ninety years of age in 1941, or more probably their sister Gladys, though she would still have been under sixty. Whoever had died, however, the family had become distanced, possibly even estranged, from each other or the Public Trustee would not have been involved.

Although the Harts and the Pillings had lived close to each other on Courtenay Road, it is not known that Eliza Pilling and Louisa Hart had agreed that both their futures as widows lay across the Mersey in West Kirby but they were of similar ages, moved there at much the same time and may have influenced each other. In addition, Louisa came from Taporley in Cheshire and Eliza's children had been born in Birkenhead so both might feel they were returning to simpler, even happier, days.

John Rayner and Frank Rayner

Opposite the Pilling family were the Rayners at no. 16. The house had been purchased in the 1880s by John Rayner, a woollen draper from Halifax, who in 1891 aged 67 lived there with his "daughter" Ellen 34, and three sons, the younger two of whom were his assistants in the draper's shop (Charles or Chas H 24 and John J 21). The oldest son, Frank William Rayner 27, was an engineer on a sailing ship and may have found the naval part of his father's trade more appealing than the outfitting part - at least at this stage in his life. When his father John died three years later in 1894, it may have been this interest in the sea rather than the shop, engines rather than wool, that meant Frank did not automatically succeed to the business (though he was clearly left the house).

As well as John Rayner and his four adult children, his grandson Gerald Haigh then aged 12 lived with them in 1891. He had been born in Birkdale and it is far from clear whether his mother was Ellen or, less likely, whether his father was her brother Frank, or somebody else outside the household. Indeed, it is not impossible, even probable some might say, that the man he thought his "grandfather", i.e., John Rayner, was his real father.

There are some other anomalies or curiosities in the Rayner record that are worth examining further. In the 1851 Census, John Rayner and his wife Ellen, aged 27 and 24, were living in London Road, Manchester with their first child, a baby son Frederick, and somebody called John Bond, who may have been a lodger but equally might have been Ellen's father. This Census return is so faint in places that his age and occupation are unreadable. What can be discerned though is that, despite being only 27, John Rayner was recorded as a "Master employer of men" as well as a woollen draper and tailor, and well-enough off to employ a servant, even at this early stage of his career.

Ten years later John Rayner was at his brother-in-law's house at Poulton-le-Fylde, the place where his wife Ellen had been born. However, she was not there on Census night, though yet another brother-in-law was, so whatever the nature of the family gathering it seems not to have been a wedding at which the women would certainly have been present nor necessarily even a funeral,

Courtenay Road in 1900: The people who lived there

at which women usually were not in the late eighteenth and early nineteenth centuries.

In the 1871 Census John and Ellen were living in Waterloo Road, Litherland with their daughter Louisa 19 (born while her parents were still in Manchester and not long after her brother Frederick) and their three youngest sons Frank, Chas and John (then aged 7, 4 and 1 respectively). It is conceivable that Frederick was elsewhere but the likelihood must be that he had died, as had any other children born in the twelve years between Louisa's and Frank's births. Now calling himself a merchant clothier and outfitter, John and his family then employed two servants.

Ellen Rayner the wife then disappears from the Census returns and in 1881 John Rayner was at Liverpool Road, Birkdale (the place where his "grandson" Gerald Haigh had been born), with a new "daughter" Emily 25 (so not Louisa by another name for she would then have been 29) and three sons - though not the same three as in other Census returns, for the oldest at 22 was William H, a woollen draper born in Liverpool. Frank W aged 17 was an engineer's apprentice and the youngest John J an eleven year old schoolboy. In other words, Chas H (4 in 1871 and 24 in 1891) was elsewhere. There were also two visitors in the house on Census night, another woollen draper Septimus Donaldson aged 23 and Sara Warden aged 25. She had been born in Birmingham, as had the family's one servant Susannah Atkinson aged 25. As the family servant ten years later was called Susan Atkins aged 35, the likelihood is that this was the same person, inaccurately enumerated or, if different, coincidentally named.

One conclusion might be that the supposed "daughters" in 1881 and 1891, Emily 25 and Ellen 34, had become John Rayner's partners after the death of his wife Ellen in the 1870s, but because of the age gap of thirty years it was more convenient to describe them as daughter than wife in the Census. This might be a supposition too far, of course, and it may be that they were indeed his daughters, but it is also possible that they were the same person and that she was the mother of Gerald Haigh, with John Rayner his father rather than grandfather. They would not be the only family in which a child grew up believing those in the same household were more distantly-related family than they actually were.

In 1901 Frank Rayner was 37, his wife Elizabeth 33 and they and their four year old son (also called Frank) were still at no. 16 Courtenay Road. He described himself as a naval tailor and employer, probably at the Lord Street shop that his father had established, for he was listed in the 1900 edition of the Gore Directory as such,[457] though whether he owned the shop by this stage, or was running it on behalf of the uncle who had inherited it, is not clear. A creditors' notice appeared the year after his father's death, but this would be no more than ensuring any outstanding debts were settled before probate was granted on his estate. Yet, the company may have gone into decline nonetheless, for in what may be thought a desperate attempt to drum up custom, the firm advertised in the *Daily Bulletin* printed on board Cunard's RMS Ivernia on its June 1905 voyage to New York.[458]

By 1911, Frank Rayner had set up on his own as a wholesale clothier at 56B Cambridge Road, Southport. This might suggest his father's firm was once again on the slide, or that there were other disputes about Frank Rayner's management, although it could equally well imply that he preferred to be closer to the sea and/or sought a different, and perhaps less demanding, role in the trade. What it does not seem to have been is a family matter for his wife Elizabeth was there with him, though their son was not (at least on Census night, though he was still alive). The family were no longer listed in Courtenay Road and by 1914 JJ Rayner & Co had joined forces with other firms to form the Miller, Rayner & Haysom partnership, "naval outfitter [and] contractor to HMG, also at 110 Fenchurch St London, 35/36 Oxford St Southampton with factory at 49-55 Regent Rd Liverpool."[459] This suggests that the Rayner company had sacrificed some autonomy for greater security and had been rewarded with a government supply contract for military uniforms just ahead of the First World War.

Peter Marsh

The Marsh family lived at 1 Courtenay Road, one of the three eight bed houses, on the north-western corner with Oxford Road, having bought it from Astrup Cariss in 1882. As well as being the longest residents in Courtenay Road during this period, they are probably the best known in at least three senses:

- Peter Marsh was a Waterloo with Seaforth Local Board (UDC) Councillor around the turn of the twentieth century, first elected in 1899;
- one of his great-grandchildren Barrie Lees has written a book on the Marsh family for the benefit of other family members;[460] and
- the Liverpool sack business founded in 1863 (when it switched from the drapery trade) and known as Peter Marsh and Sons from 1871 is still enjoying huge success in the twenty-first century. Though the main point of contact for the company remains Bootle, the Peter Marsh group website demonstrates not only the firm's continuing growth and diversity, but provides the relevant aspects of its history and chronology.[461] It states "The founder's second son Peter Walter [Marsh of Courtenay Road] joined the family business ... in 1865 [aged about 17]. [He] fathered four sons and six daughters."

Nevertheless, there are one or two points that may be less well-known or less easily found that it is worth adding here to those recorded in these other sources or already mentioned above. For example, Marsh's daughter Salome and Charles Ryle Fay enjoyed a brief teenage romance before he went on to university.[462]

Marsh was elected a UDC Councillor in 1899 and probably served two three-year terms until the 1905 elections.[463] He had been re-elected in 1902 but increasing ill-health forced his early resignation. He had not been listed at all in the 1905/6 attendance schedule, for example, and it was his increasing illness, rather than business pressures, that had prevented him from attending. He was still only in his mid-fifties but in the previous municipal year (1904/5) he had managed to attend over half the time (36 attendances out of 67 possible). At a meeting of the General Purposes Committee in October 1903 he had complained about the 'bad condition of the carriageways of Courtenay Road and Oxford Road'. The Committee instructed the UDC surveyor to have the roads repaired.[464] Few of today's Councillors are able to pursue issues that serve their own interests quite so nakedly, but it might be argued in Marsh's favour that the outcome also benefited many others in the locality as well.

Waterloo-with-Seaforth Urban District Council 10th June 1899
Peter Marsh is one from the right in the back row © Sefton Library Service

Despite ill-health from early in the 1900s, it was October 1922 before Peter Marsh died aged 73. The *Crosby Herald* reported both his funeral and six weeks later his Will.[465] Marsh had died at home where, "after a protracted illness", he was to all intents and purposes an invalid. The Marsh company was increasingly under the control of his four sons (Atkin, Ronald, John and Harold), opening "additional factories and warehouses in London, Manchester, Belfast, Glasgow, Leith, Dundee and Calcutta" during this period or shortly after. Marsh's estate was valued at nearly £17,000 (the equivalent of about half a million pounds sterling today) and Marsh left it all to his wife and children, other than his son Atkin whom he had already made a partner in the firm. Atkin Marsh received no further legacy and was to be the driving force behind the company's expansion.

7. CONCLUSION: SIMILARITIES AND DIFFERENCES

Liverpool continues to be a city of huge inequality but this is not the only similarity it has faced across the nineteenth, twentieth and twenty-first centuries. The concepts of business cycles and cycles of deprivation are particularly evident in Liverpool's history, with the 1880s as grim as the post-WWI downturn, the 1930s even more so, as have been the long periods of unemployment and decline after 1980 and the financial crash of 2008. Those less fortunate have always suffered most, though not necessarily most visibly, and it is not just the recent recessions that have affected women, children and minorities as much as, or more than, those counted in the unemployment figures, usually men. Casual and seasonal employment has long been a hazard; today's equivalent is zero hours contracts that remove any assurance about work and therefore food on the table. Despite the substantial and widely-acknowledged problems, at the time of writing Liverpool is experiencing the roll-out of Universal Credit so, to the existing indignity of food banks, the impoverished are losing out again. The United Nations Special Rapporteur on extreme poverty and human rights reached similar conclusions in reporting on his 2018 visit to the UK as a whole.[466]

But this book is not intended to be a political tract; people's stories speak for themselves and to enable them to do so remains the overwhelming objective. Those who wish to read more, or refresh their awareness of social injustice, can look at Pat Thane's 'Divided Kingdom: A History of Britain 1900 to the Present' which demonstrates how similar are the causes of poverty today to those of 1900;[467] equally revealing is 'Genuinely Seeking Work: Mass Unemployment on Merseyside in the 1930s'.[468] Nevertheless, when the better off are given tax breaks and corporation tax is slashed, while out-sourcing companies go belly-up, taking their own employees and often those in their suppliers down with them, and the 'have nots' are expected to get by on less, the country's priorities should be questioned. The residents of Blackstock Street and Courtenay Road in 1900 and their stories not only provide another means for doing so but demonstrate that not all that much has changed in over a hundred years. To those that have shall be given, while the rest have to fight hard to retain the little with which they started.

Strong Women

If Liverpool is primarily identified with the hard graft that characterises all port cities and much manufacturing, that it has functioned effectively over the centuries has often depended on women as much as men. Children, the country's future, have always depended on strong women who put their family and their children's interests first. Men do too, even if their dependence and the support from women is not always so obvious and direct. Often unrecognised and 'behind the scenes', it is no less real for that and may be evident in community networks as well as in the home.

The stories in this book demonstrate the importance of strong and resilient women in 1900. They may have had to wait until 1928 to flex their political muscle on the same basis as men (when the voting age was equalised at 21), but their domestic and community skills already made a substantial difference to their family's prospects. All but one of the seven stories of Blackstock Street households demonstrate how they relied on strong women. In the cases of Harriet Caldwell and Mary Ann Carroll they would in time become the sole breadwinner for their children, keeping them fed as well as nurturing them physically and emotionally. Both women seem to have been deserted by their husbands but all four of Harriet Caldwell's children remained in school while Mary Ann Carroll provided a home from which her older children could go out to work. Catherine Kerr, Mary True and Sarah Hartley were strong women in different senses, with Mary True coping with the deaths of two of her six children in extreme circumstances within a few months of each other, Sarah Hartley sustaining a home for her six surviving children and an ailing husband whose earning power collapsed in his later years, and Catherine Kerr taking in lodgers to stretch her limited earnings as a tailoress as far as she could. A widowed Elizabeth Goulburn may have been the carer for a disabled son. Only Emma/Emily/Louisa McDonald seems to have been more concerned with 'front', the appearance she could project, rather than with the substance that lay behind it. In one sense she became a victim of the improved circumstances that must have exceeded her expectations as a newly-wed in Hull. The other women were making the best of their lot, illustrating the power of resilience and demonstrating, probably unconsciously, the importance of this to their children.

There were strong women in Courtenay Road as well, not least Fanny Townshend, yet the significance of women's roles is less apparent. They were wives and mothers but the day-to-day household responsibilities, perhaps those for their children as well, devolved to the servants they employed. Indeed, ensuring they selected honest and diligent servants might be thought one of their most important functions. Ann Marsh, Peter's wife, was clearly a strong woman to have borne ten children, while Eliza Pilling and Louisa Hart continued to live with (some of their) adult children after they were widowed. In both cases there could have been an (unspoken) exchange between emotional support to the mother for financial security from her, but this is perhaps no more than to say that family ties remained strong. Whether Annie Pleydell-Bouverie, Ellen Rayner, and even Emily Fay, were strong women cannot be assessed from the available evidence but this does not mean that they were not. There may have been various reasons why Annie Pleydell-Bouverie chose to live apart from her husband in her later years and this could indicate an inner strength and determination rather than its opposite.

One conclusion might be that women in Blackstock Street had a different, more elemental, strength than those in Courtenay Road. Another might be that strong women were more evident in the former, with their and their family's survival dependent on their will, or at least this being required to counter the circumstances in which they lived. Perhaps the most important conclusion though is that the significance of strong women is apparent in most of the fourteen stories.

If strong women were a common factor between many of the households in both streets, organised religion and the impact of war are others.

Organised Religion

One of the noteworthy features of Crosby today is the large number of Catholic churches, ten within the area or nearby, partly the result of the Catholic adherence of the Blundell family who were the landowners for much of the area. The closest Catholic church to

Courtenay Road today is St Edmund of Canterbury just around the corner in Oxford Road, but this was founded in 1943, as also was St Helen's, another Roman Catholic church. There were fewer Roman Catholic churches in 1900 but the importance of all religions to the residents can be seen from Table 4, showing the fifteen churches of all denominations that existed at the turn of the twentieth century (or were being built then). Two were Roman Catholic (a third was founded in 1902), six were Church of England and seven Presbyterian or otherwise non-conformist; furthermore, more than half were founded in the twenty years after 1880, reflecting a growing population as the area expanded during this period.

Name	Denomination	Date founded
St Luke, Crosby	Church of England	1749
St Peter and St Paul, Crosby	Roman Catholic	1826
Christ Church, Waterloo	Church of England	1840
Church Road, Waterloo	Congregational	1854
St John, Waterloo	Church of England	1865
St Nicholas, Blundellsands	Church of England	1871
St Andrew, Waterloo	Presbyterian	1876
Mersey Road, Crosby	Congregational	1884
St Joseph, Blundellsands	Roman Catholic	1886
St Mary the Virgin, Waterloo	Church of England	1886
Oxford Road, Waterloo	Baptist	1890
Crosby Road South, Waterloo	Welsh Calvinist Methodist	1890
Mersey Road, Crosby	Wesleyan Methodist	1891
Warren Road, Blundellsands	Presbyterian	1897
St Faith, Crosby	Church of England	1900

Table 4: Churches less than one and a half miles from Crosby in 1900[469]

Conclusion: Similarities and differences

There were twenty-six churches serving Vauxhall in 1900, of which nine were Church of England and eight Roman Catholic. The latter were St Anthony, Scotland Road, founded 1804; St Joseph, Grosvenor Street, 1845; St Augustine, Great Howard Street, 1849; Our Lady of Reconciliation, Eldon Street, 1859; St Alban, Athol Street, 1859; St Brigid, Bevington Hill, 1870; All Souls, Collingwood Street, 1872; and St Sylvester, Silvester Street, 1875.[470]

As the Vauxhall population in 1901 was about 80,000, and that of Crosby and Waterloo less than 20,000,[471] the number of Roman Catholic churches (though not necessarily the number of seats) per head of population was much the same in the two areas. However, it can be assumed that more of those living in Blackstock Street, as well as in Vauxhall as a whole, not least those whose families or themselves had come from Ireland, would be Roman Catholic and proportionately, therefore, Roman Catholics in Vauxhall may had more difficulty in accessing appropriate places of worship.

Nevertheless, and whatever their faith, organised religion would be a fixed point around which daily lives could orbit and, for some, provide succour and relief or at least an assurance of salvation and better times ahead. This might make it easier to cope with the daily ordeal. As Thomas Hardy had his heroine express it in 'Two on a Tower', "Without the Church to cling to, what have we?"[472]

Impact of War

Joining the army might offer some young men a route out of their life in Blackstock Street but few men from the next generation were old enough to serve in the Boer War 1899-1902[473] and there is no indication that any did so. The 1st Battalion of the King's Liverpool Regiment were stationed in South Africa throughout the war, including among the troops bottled up in the siege of Ladysmith from the beginning of November 1899 to the end of February 1900.[474] When the siege was lifted they were joined a month later by the 1st Voluntary Service Company, and in June 1901 by the 2nd Voluntary Service Company, but in both instances these comprised soldiers volunteering from regiments not detailed to South Africa rather than the general public or conscripts. Nevertheless, the war was closely followed with the battles being remembered in Liverpool place names, such as Kimberley Avenue and Mafeking Close, and perhaps most famously the Kop at Anfield, Liverpool's football ground, being named after the battle of Spion Kop, fought at the end of January 1900 as part of the attempt to relieve Ladysmith and becoming a rout for the British with four times as many soldiers killed as on the Boer side.[475] In addition, Liverpool residents would have been aware of the accompanying dispute between the Conservative government and the Liberal opposition about whether it was a just war, with Lloyd George and some other Liberals promoting the Boer cause. It was certainly a grim one with more British soldiers dying of disease than were killed in action.[476]

In the First World War by contrast several of the younger generation were to fight. Edmund Bishop True, John Culshaw, Joseph Hartley and John Francis Pilling have been referred to above, as has Joseph Caldwell's service soon after the war in the RNVR and Thomas Culshaw's in the merchant marine during it. In addition, CR Fay would serve in the East Kent Regiment and then the Machine Gun Corps from its formation in late 1915.[477] Most if not all of the above seem to have chosen to serve rather than being conscripted.[478] That conscription was necessary demonstrates the huge scale of the conflict, another war that the British had thought would be over by the first Christmas, for neither the regular army nor the volunteers who joined up in a first flush of enthusiasm (often in 'Pals Battalions') proved sufficient. The impact would have been felt by every family, combatant or not, for even if the Defence of the Realm Act in 1914 largely passed unnoticed, the suffering of friends and neighbours and the growing number of casualties returning from the front, some disfigured, others disabled by gas or shell-shock, was soon obvious. And rising prices, apparent by the end of 1916 for basic foodstuffs such as bread, would have been calamitous for people in Blackstock Street who struggled to get by at the best of times.[479] A four pound loaf cost 11d by that November and in 1917 the first (ineffective) rationing scheme was introduced.[480]

Choice and Stability

At first glance it is apparent that few people in either Courtenay Road or Blackstock Street stayed long in the same place. It would

Conclusion: Similarities and differences

be a mistake, however, to think that this was for similar reasons or due to similar causes. There is always a risk of "errors ... in reasoning from actions to motives",[481] but active choice is more likely to have applied to people in Courtenay Road than those in Vauxhall. Some of the latter did move elsewhere (e.g., Hugh Clyde to Largs) but there is a huge difference between taking advantage of opportunities that present themselves, lucky breaks some would call them, and bettering your conditions by creating such opportunities for yourself. Both may rely on hard work but the former is opportunistic, the latter deliberate and dependent on planning and forethought. Frequently, it depends on thrift as well, and this would not be an option in the 'hand to mouth' existence that characterised most lives in Blackstock Street. Another distinction might be between active choice and passive acceptance, or more prosaically between forging ahead and trying to keep your head above water.

Consequently, instability in Courtenay Road usually indicates an upward trajectory, whereas in Blackstock Street it would often demonstrate the fragility of a family's hold on existence. Differences in life expectancy, in education that went beyond the elementary years and in the quality of housing, underline this chasm, as must making the bonds and contacts that could prove useful later. It was not necessarily aspiration that was different, for the drive to optimise one's conditions is common to nearly everybody, but the circumstances, including others' expectations, that made this more or less achievable. Somebody watching from outside might attribute differences to personality; those in it would be aware that situation was at least as significant. It was not the will that was lacking for most people in Blackstock Street, though it might have been diluted or ground down over time, but almost never did this combine with the circumstances that would enable it to be realised. Change was something that happened to you and of which you made the best. In Courtenay Road, by contrast, will and circumstances were more often aligned and, pointing in the same direction, reinforced each other.

NOTES

[1] Marilyn Silverman, 'An Irish Working Class: Explorations in Political Economy and Hegemony, 1800-1950', 2001, p9
[2] Pat Ayers, 'The Liverpool Docklands: Life and Work in Athol Street', 1988
[3] Tim Pat Coogan, 'The Twelve Apostles: Michael Collins, the Squad and Ireland's Fight for Freedom', 2016, p13
[4] Crosby Library archives, Waterloo-with-Seaforth Local Health Board 6th February 1893 minutes
[5] Ramsay Muir, 'A History of Liverpool', 1970, pp297-298
[6] Tony Lane, 'Liverpool: Gateway of Empire', 1987
[7] Ibid, pp128-131
[8] Quoted by Margaret Simey, 'Charitable Effort in Liverpool in the Nineteenth Century', 1951, p98
[9] PJ Waller, 'Democracy and Sectarianism: A Political and Social History of Liverpool 1868-1939', 1981, ppxv & xix
[10] John Belchem and Bryan Biggs (eds.), 'Liverpool: City of Radicals', 2011, p10
[11] James R Lewis, 'The Birth of Waterloo', 3rd edn, 1996
[12] Richard Pollard and Nikolaus Pevsner, 'Lancashire: Liverpool and the South West', 2006, pp484-487
[13] Waller, op cit, p7
[14] Ibid, p2
[15] *Liverpool Mercury* 7th July 1883
[16] Aspects of this are not dissimilar to the merchants who clustered around Abercromby Square in the heart of Liverpool fifty years earlier. See R Lawton, "The population of Liverpool in the mid-nineteenth century", *Transactions of the Historic Society of Lancashire and Cheshire*, 1955, vol. 107, pp89-120 (p95).
[17] Ibid, p5 based in part on BG Orchard 'The Clerks of Liverpool', 1871 which covered 17,400 clerks then in the city. Ten years later Henry Arnold described himself as a ship broker's clerk and had moved to one of the three larger houses on the other side of Courtenay Road.
[18] Jonathan Bennison, 'Map of the town and port of Liverpool', 1835
[19] Thomas Ellison, 'The Cotton Trade of Great Britain', 1968, p168
[20] Alan Smith, "The Herculaneum china and earthenware manufactory, 1796-1840", *Industrial Archaeology*, 1969, 6, pp13-27 (p18)
[21] Perhaps due to the 1846 Sanitary Act requirement that there be no more than eight houses per court with any more resulting in the basic separation of 15 feet between the sides of the court being increased by one foot per house. A Errazurez, "Some types of housing in Liverpool, 1785-1890", *Town Planning Review*, 1946, 19, pp57-68
(These requirements primarily applied to new build after the 1842 Liverpool Building Act, as well as to improvements to existing courts. There was no legal duty to change existing ones.)

[22] From Vauxhall Road in the west: Battersby Place, Canning Place, Menai Place, Providence Place, Economy Place, Mary's Place and near the other end of the street, next to The Grapes, Margaret's Place.

[23] John Finch, 'Statistics of Vauxhall Ward, Liverpool: The condition of the working class in Liverpool in 1842', 1842, p26 refers to nine in all including No.59.

[24] 'Reports Addressed to the Committee of the Liverpool Domestic Mission Society by their Ministers to the Poor and Presented at the Twenty-Second Annual General Meeting of the Society', Liverpool, Ellerbeck and Co., 1859, p15

[25] Pat O'Mara, 'The Autobiography of a Liverpool Irish Slummy', 1934

[26] Martha Kanya-Forstner, 'The Politics of Survival: Irish Women in Outcast Liverpool 1850-1890', Liverpool University PhD thesis, 1997, p69

[27] Ibid, p66

[28] *Liverpool Mercury* 2nd July 1852

[29] *Liverpool Mercury* 6th March 1857

[30] *Liverpool Mercury* 11th April 1867

[31] On his death the Nicholson tannery was sold: *Bristol Mercury* 13th May 1865.

[32] Summer Seat is thought to have derived its name when it "offered uninterrupted views of the river and Cheshire Coast", becoming a popular picnic spot in the early nineteenth century as a result. Terry Cooke, 'Scotland Road: The Old Neighbourhood', Birkenhead, Countywise, 1987, p16

[33] Bernard McPoland, a cotton dealer, had his office at 9 Naylor Street but lived at Crosby Lodge, Waterloo from before 1891 to his death in 1928 in his late 80s.

[34] *Times* 16th December 1874
Also John E Archer, "The press, the cornermen and Liverpool's 'Tithebarn-Street outrage' of 1874", *Transactions of the Historic Society of Lancashire and Cheshire*, 2011, 160, pp117-142

[35] Peter Hyland, 'The Herculaneum Pottery: Liverpool's Forgotten Glory', 2005

[36] Hyland, op cit, pp178-180; Smith, op cit, p23. Also, Joseph Mayer, "On the history of the art of pottery in Liverpool", *Transactions of the Historic Society of Lancashire and Cheshire*, 1854-55, 7, pp178-210 (pp203-207)

[37] *Bristol Mercury* 2nd, 9th and 16th August, 20th September, 11th October, 22nd November 1845

[38] *Preston Guardian* 27th May 1848

[39] *Morning Post* 9th November 1846; *Liverpool Mercury* 3rd April and *Berrow's Worcester Journal* 12th April 1849

[40] *Liverpool Mercury* 24th April 1849

[41] Arthur Freeling, 'The Railway Companion from London to Birmingham, Liverpool, and Manchester: With Guides to the Objects Worthy of Notice in Liverpool, Manchester, and Birmingham', 1841

[42] John K Walton and Alastair Wilcox (eds.), 'Low Life and Moral Improvement in Mid-Victorian England: Liverpool through the Journalism of Hugh Shimmin', 1991, pp101-102
[43] *Liverpool Mercury* 5th May 1843
[44] *Liverpool Mercury* 21st February 1845
[45] *Liverpool Mercury* 19th September 1845 and 9th January 1846
[46] *Liverpool Mercury* 13th July 1847
[47] Waller, op cit, p83
[48] Finch was a close follower of Robert Owen, even to the extent of being one of the prime movers in the Owenite community in Hampshire, Harmony Green. See, for example, Rose chapter in Harold R Hikins (ed.), 'Building the Union: Studies on the Growth of the Worker's Movement, Merseyside, 1756-1967', 1973, pp31-52.
[49] Harold Hikins introduction to John Finch (ed.), 'Statistics of Vauxhall Ward, Liverpool: The Conditions of the Working Class in Liverpool 1842', 1986 (orig. 1841), p. vi
EJ Hobsbawm, 'Labouring Men: Studies in the History of Labour', 1964, pp75-76 cites some of Finch's Vauxhall statistics alongside other contemporary comparisons.
[50] Waller, op cit, p59
[51] Finch, op cit, p27
[52] Of whom, 101 employed 4+ days/week and 63 3 days/week; 518 unemployed or employed <3 days/week; 101 not known
[53] Lawton, op cit, p95 makes the similar point that Liverpool's limited industry was restricted to sugar refining, soap and salt manufacture.
[54] Table 6 in Finch, op cit, pp32-33 identified 22 categories of earnings: none, 1s to 3s, 3s to 20s in seventeen increments of one shilling each, 20s to 30s in two increments of 5s each and 30s to 40s. Finch's table is therefore much more sensitive than is Table 1b.
[55] The average family size in Blackstock Street was 3.9 people, against 4 for the ward as a whole. This makes only a marginal difference for the average family but the larger the family the greater the poverty, and some would be very large indeed.
[56] Caird 1852 cited in John Burnett (ed.), 'Useful Toil: Autobiographies of Working People from the 1820s to the 1920s', 1974, p29,
[57] It is impossible to be more precise for Blackstock Street because of the absence of actual information per family.
[58] Table 9 in Finch, op cit, p36
[59] Ibid, p12
[60] James Samuelson, 'The Lament of the Sweated', 1903, p19
[61] Finch, op cit, p12 and Table 10, p37
[62] Ibid, pp14 and 41-49
[63] Ibid, pp14-15
This was at the corner of Vauxhall Road and Freemasons Row, four streets south of Blackstock Street.

Notes

[64] Ibid, pp15-16

[65] In his diary for 18th November 1875 the 15th Earl of Derby recorded the Cabinet discussing a forthcoming Education Bill and agreeing that "all children working for wages from 5 to 13 should have to have a certificate of being able to read, write and cypher: but numerous exceptions will be necessary". John Vincent (ed.), 'The Diaries of Edward Henry Stanley, 15th Earl of Derby (1826-1893) Between September 1869 and March 1878', vol. 4, 1994, p254

[66] JN Tarn, "Housing in Liverpool and Glasgow: The growth of civic responsibility", *Town Planning Review*, 1969, 39, pp319-334

[67] It should be noted that the house numbers ascribed in the 1851 Census bear no relation to those in the 1853 Gore Directory. For example, Timothy Rimmer, one of the shoe-makers, was listed in the Census at 17 whereas Gore's Directory puts him at number 9.

[68] PE Razzell and RW Wainwright (eds), 'The Victorian Working Class: Selections from Letters to the *Morning Chronicle*', 1973, pxxii; Letter VI

[69] By the 1890s, there was very little housing left in Oriel Street yet the huge number of courts in Paul Street remained.

[70] 'Thirteenth Annual Report of the Poor Law Commissioners', House of Commons 1847: Appendix A, Report No. 8 by Alfred Austin 'Relief of Irish Poor in Liverpool', pp110-116

[71] Returns of the number of Irish poor removed from the parish of Liverpool to Ireland since January 1849, House of Commons, 1854, LV, paper no 374

[72] Muir, op cit, p316

[73] Iain C Taylor, "The insanitary housing question and tenement dwellings in nineteenth century Liverpool", pp41-87 in Anthony Sutcliffe (ed.), 'Multi-Storey Living: The British Working Class Experience', 1974

[74] Ibid, pp77 & 78

[75] Ibid, p80

[76] Lawton, op cit, p93

[77] Ibid, pp101 & 104

[78] Kanya-Forstner, 1997, op cit, p60

[79] It can be assumed that both worked at the lime works then at the end of Blackstock Street.

[80] *Glasgow Herald* 24th July 1886

[81] Graeme Milne, 'People, Place and Power on the Nineteenth Century Waterfront', 2016

[82] https://www.thegazette.co.uk/London/issue/21484/page/2750/data.pdf - accessed 6th October 2017

[83] http://www.pastscape.org.uk/ - accessed 20th October 2017

[84] *Liverpool Mercury* 17th, 21st and 31st January, 4th, 14th, 18th and 28th February, 4th, 14th, 18th and 28th March, 1st and 11th April 1851

[85] http://discovery.nationalarchives.gov.uk/details/r/a3a64b4f-403f-4f90-80ef-b541d43a66f7 - accessed 20th October 2017

[86] Smyth Bros of 37 Blackstock Street claimed that they had done all they could, whereas the prosecution said the appliances at the furnace meant there need be no smoke at all. *Liverpool Mercury* 27th July 1855
A few years previously Smyth Bros had bought, though perhaps unwittingly, two hides that had been stolen. *Liverpool Mercury* 7th December 1847
[87] *Liverpool Mercury* 8th & 10th November 1856
[88] *Liverpool Mercury* 12th October 1871
[89] Richard Hawes, "The municipal regulation of smoke pollution in Liverpool, 1853-1866", *Environment and History*, 1998, 4, pp75-90
[90] *Liverpool Mercury* 12th May 1864 and 15th March 1866
[91] *Leicester Chronicle and the Leicestershire Mercury* 11th April 1896
[92] *Liverpool Mercury* 17th September 1891
Among those present when the foundation stone was laid was Rev Charles Garrett. *Liverpool Mercury* 1st October 1890
[93] Crosby Library archives, Waterloo-with-Seaforth Local Health Board 4th August 1874 minutes
[94] *Bristol Mercury and Daily Post* and *Standard* 25th April, *Star* 28th April 1896 The total net personalty was £76,600 or about £5m today.
[95] *Morning Post* 11th June 1896
[96] *Liverpool Mercury* 24th December 1852
[97] *Morning Post* 26th January 1855
[98] *Daily News* and *Standard* 10th January, *Belfast Newsletter*, *Morning Post* and *John Bull* 12th January 1852
[99] *Dundee Courier* 13th, *Bradford Observer* 14th, *Hull Packet* 15th, *North Wales Chronicle*, *York Herald*, *Leicester Chronicle*, *Huddersfield Chronicle and West Yorkshire Advertiser* 16th, *Lloyd's Weekly Newspaper* 17th and *John Bull* 18th April 1859
[100] *Liverpool Mercury* 16th and *Preston Guardian* 19th July 1856
[101] *Liverpool Mercury* 3rd and *Freeman's Journal* 4th February 1859
[102] Thomas Burke, 'Catholic History of Liverpool', 1910, pp122-123
[103] *Liverpool Review* 23rd October 1886, p7
[104] *Liverpool Mercury* and *Morning Post* 21st, *Freeman's Journal* 24th and *Hull Packet and East Riding Times* 28th January 1853
[105] *Liverpool Mercury* 20th, *Daily News* and *Morning Post* 21st, *Belfast Newsletter* 23rd, *York Herald* 25th and *Lloyd's Weekly Newspaper* 26th September 1858
[106] *Liverpool Mercury* 18th October 1856
According to http://www.bbc.co.uk/news/uk-england-merseyside-33148863 "Records show humpbacks were last seen in the bay in 1938 and 1863." - accessed 26th October 2017
[107] Asa Briggs, 'The Age of Improvement, 1783-1867', 2nd ed., 2000 (orig. 1959), p431

Notes

[108] Diary entry for 19th May 1878 in John Vincent (ed.), 'The Diaries of Edward Henry Stanley, 15th Earl of Derby (1826-1893) Between 1878 and 1893: A Selection', 2003, p16
[109] Ibid, p57 - Diary entry for 19th November 1878
[110] Ibid, p65 - Diary entry for 17th December 1878
[111] *Morning Post* 23rd and *Liverpool Mercury* 24th January 1866
[112] http://victorianpress.wixsite.com/liverpoolporcupine/single-post/2015/05/26/Independence-for-Lancashire - accessed 27th October 2017
[113] *Liverpool Mercury* 15th June 1858 and 14th May 1867
[114] *Liverpool Mercury* 7th June 1866
[115] *Leeds Mercury* and *Liverpool Mercury* 12th September 1868
[116] *Liverpool Mercury* 24th November 1869
[117] *Glasgow Herald* 8th and 19th, *Standard* 9th, *Nottinghamshire Guardian* 12th, *Ipswich Journal* 13th and *Manchester Times* 20th August 1870
[118] *Times* 8th April 1873; also, *The Wrexham Advertiser, Denbighshire, Flintshire, Cheshire, Shropshire, Merionethshire, and North Wales Register* 12th April 1873
[119] *Bradford Observer* 2nd and *Huddersfield Daily Chronicle* 4th June 1873
[120] *Liverpool Mercury* 9th September 1873
[121] *Bristol Mercury* 21st April and 28th, *Glasgow Herald* 20th & 27th July 1855
[122] *Glasgow Herald* 25th July and 8th August 1856
[123] *Liverpool Mercury* 28th March 1866; also *Times* 20th February 1866
[124] *Glasgow Herald* 17th February 1873
[125] *Glasgow Herald* 22nd and 29th January, *Bristol Mercury* 12th February 1876
[126] *Liverpool Mercury* 28th & 30th September, 3rd October 1878
[127] *Sheffield and Rotherham Independent* 20th January 1880
[128] *Morning Post* 29th April 1858
[129] *Liverpool Mercury* 13th July 1878
[130] He was also a director of the Imperial Marine Insurance Company whose head office was in Liverpool but had another at Cornhill in London. *Pall Mall Gazette* 5th, 6th, 7th, 9th, *Standard* 5th, 6th, 8th, *Freeman's Journal* 8th, *Liverpool Mercury* 12th December 1871.
Battersby would give £1000 towards the endowment of a maths professorship at University College, Liverpool. *Liverpool Mercury* 4th May 1882
[131] *Liverpool Mercury* 4th, 14th June and 26th, 30th July 1878
The mustard mill at the end of the street was also up for sale in 1878. *Liverpool Mercury* 17th January and *Sheffield and Rotherham Independent* 22nd February 1878
[132] *Liverpool Mercury* 4th October 1878
[133] *Liverpool Mercury* 16th November 1880

[134] Including the formation in 1889 of the Mersey Quay and Railway Carters Union with 3000 members initially. Arthur Marsh and Victoria Ryan, 'Historical Directory of Trade Unions: vol.3', 1987, pp249-250
[135] *Liverpool Mercury* 4th December 1874
[136] *Liverpool Mercury* 15th February 1877 In both cases the application was to be made to J Mills at 1 Blackstock Street.
[137] *Liverpool Mercury* 14th November 1878
[138] *Liverpool Mercury* 7th September 1878
[139] *Liverpool Mercury* 23rd September 1878
[140] *Manchester Times* 16th August 1879
[141] *Liverpool Mercury* 18th August 1879
[142] *Liverpool Mercury* 11th November 1879
[143] *Liverpool Mercury* 30th April 1884
[144] *Liverpool Mercury* 23rd July 1884
Another example was the 'Beautiful Warrington Society' in which the local soap company Crosfield's participated in the 1890s. AE Musson, 'Enterprise in Soap and Chemicals: Joseph Crosfield & Sons Ltd, 1815-1965', 1965, p152
[145] The lard and oil refinery at number 6, for example, was advertised for sale in March 1882 (*Liverpool Mercury* 13th March 1882) while the wood importers RG Tickle and Son moved to the yard at numbers 33-37 that September when their lease at 77-81 Naylor Street expired (*Liverpool Mercury* 5th, 8th and 15th September 1882).
[146] *Liverpool Mercury* 17th November 1869 when an eleven-month old baby died in one of the courts when it was left in a drawer on the floor overnight.
[147] *Freeman's Journal* 16th January 1880
[148] Diary entry for 12th January 1880 in Vincent, op cit, 2003, p205 Derby was chairman of the Liverpool bench for many years and Vincent comments that "His knowledge of drink, Irishmen and working class violence was therefore extensive and peculiar". Ibid, pxi
Yet Derby had noted previously on 14th January 1879 that the assizes at Kirkdale had tried "hardly any assaults: which is due to hard times and consequent enforced sobriety". Ibid, p88
Three months later, and well before the severe slump of the mid-1880s, Derby added "Police reports show a decrease of petty offences due to lower wages, and their consequence less beer". Ibid, 22nd April 1879, p119
[149] Diary entry for 20th June 1878 in Vincent, op cit, 2003, p25
[150] N Hockenhull, 'Waterloo with Seaforth Local Board of Health: The Beginning', Paper read to Crosby and District History Society, March 1955, pp2 & 3A
[151] John Marshall, 'The Lancashire and Yorkshire Railway: vol. 1', 1969, pp150-153
[152] Ibid, p153
[153] Hugh Gault, 'The Quirky Dr Fay: A Remarkable Life', 2011

Notes

[154] CR Fay, 'Huskisson and His Age', 1951, p20n
[155] Crosby Library archives, Waterloo-with-Seaforth Local Health Board 4th February 1867 & 3rd May 1869 minutes
[156] Ibid, 7th April 1873 and 5th July 1875 minutes
[157] https://www.thegazette.co.uk/London/issue/25855/page/5121/data.pdf - accessed 18th January 2018
[158] http://www.costain.com/about-us/our-history/ - accessed 18th January 2018
[159] Crosby Library archives, Waterloo-with-Seaforth Local Health Board 4th & 22nd December 1876 minutes
[160] Ibid, 4th April 1878 minutes
[161] Ibid, 6th September 1880 minutes
[162] *Liverpool Mercury* 13th, 14th, 19th, 21st, 27th, 30th January & 2nd, 3rd, 5th February 1863
[163] *Freeman's Journal* 31st May 1881, *Liverpool Mercury* 14th July and *Cheshire Observer* 9th September 1882
[164] *Liverpool Mercury* 25th February 1880
[165] Crosby Library archives, Waterloo-with-Seaforth Local Health Board 2nd August 1880 minutes
[166] *Liverpool Mercury* 20th March & 11th April 1882
[167] *Liverpool Mercury* 23rd, 27th, 28th & 29th March 1882
[168] *Liverpool Mercury* 16th May 1882
[169] *Liverpool Mercury* 19th, 28th September & 4th October 1882
[170] Barrie Lees, personal communication, 15th November 2017
[171] In the Bible Salomé was the step-daughter of Herod (he had married her mother), danced for him and sought the beheading of John the Baptist, already Herod's prisoner, when her dancing pleased Herod. She was also the mother of the disciples James and John and was present at Christ's crucifixion.
[172] *Liverpool Mercury* 11th February and 9th May 1890
[173] *Liverpool Mercury* 24th October 1892
On this occasion they also specified that applicants be Protestant.
[174] *Journal of the Society of Arts*, 10th February 1858, 6, pp204-205; *The Athenaeum* 14th May 1859
[175] *Times* 30th July 1883
[176] *Morning Post* 3rd November 1884
[177] *Liverpool Mercury* 13th March 1883
[178] *Edinburgh Gazette*, 25th December 1883 bankruptcy of Astrup Cariss, 35A Castle St, accountant and residing at 60 Hope St, Liverpool; *Liverpool Mercury* 21st January 1884
[179] *Liverpool Mercury* 3rd January 1884; on 30th November 1883 the newspaper reported that he had left the City some time ago.
[180] *Liverpool Mercury* 12th March 1884
[181] National archives DRO 7/11, 21st October 1884
[182] *Liverpool Mercury* 31st October 1884

[183] *Liverpool Mercury* 25th, 28th April, 1st May 1885
[184] *Liverpool Mercury* 6th May 1885
[185] *Liverpool Mercury* 8th May 1885
[186] *Liverpool Mercury* 8th October 1886
[187] *Liverpool Mercury* 20th March, 1st, 5th, 19th April, 13th September 1890
[188] *Liverpool Mercury* 1st July 1892
[189] *Morning Post* 1st July 1887
[190] *Morning Post* 11th January 1888
[191] *Morning Post* 25th January 1889
[192] *Liverpool Mercury* 9th, 11th, 14th, 16th, 18th, 26th April, 3rd May, 12th 18th, 24th, 28th September and 1st October 1894
[193] *Liverpool Mercury* adverts August and September 1886, January 1887 and January, May and August 1892
[194] *Liverpool Mercury* 7th July 1894
[195] *Liverpool Mercury* 11th January 1895
[196] *Liverpool Mercury* 11th February 1895
[197] *Liverpool Mercury* 1st September and 28th October 1885
[198] Waterloo Directory for 1888
[199] *Liverpool Mercury* 13th & 14th April 1892
[200] *Preston Guardian* 21st May 1892
[201] *Liverpool Mercury* 30th November 1895
[202] *Derby Mercury* 25th November 1896
[203] *Times* 28th June and 16th July 1907
[204] *Liverpool Mercury* 3rd, 4th and 5th May 1894
[205] *The Standard* 1st February 1895
[206] *Liverpool Mercury* 9th February 1895
[207] Mona Hearn, 'Below Stairs: Domestic Service Remembered in Dublin and Beyond, 1880-1922', 1993 notes that employers took care when choosing a servant and probably looked for literate people (p12).
[208] Jose Harris, 'Private Lives, Public Spirit: A Social History of Britain, 1870-1914', 1993, p19
[209] *Liverpool Mercury* 30th July, *Manchester Times* 31st July, *Lancaster Gazette* and *Blackburn Standard* both 1st August 1891
[210] John Furnival, 'Children of the Second Spring: Father James Nugent and the Work of Child Care in Liverpool', 2005, p227 'Second Spring' was Cardinal Newman's term for the 1850 revival of the Catholic hierarchy.
[211] Francis Devas, 'Mother Mary Magdalen of the Sacred Heart (Fanny Margaret Taylor) Foundress of the Poor Servants of the Mother of God 1832-1900', 1927, p283
[212] A Liverpool refuge for prostitutes had been suggested to the 15th Earl of Derby in 1884. He had suggested Ormskirk instead "inasmuch as a crowded town is hardly the right place for such an institution". Diary entry for 27th December 1884 in Vincent, op cit, 2003, p731

[213] Liverpool Records Office 331.137 COM 'Full Report of the Commission of Inquiry into the subject of the Unemployed in the city of Liverpool', *Liverpool Post and Echo*, 1894
None lived in Blackstock Street
[214] Liverpool Records Office 361 CEN 3/1 William Grisewood, 'The Poor of Liverpool and What is Done for Them', 1899
[215] Joe Holland, 'Modern Catholic Social Teaching: The Popes Confront the Industrial Age 1740-1958', 2003, p183
[216] Richard L Camp, 'The Papal Ideology of Social Reform: A Study in Historical Development, 1878-1967', 1969, p79
[217] John Belchem, "The Liverpool-Irish enclave", *Immigrants and Minorities*, 1999, 18 (2&3), pp128-146 (p135).
[218] Martha Kanya-Forstner, "Defining womanhood: Irish women and the Catholic church in Victorian Liverpool", *Immigrants and Minorities*, 1999, 18 (2&3), pp168-188 (p169)
[219] Ibid, p173
[220] See http://www.welldoers.org/ - accessed 30th January 2018
At 119-133 Limekiln Lane, a ten minute walk and half a mile from the eastern end of Blackstock Street.
[221] St Saviour's Refuge, Paul Street, at https://www.wearenugent.org/about/background/ - accessed 22nd February 2018. In 1901 Census at 41 Bevington Bush, between eastern end of Blackstock Street and Paul Street.
Further details at http://www.childrenshomes.org.uk/list/MH4.shtml - accessed 20th February 2018
[222] Devas, op cit, p283; Furnival, op cit, pp230-231 provides further detail.
[223] Liverpool Metropolitan Cathedral Archdiocesan archives CHC/S7/16/A/3 St Saviour's Refuge Paul Street, Correspondence, Reports, Financial and Property matters 1878 – 1932
[224] Lindsey Earner-Byrne, 'Letters of the Catholic Poor: Poverty in Independent Ireland, 1920-1940', 2017, p216
[225] Diary entry for 22nd January 1881 in Vincent, op cit, 2003, p299
Derby records that there were 22 degrees of frost in 1881, people froze to death and the Mersey was iced enough for at least one person to walk across. The winter was the worst since 1861, he thought, and that did not last so long.
Martha Kanya-Forstner, 1999, op cit, p173 singles out 1878 as another harsh winter "when thousands of casual labourers were thrown out of work".
[226] Neil Parsons, 'King Khama, Emperor Joe and the Great White Queen: Victorian Britain Through African Eyes', 1998, pp28-29
[227] *Liverpool Mercury* 15th December 1894
[228] *Liverpool Mercury* 25th December 1894
[229] *Liverpool Mercury* 31st December 1894
[230] *Liverpool Mercury* 1st & 2nd January 1895

[231] *Liverpool Mercury* 11th January 1895
[232] *Liverpool Mercury* 14th January 1895
[233] *Liverpool Mercury* 15th January 1895
[234] *Liverpool Mercury* 16th January 1895
[235] *Liverpool Mercury* 24th January 1895
[236] *Liverpool Mercury* 31st January 1895
[237] *Liverpool Mercury* 1st February 1895
[238] *Liverpool Mercury* 7th February 1895
[239] Garrett had inducted Arthur Wood, Kingsley Wood's father, into the Wesleyan Methodist Church and Arthur Wood was invited by the Mission to succeed Garrett in 1900. Wood declined, deciding that his commitments in London and at Wesley's Chapel in the City Road prevented him. See Hugh Gault, 'Making the Heavens Hum: Kingsley Wood and the Art of the Possible 1881-1924', 2014, p20.
[240] *Liverpool Mercury* 18th February 1895
[241] Ibid, letter from E Valentine Smith
[242] 'Report of the Royal Commission on Alien Immigration', London, HMSO, 1903, p14, para 93
[243] Ibid, p21 para 139
[244] Ibid, p27 para 170
[245] PJ Waller, 'Town, City and Nation: England 1850-1914', 1983, p284
[246] Mike Morris, Tony Wailey & Andrew Davies (eds.), 'George Garrett: Ten Years On the Parish', 2017, p59
[247] Liverpool Records Office 352.4 HEA Medical Officer of Health report for 1900
[248] Ayers, op cit, p8
[249] Ibid, p35
[250] Silverman, op cit; Earner-Byrne, op cit, pp190-196 for example
According to the 1901 Census, about 14.5% of married or widowed women in Liverpool were employees. This is almost certainly an under-estimate.
[251] Melanie Tebbutt, 'Making Ends Meet: Pawnbroking and Working-Class Credit', 1983, p54
[252] 'Report by the Joint Select Committee of the House of Lords and the House of Commons on the Moneylenders Bill ...', London, HMSO, 1925
The committee heard eight days of evidence with Keeling's testimony on 19th June 1925 reported in paras 900-944 and Payne's on 24th June in paras 1395-1465.
References to Liverpool appear 46 times in the report.
[253] 'Report of an Enquiry by the Board of Trade into Working-Class Rents, Housing and Retail Prices', Cd 3864, London, HMSO, 1908; 'Report of an Enquiry by the Board of Trade into Working-Class Rents and Retail Prices', Cd 6955, London, HMSO, 1913
[254] Ibid, p277
[255] Waller, 1981, op cit, p81; George Chandler, 'Liverpool', 1957, p418

[256] Waller, 1981, op cit, pp41-42
[257] Ibid, p45
[258] Ibid, p59
[259] A marine insurance broker and writer on the subject who, according to his DNB entry, had set up his own company Court and McArthur in 1874 at the age of 30. It had offices at Exchange Buildings, Liverpool and in London.
[260] LW Brady, 'TP O'Connor and the Liverpool Irish', 1983, pp143 & 145 also refers to the Liberals losing Exchange to a "Unionist" (i.e., Liberal Unionist) in 1895 and an "unsuccessful intervention" by O'Connor's party colleagues in the 1897 by-election, though the latter had an impact in reducing the "Unionist" majority to 54.
[261] Waller, 1981, op cit, p100
[262] Ibid, p137
[263] Brady, op cit, p26 Also see p2 above.
[264] Waller, 1981, op cit, pp160-162
[265] Freddy O'Connor, 'A Pub on Every Corner: vol.3 - North Liverpool', 1998, p3
[266] Martha Kanya-Forstner, 1999, op cit, p177 She refers to church anxiety about this as far back as 1850.
[267] Liverpool Record Office 347/JUS/1/1/52 1895-1896
Strangely there is no mention of the Green Flag Vaults in these licensing records.
[268] Liverpool Record Office M380 PWK 18/1/5
[269] Halsbury's Laws of England (4th edition), 2004: 35(1)71 referring to arbitration (ultimately decided by the Court of Appeal notes 11 and 12 under the 1890 Partnership Act) and 7(2)1599 referring to the procedure for rectifying registration (a 1902 Court of Chancery case note 7).
Also quoted as case law in three High Court and one Supreme Court (Law Lords) cases. See legal reports in *Times* 9th December 1901, 19th February 1902, 27th July and 13th August 1906.
[270] Liverpool Record Office M380 PWK 18/5/1; Norman Barber, 'A Century of British Brewers 1890-1990', 1994, p67
[271] http://breweryhistory.com/wiki/index.php?title=List_of_Robert_Cain_Pubs - accessed 22nd November 2017
[272] www.merseypub.com/guide/pu101.htm - accessed 10th August 2017
[273] O'Connor, op cit, p28
[274] *Liverpool Mercury* 7th March 1874
[275] Published with the agreement of the Bluecoat Press 18th February 2019
[276] Tebbutt, op cit, p43
[277] Ibid, p2
[278] Eventually under a revised Act of 1872 that specified charges, interest rates and rules on selling unredeemed items. Tebbutt, op cit, p8
[279] Tebbutt, op cit, p10

[280] Ibid, p11
[281] Ayers, op cit, pp64-68
[282] David Vincent, 'Poor Citizens: The State and the Poor in Twentieth Century Britain', 1991, p4
[283] For example, Graeme Milne, "Maritime city, maritime culture? Representing Liverpool's waterfront districts since the mid-nineteenth century", pp88-108 in Mike Benbough-Jackson and Sam Davies (eds.), 'Merseyside: Culture and Place', 2011. On p91 Milne refers to the report the Chief Constable Nott-Bower made to Liverpool Council on the crackdown.
[284] John Benson, 'The Penny Capitalists: A Study of Nineteenth-Century Working-class Entrepreneurs', 1983, p70
[285] Furnival, op cit, p228
[286] See DNB entry for Fanny Taylor
"By 1900 [the Order] had women's refuges in Streatham, Soho, Brentford, and Liverpool; orphanages in Roehampton and Brentford; homes for the elderly in Dublin and Rathdown Union; a hostel in Paris; schools in Rome and Cork; and, its most ambitious undertaking, Providence Hospital, a free industrial hospital in St Helens, Lancashire."
[287] Paula Bartley, 'Prostitution: Prevention and Reform in England, 1860-1914', 2000, pp54 & 166-167
[288] At 55 Bidston Road, Oxton just to the north of Shrewsbury Road, Birkenhead, where he died in 1936.
https://www.thegazette.co.uk/London/issue/34286/page/3321/data.pdf - accessed 26th March 2018
[289] *Liverpool Mercury* 8th October 1880
[290] Also in HM Luft, 'A History of Merchant Taylors' School, Crosby 1600-1970', 1970, p229. My thanks to Trevor Hildrey the School's archivist for this information.
[291] GB1752.LBC/2/99 Meetings of the Northern Soapmakers Association (including 17th April 1901) and GB1752.LBC/2/101 Soapmakers Association 34th Annual Report, June 1901, p98, both Unilever Collections, Unilever, Arts, Archives and Records Management, Port Sunlight.
[292] Musson, 1965, op cit, p143
[293] GB1752.JCS/WG/2/3/1 including Gossage's AGM on 25th July 1911 where JJ and GR Crosfield and Jones were confirmed as Directors for the next three years. Unilever Collections, Unilever, Arts, Archives and Records Management, Port Sunlight.
[294] AE Musson, 'The Growth of British Industry', 1981 (orig. 1978), pp249-250
Brewing was one of the most obvious examples of this trend, while British Oil and Cake Mills brought together seventeen firms in 1899.
[295] Charles Wilson, 'The History of Unilever: A Study in Economic Growth and Social Change', vol. I, 1954, p77

[296] *Times* 13th October 1906; HR Edwards, 'Competition and Monopoly in the British Soap Industry', 1962, p166
[297] Unilever Information Guide No.4, 'The Formation of Unilever', Port Sunlight, UARM, undated, p12
[298] WH Lever DNB entry
[299] GB 1752.JCS/WG/4/1/7: *Daily Telegraph* 15th December 1908, *Times* 11th April 1910, Unilever Collections, Unilever, Arts, Archives and Records Management, Port Sunlight.
[300] Unilever Information Guide No.4
[301] *Liverpool Mercury* 5th May 1897
[302] GB1752.EFL/JW/1/20/2/16, Letters between Briggs and Joseph Watson, 19th to 28th September 1906, Unilever Collections, Unilever, Arts, Archives and Records Management, Port Sunlight. Briggs' letter of 19th September 1906 included the shares in Lever Bros or cash alternative that he would accept.
[303] See Deacon's DNB entry for further detail
[304] *Birmingham Daily Post* 7th and 9th March, and *Sheffield and Rotherham Independent* 6th, 7th, 9th-11th March 1891
[305] *Sheffield and Rotherham Independent* 25th, 30th & 31st May, 5th & 6th December 1892
[306] *Hampshire Advertiser* 30th May 1891
[307] For example, *The Graphic* 12th & 26th September, 24th October, 21st November, 5th & 19th December 1891, 2nd January, 13th February, 12th March, 9th April & 7th May 1892
[308] Diary entry for 25th December 1884 in Vincent, op cit, 2003, p730
[309] Diary entry for 25th December 1885 in Vincent, op cit, 2003, p819
[310] *Liverpool Mercury* 24th July, 7th & 10th August, 9th September 1891
[311] *Liverpool Mercury* 22nd January & 24th February 1892
[312] *Liverpool Mercury* 20th November 1894
[313] *Liverpool Courier* 2nd, 13th & 15th January 1897; *Liverpool Mercury* 10th, 19th & 25th May 1897
[314] *Liverpool Mercury* 14th January 1897
[315] *Times* 13th & 23rd February 1899
[316] *Liverpool Mercury* 23rd March 1897
[317] Gore's Directory of Liverpool and Birkenhead 1900 Part 2: Alphabetical Directory, p1248 at http://specialcollections.le.ac.uk/cdm/compoundobject/collection/p16445col14/id/278535/rec/7 , https://archive.org/stream/listofmembers1901instuoft/listofmembers1901instuoft_djvu.txt and https://patents.google.com/patent/US848704A/en
- all accessed 11th April 2018
[318] See R Bean chapter on new unionism, pp99-118 in Hikins, 1973, op cit.
[319] Arthur Marsh and John B Smethurst, 'Historical Directory of Trade Unions: vol.5', 2006, pp196-197

The Union did not last long as membership dwindled through the 1890s. It was dissolved in 1904 and the remaining members absorbed into the Amalgamated Union of Co-operative Employees in 1905.

[320] *Liverpool Mercury* 4th June 1891
[321] *Liverpool Mercury* 16th June 1891
[322] *Liverpool Mercury* 8th April 1892
[323] *Liverpool Mercury* 17th & 21st June 1892
[324] *Liverpool Mercury* 13th August 1894
[325] *Liverpool Mercury* 1st January 1896
[326] *Leeds Mercury* 18th September 1900
[327] Harold W Brace, 'History of Seed Crushing in Great Britain', 1906 lists them in Appendix A pp139-144.
[328] Ibid, p142 Though the *Liverpool Mercury* never refers to it by this name, or indeed at all.
[329] BOCM Prospectus *London Evening News* 11th and *Daily Mail* 13th July 1899
Other Directors with firms based (at least in part) in Liverpool were BW Cox of Phoenix Oil and FC Liversedge of W&WH Stead.
[330] Evelyn Hubbard, "American 'Trusts' and English combinations", *Economic Journal*, 1902, 12, pp159-176 (p171)
[331] HW Macrosty, "Business aspects of British Trusts", *Economic Journal*, 1902, 12, pp347-366; *New York Times* article on "English oil combination" 14th July 1899, p3
[332] *Economist* 15th February 1908, p324
[333] Wilson, op cit, pp278-282
[334] Brace, op cit, p11; JW Pearson, "The seed crushing industry", *Journal of the Royal Society of Arts*, 12th December 1919, pp50-62 (pp57-59) JW Pearson was then the BOCM Chairman and Managing Director.
[335] Brace, op cit, p142
[336] *Morning Post* 24th June 1895
[337] *Cheshire Observer* 21st December 1895
They repeated this in subsequent years and by 1898 had expanded to awards at a Burnley show. *Weekly Standard and Express* 17th December 1898
[338] *Staffordshire Advertiser* 8th December 1900
[339] Brace, op cit, p142
[340] John L Garbutt (ed.), 'Manbré and Garton Ltd 1855-1955: A Hundred Years of Progress', 1955, pp11, 22 & 26
[341] Philippe Chalmin, 'The Making of a Sugar Giant: Tate & Lyle 1859-1989', 1990, p63
[342] Christine Clark, 'The British Malting Industry Since 1830', 1998, pp113 & 114
[343] *Liverpool Mercury* 29th June and 24th August 1882, the former along with Smyth Bros.

Notes

[344] *Huddersfield Chronicle*, *Morning Post* and *Liverpool Mercury* 24th July 1885; *Sheffield and Rotherham Independent* and *Huddersfield Chronicle and West Yorkshire Advertiser* 25th July 1885

[345] *Cheshire Observer* 5th July 1884

[346] *Liverpool Mercury* 16th March 1897 and many other reports.

[347] *Liverpool Mercury* 7th December 1897

[348] Addendum B to 'Report to the Local Government Board on Recent Epidemic Arsenical Poisoning Attributed to Beer', Cd 459, London, HMSO, 1901

[349] *Yorkshire Evening Post* 5th and *Manchester Courier and Lancashire General Advertiser* 6th February 1901

[350] Royal Commission on Arsenical Poisoning: Minutes of Evidence vol. 1 - 1901 [Cd 1845] and vol. II - 1902-3 [Cd 1869]; Final Report [Cd 1848], London, HMSO, 1903

[351] *Yorkshire Evening Post* 11th April 1902

[352] Kelly's Directory of the Leather Trades, 8th edn., 1899, pp872 & 997

[353] James Samuelson, 'The Lament of the Sweated', 1903, pp11-15 and 'The Children of Our Slums', 1911, pp3-5

Lawrence Feehan, 'Charitable Effort, Statutory Authorities and the Poor in Liverpool c1850-1914', Liverpool University PhD thesis, 1987, notes that "… the levels [of slum mortality] reached by Scotland and Vauxhall Wards by 1914 were hardly better than Abercromby Ward had achieved by the early 1870s". (p ix)

[354] *Liverpool Mercury* 22nd July 1890 & 19th July 1892

[355] House no.9 and four properties in court 3 adjoining were advertised in the *Liverpool Mercury* 13th May 1892: "Freehold. Rental £56 11s; chief £10."

When one of the court properties was available again, surprisingly it too was advertised: "4 In 3 Court … Very respectable. Key at 9 Blackstock Street". *Liverpool Mercury* 4th January 1894

[356] Michael O'Neill, St Anthony's archivist, personal communication 8th June 2018

[357] *Liverpool Review* 1st March 1890, p11 "The carters' new union: A glimpse of the life and work of Liverpool carters" (i.e., Mersey Quay and Railway Carters Union formed 1889)

[358] https://maps.nls.uk/view/126523106#zoom=5&lat=5032&lon=4527&layers=BT - accessed 22nd May 2018

[359] Liverpool Records Office 352/MIN/HEA II/34/6 'Working conditions for Corporation carters 1910-1920'

[360] *Liverpool Review* 8th March 1890, p14 "Thirty victories for the carters' union" from Secretary of the Union in response to 1st March article

[361] Feehan, op cit, p486 - Table 20a: Number and percentage of applications [for relief] from certain Liverpool trades

[362] Pamela Horn, 'The Rise and Fall of the Victorian Servant', 1990 (orig. 1975), pp172-173
[363] 'The Autobiography of a Charwoman, as Chronicled by Annie Wakeman', 1906
[364] http://www.merseyserollofhonour.co.uk/get2.php?cwgc=3038867 - accessed 29th May 2018
[365] Donald McCormick, 'The Mystery of Lord Kitchener's Death', 1959, pp19 & 22
[366] Ibid pp29-30
[367] 737 deaths according to https://www.scotsman.com/news/truth-behind-the-sinking-of-hms-hampshire-revealed-1-4146171 - accessed 29th May 2018
[368] McCormick, op cit, pp20 & 30
[369] *Liverpool Daily Post* 5th June 1917
[370] *Liverpool Daily Post, Liverpool Echo* 9th August 1917
[371] Linda Grant, "Women's work and trade unionism in Liverpool 1890-1914", *North West Labour History Society Bulletin*, 1980/81, 7, pp65-83 (p69)
[372] Krista Cowman, 'Mrs Brown is a Man and a Brother', 2004, pp27-29
[373] Grant, op cit, p69
[374] Ibid
[375] Arthur Marsh and Victoria Ryan, 'Historical Directory of Trade Unions: vol.4', 1994, pp42-424 and 447-449
[376] Grant, op cit, p70
[377] *Liverpool Mercury* 16th and 24th June 1890
[378] *Wigan Observer and District Advertiser* 5th October 1907
[379] National archives mercantile marine ribbon and British medal ribbon issued 19th August 1919 to Thomas Culshaw born 1884 - accessed 18th June 2018.
[380] National archives Liverpool regiment Private 74567 (enlisted 6th June 1916); Labour Corps 49908 April/May 1917 - accessed 24th May 2018.
[381] As in the Manchester example in Waller, 1983, op cit, p303.
[382] Crosby Library archives, Waterloo-with-Seaforth Local Health Board 28th August 1900 Health Committee minutes (p148 in 1900/01 minute book)
[383] *Police Gazette* 13th July 1917 CRO No. 6367-16
[384] http://www.liverpoolmuseums.org.uk/mol/visit/galleries/soldiers/research/kingsreg/index.aspx - accessed 5th July 2018
[385] National archives medal card WO 372/9/66022: Liverpool Regiment (No. 62161), Labour Corps (No. 40421)
[386] John Starling and Ivor Lee, 'No Labour, No Battle: Military Labour During the First World War', 2009, p327
[387] Ibid, pp159-161

Notes

[388] Also in Jennifer Stanistreet and Andrew Farthing, 'Crosby in Camera', Sefton Council, 1995. Crosby library reference TR37.
[389] Gault, 2011, op cit, p28 Original reports in *Times* 16th, 17th and 22nd July 1903
[390] Crosby Library archives
[391] Hugh Gault, 'Kingsley Wood: Scenes from a Political Life 1925-1943', 2017, pp174-185
[392] See https://archiveshub.jisc.ac.uk/search/archives/50a5d416-8fc1-3a00-9345-9f16d7b07b73 - accessed 2nd July 2018. There remained some private telephone services, for example in Hull.
[393] It was under this name that the company sponsored a prize at the Blackburn cattle show *Weekly Standard and Express* 22nd December 1900. This was not Liverpool Vesta Cake Company, which extensively adopted this promotional gambit, for it is identified separately in the telephone directory.
[394] No doubt claiming to be older than your chronological age did happen but it is much rarer.
[395] Crosby Library archives, Waterloo-with-Seaforth Local Health Board 4th June 1883 minutes (p186 in 1882 to 1885 minute book)
[396] Ibid, 2nd July 1883 minutes (p194)
[397] Ibid, 5th April 1886 minutes (p52 in 1885 to 1892 minute book)
[398] Ibid, 5th July 1886 (p83)
[399] Ibid, 2nd May 1887 (p171)
[400] When this map was updated in 1908, the trees had been cut down.
[401] A Conservative grouping set up in 1883 by Disraeli's admirers to honour his memory. The primrose was Disraeli's favourite flower.
[402] Cowman, op cit, pp43 & 46
[403] *Liverpool Mercury* 11th June 1890
[404] For example: http://hastingschronicle.net/features/the-ragged-trousered-philanthropists-a-new-introduction/ - accessed 17th July 2017; http://www.unionhistory.info/ragged/tressell.php - accessed 10th July 2018
[405] Charles Ryle Fay, 'Round About Industrial Britain 1830-1860', Toronto, University of Toronto Press, 1952, pp102-103 note
[406] See Gault, 2011, op cit, p13 for further details.
[407] Bosdin Leech, 'History of the Manchester Ship Canal from Its Inception to Its Completion: 2 vols.', Manchester, Sherratt and Hughes, 1907, vol. 1, pp89, 208
[408] Diary entry for 11th August 1882 in Vincent, op cit, 2003, p453
[409] Leech, op cit, vol. 2, p226
[410] Francis E Hyde, 'Liverpool and the Mersey: An Economic History of a Port', Newton Abbot, David & Charles, 1971, p57
[411] Graeme Milne, 'Trade and Traders in Mid-Victorian Liverpool: Mercantile Business and the Making of a World Port', Liverpool, Liverpool University Press, 2000, pp105-107, 118-121, 131

Also, Peter N Davies, 'Henry Tyrer: A Liverpool Shipping Agent and His Enterprise, 1879-1979', London, Croom Helm, 1979

[412] Gore 1900 Pt2 [Alphabetical Directory], p275 http://specialcollections.le.ac.uk/cdm/compoundobject/collection/p16445col l4/id/278535/rec/18 - accessed 13th July 2018

[413] Gore 1900 Pt1 [Street List and Street Directory], p257 http://specialcollections.le.ac.uk/cdm/compoundobject/collection/p16445col l4/id/278528/rec/9 -accessed 13th July 2018
The coal merchant Archibald Bathgate (see 11 Courtenay Road in Table 2) also had offices in this street.

[414] *Manchester Evening News* 11th December 1903

[415] *Manchester Courier and Lancashire General Advertiser* 4th January 1904

[416] Crosby Library archives, Waterloo-with-Seaforth Local Health Board 3rd February 1896 minutes (p417 in 1892 to 1898 minute book)

[417] Crosby Library archives, Waterloo-with-Seaforth Local Health Board 1st June 1898 General Purposes Committee (p67 in 1898-1899 minute book)

[418] FWS Craig (ed.), 'British Parliamentary Election Results 1885-1918', London, Macmillan, 1974

[419] Letter from Charles Ryle Fay to his King's College, Cambridge tutor Oscar Browning 10th February 1902, King's College, Cambridge archives OB/1/553/C

[420] Undated letter from Charles Ryle Fay to Oscar Browning, King's College, Cambridge archives OB/1/553/C

[421] Charles Carver Miller was a partner in Harley & Miller of 36-39 St John Wholesale Fish Market and 4 Gloucester Street, Liverpool (Gore 1900 Pt2 [Alphabetical Directory], p596)

[422] Ordnance Survey map Lancashire XCVIII.8 (revised 1907, published 1908): https://maps.nls.uk/view/126521981 - accessed 16th July 2018

[423] This was the address of the next of kin of James Kelly, born in England but a private in the Canadian Expeditionary Force despatched to fight in WWI in early 1917. http://data2.archives.ca/e/e444/e011087783.pdf 213th Battalion -2nd Reinforcing Draft
The house at 1 Agnes Road still exists and stands manse-like next to Blundellsands and Crosby railway station.

[424] Jacob Radnor (Pleydell-Bouverie), 'A Huguenot Family (Des Bouverie, Bouverie, Pleydell-Bouverie) 1536-1889', Winchester, Foxbury Press, 2001, p60

[425] 'Brevet' is a nominal rank without the increased pay that would normally result.

[426] 'A History of the Scottish Highlands, Highland Clans and Highland Regiments', p686
Digitised in 2012, see
https://archive.org/stream/historyofscottis008kelt/historyofscottis008kelt_dj vu.txt and

http://www.electricscotland.com/history/genhist/historyofscottish08.pdf - accessed 17th July 2018

[427] The other sons were Frederick (1849-1893), Charles (1850-1921), Henry (1854-1930) and Cecil (1856-1877), all of whom died childless. The funeral of Charles, a Captain in the Royal Navy, was reported in the *Hampshire Telegraph* 25th February 1921.

[428] She was the daughter of A Gibson and the widow of J Edwards, according to Burke's Peerage. Neither is traceable in the Census records for England.

[429] Gore 1900 Pt2 [Alphabetical Directory], p86 http://specialcollections.le.ac.uk/cdm/compoundobject/collection/p16445coll4/id/278535/rec/18 - accessed 18th July 2018 Nor is he listed in the Gore Trade Directory as a cotton dealer or merchant.

[430] *Hampshire Chronicle* 10th April 1904

[431] Ordnance Survey map Lancashire LXXV.13 (revised 1908-9, published 1911): https://maps.nls.uk/view/126518927 - accessed 18th July 2018

[432] *Liverpool Daily Post* 30th January 1918

[433] 'Gore's Directory of Liverpool and Its Environs', 1853, pp136,137, 598 http://specialcollections.le.ac.uk/cdm/compoundobject/collection/p16445coll4/id/112369/rec/34 - accessed 25th July 2018

[434] *Liverpool Mercury* 8th October 1864

[435] In the same Census the bonnet warehouse at no.29 also housed five draper's assistants, all describing themselves as shopmen,

[436] Kelly Directory of Liverpool 1894, p265

[437] *Huddersfield Daily Chronicle* 4th and *Huddersfield Chronicle and West Yorkshire Advertiser* 6th November 1880

[438] *Liverpool Mercury* 4th December 1882: Liquidation of William Townshend merchant and ship-owner at 17 Adelaide Terrace and B, Queen's Insurance Buildings, 10 Dale Street.

[439] *Liverpool Mercury* 13th May 1885

[440] Kelly Directory of Liverpool 1894, pp377-378, 508

[441] The Townshend family tree constructed by David Richards gives further information for the family at https://gw.geneanet.org/newlandrichards?lang=en&p=william&n=townshend&oc=2 - accessed 24th July 2018.

[442] Gore 1900 Pt2 [Alphabetical Directory], p685

[443] National archives: BT 31/5225/35455 Company No: 35455; John Pilling Ltd. Incorporated in 1891. Dissolved before 1916; BT 31/15860/54671 Company No: 54671; John Pilling Ltd. Incorporated in 1897. Dissolved between 1916 and 1932 - both accessed 10th September 2018.

[444] Jacqui Adams, Secretary to the Pilling Trust, personal communication, 8th October 2018

[445] There were many newspaper reports of what was clearly a notorious affair, not least because the women were acquitted and then sued the hotel for false imprisonment.

[446] https://maps.nls.uk/view/126437614 Cheshire XII.11 published 1899 and https://maps.nls.uk/view/114581398 Cheshire XII.11 published 1911 - both accessed 18th September 2018
[447] National archives WO 374/54195 - accessed 11th September 2018 Further information on his military career may be available at The Museum of Liverpool. http://www.liverpoolmuseums.org.uk/mol/visit/galleries/soldiers/research/kingsreg/ - accessed 11th September 2018
[448] They certainly lived there by 1888 for they were listed in the Waterloo Directory that year. See Table 2 on p35.
[449] Gore 1900 Pt2 [Alphabetical Directory], pp364 & 381
See https://maps.nls.uk/view/126523136 - accessed 19th September 2018
[450] *Liverpool Daily Post* 29th August 1881
[451] *Liverpool Daily Post* and *Western Daily Press* both 11th August 1891 Both publications agreed on the venue, the Public sale room, Exchange Station Buildings, Tithebarn Street, but the *Western Daily Press* advert referred to 3000 hides only. One or other was clearly a misprint.
[452] *Public Ledger and Daily Advertiser* 11th July 1897
[453] *Globe* and *Daily Telegraph & Courier* both 10th November 1910 George Heyworth retired from the company in 1916, living for another twenty-four years until 1940 when aged 84 he collapsed and died during a service at Sefton Park Presbyterian church. He had been a church elder and a keen Liverpool philanthropist so the company must have done well. *Liverpool Echo* and *Liverpool Evening Express* both 15th July 1940
[454] 'The British Isles : A Guide for Overseas Visitors, taking in the American pilgrim shrines, the principal show-places and others famed for their history, beauty, or literary associations', London, EJ Burrow, 1900, p246
[455] See https://www.flickr.com/photos/internetarchivebookimages/14784009415/ - accessed 19th September 2018 No known copyright restrictions.
[456] *Liverpool Echo* 25th Feb 1941
[457] Of JJ Rayner & Sons naval contractors, merchant tailors, drapers and general outfitters 24 Lord St in Gore 1900 Pt2 [Alphabetical Directory], p713. They also had other premises at 51-55 Regent Road and 24 Derby Road, Bootle, though it is not clear whether these were additional shops, offices or warehouses.
[458] https://www.gjenvick.com/VintageMagazines/Maritime/CunardLine/CunardDailyBulletin/1905-06-28-CunardDailyBulletin-Ivernia.html - accessed 25th September 2018
[459] *Times* 12th October 1914
[460] Barrie Lees, personal communication, 8th June 2017
[461] http://petermarsh.co.uk/timeline/ - accessed 24th September 2018
[462] Barrie Lees, personal communications, October 2011

[463] When re-elected for North Ward on 7th April 1902, he received almost twice the votes of his opponent.
[464] Waterloo-with-Seaforth Local Health Board 16th October 1903 minutes (p223 in 1902-1903 minute book)
[465] *Crosby Herald* 28th October 1922, pp4 & 6 and 2nd December 1922, p4.
[466] 'Statement on visit to the United Kingdom', by Professor Philip Alston, United Nations Special Rapporteur on extreme poverty and human rights, November 2018
[467] Pat Thane, 'Divided Kingdom: A History of Britain 1900 to the Present', 2018
[468] Sam Davies, Pete Gill, Linda Grant, Martyn Nightingale, Ron Noon & Andy Shallice (members of Merseyside Socialist Research Group), 'Genuinely Seeking Work: Mass Unemployment on Merseyside in the 1930s', 1992
[469] https://www.genuki.org.uk/nearby-churches/53.484993%2C-3.038314%2C3 - accessed 22nd January 2019
Other churches founded in Crosby soon after 1900 included St Thomas of Canterbury, Waterloo, Roman Catholic, 1902 and United Free Baptist Church, Waterloo 1910.
[470] https://www.genuki.org.uk/nearby-churches/53.417984%2C-2.990035%2C3 - accessed 22nd January 2019 This website dates the founding of Our Lady of Reconciliation, Eldon Street as 1854.
[471] https://www.british-history.ac.uk/vch/lancs/vol3/pp91-95 - accessed 22nd January 2019
"The population in 1901 was 7,555, and that of Waterloo 9,839."
[472] Thomas Hardy, 'Two on a Tower', 2012 (orig. 1882), p157
[473] Only James and Robert Goulburn in Blackstock Street, the two older Townshend sons, Henry and William, and Harold Marsh in Courtenay Road, were old enough to have served in the Boer War 1899-1902. All the other men of the next generation were born in 1883 or later.
[474] 'Historical Record of the King's Liverpool Regiment of Foot …' (3rd edn), 1904, ppxxxviii-xxxix, 211ff
[475] https://www.zulu.org.za/destinations/battlefields/information/the-battle-of-spionkop-spioenkop-M57864 - accessed 1st February 2019
[476] Five times as many, for example, in the case of Lancashire Regiments: John Downham, 'Red Roses on the Veldt: Lancashire Regiments in the Boer War, 1899-1902', 2000, pp307-325
[477] Gault, 2011, op cit, pp63-88
[478] Conscription was introduced for all single men aged between 18 and 41 by the Military Service Act in January 1916 and extended to married men in May that year.
[479] Michael McDonagh, 'In London During the Great War', 1935, p176
[480] Arthur Marwick, 'The Deluge: British Society and the First World War', 1965, pp193 & 196
[481] Hardy, op cit, p272

BIBLIOGRAPHY

Primary Sources

Archives
King's College, Cambridge
>Letter from Charles Ryle Fay to Oscar Browning 10th February 1902
>Letter from Charles Ryle Fay to Oscar Browning undated

Liverpool Metropolitan Cathedral Archdiocesan archives
>St Saviour's Refuge Paul Street, Correspondence, Reports, Financial and Property matters 1878-1932

Liverpool Records Office
>'Full Report of the Commission of Inquiry into the subject of the Unemployed in the city of Liverpool', *Liverpool Post and Echo*, 1894
>Licensing records 1895-1896
>Medical Officer of Health report for 1900
>Robert Cain & Sons Ltd Corporate Records
>Robert Cain & Sons Ltd Property Records
>William Grisewood, 'The Poor of Liverpool and What is Done for Them', 1899
>'Working conditions for Corporation carters 1910-1920'

National archives
>Hercules Permanent Benefit Building Society, Statutory Declaration of changes in Trusteeship, 21st October 1884
>Liverpool Regiment (No. 62161), Labour Corps (No. 40421)
>Liverpool regiment Private 74567 (enlisted 6th June 1916); Labour Corps 49908 April/May 1917
>Mercantile marine ribbon and British medal ribbon issued 19th August 1919 to Thomas Culshaw
>Pilling companies: BT 31/5225/35455 Company No: 35455; BT 31/15860/54671 Company No: 54671

Sefton Local History/Crosby Library archives
>Waterloo Directory 1888
>Waterloo-with-Seaforth Local Health Board:
>>4th February 1867 & 3rd May 1869 minutes (pp400 & 474 in July 1856 to January 1870 minute book)
>>7th April 1873 & 5th July 1875 minutes (pp123 & 187 in February 1870 to December 1881 minute book)
>>4th August 1874 minutes (p159 in 1870 to 1881 minute book)
>>4th & 22nd December 1876 minutes (pp225 & 226 in February 1870 to December 1881 minute book)
>>4th April 1878 (p264 in February 1870 to December 1881 minute book)

Bibliography

    2nd August 1880 minutes (p343 in February 1870 to December 1881 minute book)
    6th September 1880 (p345 in February 1870 to December 1881 minute book)
    4th June & 2nd July 1883 minutes (pp186 &194 in 1882 to 1885 minute book)
    5th April & 5th July 1886 & 2nd May 1887 minutes (pp52, 83 & 171 in 1885 to 1892 minute book)
    6th February 1893 minutes (p40 in 1892 to 1898 minute book)
    3rd February 1896 minutes (p417 in 1892 to 1898 minute book)
    1st June 1898 General Purposes Committee (p67 in 1898-1899 minute book)
    28th August 1900 Health Committee minutes (p148 in 1900/01 minute book)
    16th October 1903 minutes (p223 in 1902-1903 minute book)
Unilever Collections, Unilever Art, Archives and Records Management
    Gossage's AGM, 25th July 1911
    Letters between Briggs and Joseph Watson 19th to 28th September 1906
    Meetings of the Northern Soapmakers Association (including 17th April 1901)
    Soapmakers Association 34th Annual Report, June 1901

Books and Other Contemporary Documents

'The Autobiography of a Charwoman, as Chronicled by Annie Wakeman', London, Routledge, 1906

Bennison, Jonathan, 'Map of the town and port of Liverpool', Liverpool, 1835

'The British Isles : A Guide for Overseas Visitors, taking in the American pilgrim shrines, the principal show-places and others famed for their history, beauty, or literary associations', London, EJ Burrow, 1900

Finch, John, 'Statistics of Vauxhall Ward, Liverpool: The condition of the working class in Liverpool in 1842', Liverpool, Walmsley, 1842

Freeling, Arthur, 'The Railway Companion from London to Birmingham, Liverpool, and Manchester: With Guides to the Objects Worthy of Notice in Liverpool, Manchester, and Birmingham', London, Whittaker and Co., 1841

'Historical Record of the King's Liverpool Regiment of Foot ...' (3rd edn), Enniskillen, William Trimble, 1904

Orchard, BG, 'The Clerks of Liverpool', Liverpool, J Collinson, 1871

'Report by the Joint Select Committee of the House of Lords and the House of Commons on the Moneylenders Bill ...', London, HMSO, 1925

'Report from the Select Committee on the Liverpool Election Petition; with the Minutes of Proceedings', 21st June 1853

'Report of an Enquiry by the Board of Trade into Working-Class Rents and Retail Prices', Cd 6955, London, HMSO, 1913

'Report of an Enquiry by the Board of Trade into Working-Class Rents, Housing and Retail Prices', Cd 3864, London, HMSO, 1908

'Report of the Royal Commission on Alien Immigration', London, HMSO, 1903

'Reports Addressed to the Committee of the Liverpool Domestic Mission Society by their Ministers to the Poor and Presented at the Twenty-Second Annual General Meeting of the Society', Liverpool, Ellerbeck and Co., 1859

'Report to the Local Government Board on Recent Epidemic Arsenical Poisoning Attributed to Beer', Cd 459, London, HMSO, 1901

Returns of the number of Irish poor removed from the parish of Liverpool to Ireland since January 1849, House of Commons, 1854, LV, paper no 374

Royal Commission on Arsenical Poisoning: Minutes of Evidence vol. 1 - 1901 [Cd 1845] and vol. II - 1902-3 [Cd 1869]; Final Report [Cd 1848], London, HMSO, 1903

Samuelson, James,
    'The Lament of the Sweated', London, PS King, 1903
    'The Children of Our Slums', Liverpool, Liverpool Booksellers Co., 1911

'Thirteenth Annual Report of the Poor Law Commissioners', House of Commons 1847: Appendix A, Report No. 8 by Alfred Austin 'Relief of Irish Poor in Liverpool'

Newspapers
Belfast Newsletter 12th January 1852; 23rd September 1858
Berrow's Worcester Journal 12th April 1849
Birmingham Daily Post 7th and 9th March
Blackburn Standard 1st August 1891
Bradford Observer 14th April 1859; 2nd June 1873
Bristol Mercury 2nd, 9th and 16th August, 20th September, 11th October, 22nd November 1845; 21st April and 28th July 1855; 13th May 1865; 12th February 1876
Bristol Mercury and Daily Post 25th April 1896
Cheshire Observer 9th September 1882; 5th July 1884; 21st December 1895
Crosby Herald 28th October and 2nd December 1922
Daily Mail 13th July 1899
Daily News 10th January 1852; 21st September 1858
Daily Telegraph 15th December 1908 (in Unilever Collections)
Daily Telegraph & Courier 10th November 1910
Derby Mercury 25th November 1896
Dundee Courier 13th April 1859
Edinburgh Gazette, 25th December 1883

Bibliography

Freeman's Journal 24th January 1853; 4th February 1859; 8th December 1871; 16th January 1880; 31st May 1881
Freeman's Journal and Daily Commercial Advertiser 4th and 9th November 1893
Glasgow Herald 20th and 27th July 1855; 25th July and 8th August 1856; 8th and 19th August 1870; 17th February 1873; 22nd and 29th January 1876; 24th July 1886
Globe 10th November 1910
The Graphic 12th and 26th September, 24th October, 21st November, 5th and 19th December 1891; 2nd January, 13th February, 12th March, 9th April and 7th May 1892
Hampshire Advertiser 30th May 1891
Hampshire Chronicle 10th April 1904
Hampshire Telegraph 25th February 1921
Huddersfield Daily Chronicle 24th July 1885; 4th November 1880
Huddersfield Chronicle and West Yorkshire Advertiser 16th April 1859; 25th July 1885; 6th November 1880
Huddersfield Daily Chronicle 4th June 1873
Hull Packet 15th April 1859
Hull Packet and East Riding Times 28th January 1853
Ipswich Journal 13th August 1870
John Bull 12th January 1852; 18th April 1859
Lancaster Gazette 1st August 1891
Leeds Mercury 12th September 1868; 18th September 1900
Leicester Chronicle 16th April 1859
Leicester Chronicle and the Leicestershire Mercury 11th April 1896
Liverpool Courier 2nd, 13th and 15th January 1897
Liverpool Daily Post 29th August 1881; 11th August 1891; 5th June and 9th August 1917; 30th January 1918
Liverpool Echo 9th August 1917; 15th July 1940; 25th February 1941
Liverpool Evening Express 15th July 1940
Liverpool Mercury 5th May 1843; 21st February and 19th September 1845; 9th January 1846; 13th July and 7th December 1847; 3rd and 24th April 1849; 17th, 21st and 31st January, 4th, 14th, 18th and 28th February, 4th, 14th, 18th and 28th March, 1st and 11th April 1851; 2nd July and 24th December 1852; 21st January 1853; 27th July 1855; 16th July, 18th October, 8th and 10th November 1856; 6th March 1857; 15th June and 20th September 1858; 3rd February 1859; 13th, 14th, 19th, 21st, 27th and 30th January, 2nd, 3rd, and 5th February 1863; 12th May and 8th October 1864; 24th January, 15th and 28th March, 7th June 1866; 11th April and 14th May 1867; 12th September 1868; 17th and 24th November 1869; 12th October and 12th December 1871; 9th September 1873; 7th March and 4th December 1874; 15th February 1877; 17th January, 4th and 14th June, 13th, 26th and 30th July, 7th, 23rd, 28th and 30th September, 3rd and 4th October, 14th November 1878; 18th August and 11th

November 1879; 25th February, 8th October and 16th November 1880; 13th, 20th, 23rd, 27th, 28th and 29th March, 11th April, 4th and 16th May, 29th June, 14th July, 24th August, 5th, 8th, 15th, 19th and 28th September, 4th October and 4th December 1882; 13th March, 7th July and 30th November 1883; 3rd and 21st January, 12th March, 30th April, 23rd July, 21st and 31st October 1884; 25th and 28th April, 1st, 6th, 8th and 13th May, 24th July, 1st September and 28th October 1885; 8th October 1886; 11th February, 20th March, 1st, 5th and 19th April, 9th May, 11th, 16th and 24th June, 22nd July, 13th September and 1st October 1890; 4th and 16th June, 24th and 30th July, 7th and 10th August, 9th and 17th September 1891; 22nd January, 24th February, 8th, 13th and 14th April, 17th and 21st June, 1st and 19th July, 24th October 1892; 4th January, 9th, 11th, 14th, 16th, 18th and 26th April, 3rd, 4th and 5th May, 7th July, 13th August, 12th 18th, 24th and 28th September, 1st October, 20th November, 15th, 25th and 31st December 1894; 1st, 2nd, 11th, 14th, 15th, 16th, 24th and 31st January, 1st, 7th, 9th, 11th and 18th February and 30th November 1895; 1st January 1896; 14th January, 16th and 23rd March, 5th, 10th, 19th and 25th May and 7th December 1897

Liverpool Review 23rd October 1886; 1st and 8th March 1890

Lloyd's Weekly Newspaper 26th September 1858; 17th April 1859

London Evening News 11th July 1899

Manchester Courier and Lancashire General Advertiser 6th February 1901; 4th January 1904

Manchester Evening News 11th December 1903

Manchester Times 20th August 1870; 16th August 1879; 31st July 1891

Morning Post 9th November 1846; 12th January 1852; 21st January 1853; 26th January 1855; 29th April and 21st September 1858; 23rd January 1866; 3rd November 1884; 24th July 1885; 1st July 1887; 11th January 1888; 25th January 1889; 24th June 1895; 11th June 1896

New York Times 14th July 1899

North Wales Chronicle 16th April 1859

Nottinghamshire Guardian 12th August 1870

Pall Mall Gazette 5th, 6th, 7th and 9th December 1871

Preston Guardian 27th May 1848; 19th July 1856; 21st May 1892

Public Ledger and Daily Advertiser 11th July 1897

Sheffield and Rotherham Independent 22nd February 1878; 20th January 1880; 25th July 1885; 6th, 7th, 9th-11th March 1891; 25th, 30th & 31st May, 5th and 6th December 1892

Staffordshire Advertiser 8th December 1900

Standard 10th January 1852; 9th August 1870; 5th, 6th and 8th December 1871; 1st February 1895; 25th April 1896

Star 28th April 1896

Times 20th February 1866; 8th April 1873; 16th December 1874; 30th July 1883; 13th and 23rd February 1899; 9th December 1901; 19th

Bibliography

February 1902; 16th, 17th and 22nd July 1903; 27th July, 13th August and 13th October 1906; 28th June and 16th July 1907; 11th April 1910 (in Unilever Collections); 12th October 1914
Weekly Standard and Express 17th December 1898; 22nd December 1900
Western Daily Press 11th August 1891
Wigan Observer and District Advertiser 5th October 1907
Wrexham Advertiser, Denbighshire, Flintshire, Cheshire, Shropshire, Merionethshire, and North Wales Register 12th April 1873
York Herald 25th September 1858; 16th April 1859
Yorkshire Evening Post 5th February 1901; 11th April 1902

Periodicals and Specialist Publications
The Athenaeum 14th May 1859
Journal of the Society of Arts, 10th February 1858, 6, pp204-205
Kelly's Directory of the Leather Trades, 8th edn., London, Kelly's Directories, 1899
Kelly Directory of Liverpool 1894
Police Gazette 13th July 1917

Secondary Sources

Books
Ayers, Pat, 'The Liverpool Docklands: Life and Work in Athol Street', Liverpool, Docklands History Books, 1988
Barber, Norman, 'A Century of British Brewers 1890-1990', New Ash Green Kent, Brewery History Society, 1994
Bartley, Paula, 'Prostitution: Prevention and Reform in England, 1860-1914', London, Routledge, 2000
Belchem, John and Biggs, Bryan (eds.), 'Liverpool: City of Radicals', Liverpool, Liverpool University Press, 2011
Benbough-Jackson, Mike and Davies, Sam (eds.), 'Merseyside: Culture and Place', Newcastle, Cambridge Scholars, 2011
Benson, John, 'The Penny Capitalists: A Study of Nineteenth-Century Working-class Entrepreneurs', Dublin, Gill & Macmillan, 1983
Brace, Harold W, 'History of Seed Crushing in Great Britain', London, Land Books, 1906
Brady, LW, 'TP O'Connor and the Liverpool Irish', London, Royal Historical Society, 1983
Briggs, Asa, 'The Age of Improvement, 1783-1867', 2nd ed., London, Longman, 2000 (orig. 1959)
Burke, Thomas, 'Catholic History of Liverpool', Liverpool, C Tinling & Co., 1910
Burnett, John (ed.), 'Useful Toil: Autobiographies of Working People from the 1820s to the 1920s', London, Allen Lane, 1974

Camp, Richard L, 'The Papal Ideology of Social Reform: A Study in Historical Development, 1878-1967', Leiden, EJ Brill, 1969
Chalmin, Philippe, 'The Making of a Sugar Giant: Tate & Lyle 1859-1989', London, Harwood Academic Publishers, 1990
Chandler, George, 'Liverpool', London, Batsford, 1957
Clark, Christine, 'The British Malting Industry Since 1830', London, Hambledon Press, 1998
Coogan, Tim Pat, 'The Twelve Apostles: Michael Collins, the Squad and Ireland's Fight for Freedom', London, Head of Zeus, 2016
Cowman, Krista, 'Mrs Brown is a Man and a Brother', Liverpool, Liverpool University Press, 2004
Craig, FWS (ed.), 'British Parliamentary Election Results 1885-1918', London, Macmillan, 1974
Davies, Peter N, 'Henry Tyrer: A Liverpool Shipping Agent and His Enterprise, 1879-1979', London, Croom Helm, 1979
Davies, Sam, Gill, Pete, Grant, Linda, Nightingale, Martyn, Noon, Ron & Shallice, Andy, 'Genuinely Seeking Work: Mass Unemployment on Merseyside in the 1930s', Birkenhead, Liver Press, 1992
Devas, Francis, 'Mother Mary Magdalen of the Sacred Heart (Fanny Margaret Taylor) Foundress of the Poor Servants of the Mother of God 1832-1900', London, Burns Oates & Washbourne, 1927
Downham, John, 'Red Roses on the Veldt: Lancashire Regiments in the Boer War, 1899-1902', Lancaster, Carnegie Publishing, 2000
Earner-Byrne, Lindsey, 'Letters of the Catholic Poor: Poverty in Independent Ireland, 1920-1940', Cambridge, Cambridge University Press, 2017
Edwards, HR, 'Competition and Monopoly in the British Soap Industry', Oxford, Clarendon Press, 1962
Ellison, Thomas, 'The Cotton Trade of Great Britain', London, Frank Cass, 1968 (orig. 1886)
Fay, Charles Ryle,
'Huskisson and His Age', London, Longmans Green & Co., 1951
'Round About Industrial Britain 1830-1860', Toronto, University of Toronto Press, 1952
Finch, John (ed.), 'Statistics of Vauxhall Ward, Liverpool: The Conditions of the Working Class in Liverpool 1842', Liverpool, Toulouse Press, 1986 (orig. 1841)
Furnival, John, 'Children of the Second Spring: Father James Nugent and the Work of Child Care in Liverpool', Leominster, Gracewing, 2005
Garbutt, John L (ed.), 'Manbré and Garton Ltd 1855-1955: A Hundred Years of Progress', London, Hazell, Watson & Viney, 1955
Gault, Hugh,
'Making the Heavens Hum Pt1: Kingsley Wood and the Art of the Possible 1881-1924', Cambridge, Gretton Books, 2014
'Making the Heavens Hum Pt2 - Kingsley Wood: Scenes from a Political Life 1925-1943', Cambridge, Gretton Books, 2017

Bibliography

'The Quirky Dr Fay: A Remarkable Life', Cambridge, Gretton Books, 2011

Halsbury's Laws of England (4th edition), London, LexisNexis UK, 2004

Hardy, Thomas, 'Two on a Tower', London, Penguin English Library, 2012 (orig. 1882)

Harris, Jose, 'Private Lives, Public Spirit: A Social History of Britain, 1870-1914', Oxford, OUP, 1993

Hearn, Mona, 'Below Stairs: Domestic Service Remembered in Dublin and Beyond, 1880-1922', Dublin, Lilliput Press, 1993

Hikins, Harold R (ed.), 'Building the Union: Studies on the Growth of the Worker's Movement, Merseyside, 1756-1967', Liverpool, Toulouse Press, 1973

Hobsbawm, EJ, 'Labouring Men: Studies in the History of Labour', London, Weidenfeld and Nicolson, 1964

Holland, Joe, 'Modern Catholic Social Teaching: The Popes Confront the Industrial Age 1740-1958', New York, Paulist Press, 2003

Horn, Pamela, 'The Rise and Fall of the Victorian Servant', Stroud, Gloucs., Alan Sutton Publishing, 1990 (orig. 1975)

Hyde, Francis E, 'Liverpool and the Mersey: An Economic History of a Port', Newton Abbot, David & Charles, 1971

Hyland, Peter, 'The Herculaneum Pottery: Liverpool's Forgotten Glory', Liverpool, Liverpool University Press, 2005

Lane, Tony, 'Liverpool: Gateway of Empire', London, Lawrence and Wishart, 1987

Leech, Bosdin, 'History of the Manchester Ship Canal from Its Inception to Its Completion: 2 vols.', Manchester, Sherratt and Hughes, 1907

Lewis, James R, 'The Birth of Waterloo', 3rd edn, Sefton Libraries, 1996

Luft, HM, 'A History of Merchant Taylors School, Crosby 1600-1970', Liverpool, Liverpool University Press, 1970

Marsh, Arthur and Ryan, Victoria,
'Historical Directory of Trade Unions: vol.3', Aldershot, Gower, 1987
'Historical Directory of Trade Unions: vol.4', Aldershot, Scolar Press, 1994

Marsh, Arthur and Smethurst, John B, 'Historical Directory of Trade Unions: vol.5', Aldershot, Ashgate, 2006

Marshall, John, 'The Lancashire and Yorkshire Railway: vol. 1', Newton Abbot, David and Charles, 1969

Marwick, Arthur 'The Deluge: British Society and the First World War', London, Bodley Head, 1965

McDonagh, Michael, 'In London During the Great War', London, Eyre and Spottiswoode, 1935

Milne, Graeme,
'People, Place and Power on the Nineteenth Century Waterfront', Aldershot, Palgrave Macmillan, 2016

'Trade and Traders in Mid-Victorian Liverpool: Mercantile Business and the Making of a World Port', Liverpool, Liverpool University Press, 2000

Morris, Mike, Wailey, Tony and Davies, Andrew (eds.), 'George Garrett: Ten Years On the Parish', Liverpool, Liverpool University Press, 2017

Muir, Ramsay, 'A History of Liverpool', Wakefield, S R Publishers, 1970, pp297-298 (orig. 1907)

Musson, AE,
'Enterprise in Soap and Chemicals: Joseph Crosfield & Sons Ltd, 1815-1965', Manchester, Manchester University Press, 1965
'The Growth of British Industry', London, Batsford, 1981 (orig. 1978)

O'Connor, Freddy. 'A Pub on Every Corner: vol.3 - North Liverpool', Liverpool, Bluecoat Press, 1998

O'Mara, Pat, 'The Autobiography of a Liverpool Irish Slummy', London, Martin Hopkinson, 1934

Parsons, Neil, 'King Khama, Emperor Joe and the Great White Queen: Victorian Britain Through African Eyes', London, University of Chicago Press, 1998

Pollard, Richard and Pevsner, Nikolaus, 'Lancashire: Liverpool and the South West', London, Yale University Press, 2006

Radnor (Pleydell-Bouverie), Jacob, 'A Huguenot Family (Des Bouverie, Bouverie, Pleydell-Bouverie) 1536-1889', Winchester, Foxbury Press, 2001

Razzell, PE and Wainwright, RW (eds), 'The Victorian Working Class: Selections from Letters to the *Morning Chronicle*', London, Frank Cass, 1973

Silverman, Marilyn, 'An Irish Working Class: Explorations in Political Economy and Hegemony, 1800-1950', Toronto, University of Toronto Press, 2001

Simey, Margaret, 'Charitable Effort in Liverpool in the Nineteenth Century', Liverpool, Liverpool University Press, 1951

Stanistreet, Jennifer and Farthing, Andrew, 'Crosby in Camera', Sefton Council, 1995

Starling, John and Lee, Ivor, 'No Labour, No Battle: Military Labour During the First World War', Stroud Gloucs., Spellmount, 2009

Sutcliffe, Anthony (ed.), 'Multi-Storey Living: The British Working Class Experience', London, Croom Helm, 1974

Tebbutt, Melanie, 'Making Ends Meet: Pawnbroking and Working-Class Credit', Leicester, Leicester University Press, 1983

Thane, Pat, 'Divided Kingdom: A History of Britain 1900 to the Present', Cambridge, Cambridge University Press, 2018

Unilever Information Guide No.4, 'The Formation of Unilever', Port Sunlight, UARM, undated

Bibliography

Vincent, David, 'Poor Citizens: The State and the Poor in Twentieth Century Britain', London, Longman, 1991

Vincent, John (ed.),
'The Diaries of Edward Henry Stanley, 15th Earl of Derby (1826-1893) Between September 1869 and March 1878', Camden Fifth Series, vol. 4, London, Royal Historical Society, 1994
'The Diaries of Edward Henry Stanley, 15th Earl of Derby (1826-1893) Between 1878 and 1893: A Selection', Oxford, Leopard's Head Press, 2003

Waller, PJ,
'Democracy and Sectarianism: A Political and Social History of Liverpool 1868-1939', Liverpool, Liverpool University Press, 1981
'Town, City and Nation: England 1850-1914', Oxford, Oxford University Press, 1983

Walton, John K and Wilcox, Alastair (eds.), 'Low Life and Moral Improvement in Mid-Victorian England: Liverpool through the Journalism of Hugh Shimmin', Leicester, Leicester University Press, 1991

Wilson, Charles, 'The History of Unilever: A Study in Economic Growth and Social Change', vol. I, London, Cassell, 1954

Articles

Archer, John E, "The press, the cornermen and Liverpool's 'Tithebarn-Street outrage' of 1874", *Transactions of the Historic Society of Lancashire and Cheshire*, 2011, 160, pp117-142

Belchem, John, "The Liverpool-Irish enclave", *Immigrants and Minorities*, 1999, 18 (2&3), pp128-146

Errazurez, A, "Some types of housing in Liverpool, 1785-1890", *Town Planning Review*, 1946, 19, pp57-68

Grant, Linda, "Women's work and trade unionism in Liverpool 1890-1914", *North West Labour History Society Bulletin*, 1980/81, 7, pp65-83

Hawes, Richard, "The municipal regulation of smoke pollution in Liverpool, 1853-1866", *Environment and History*, 1998, 4, pp75-90

Hubbard, Evelyn, "American 'Trusts' and English combinations", *Economic Journal*, 1902, 12, pp159-176

Kanya-Forstner, Martha, "Defining womanhood: Irish women and the Catholic church in Victorian Liverpool", *Immigrants and Minorities*, 1999, 18 (2&3), pp168-188

Lawton, R, "The population of Liverpool in the mid-nineteenth century", *Transactions of the Historic Society of Lancashire and Cheshire*, 1955, vol. 107, pp89-120

Macrosty, HW, "Business aspects of British Trusts", *Economic Journal*, 1902, 12, pp347-366 HW

Mayer, Joseph, "On the history of the art of pottery in Liverpool", *Transactions of the Historic Society of Lancashire and Cheshire*, 1854-55, 7, pp178-210

McCormick, Donald, 'The Mystery of Lord Kitchener's Death', London, Putnam, 1959

Menzies, EM, "The Freeman voter in Liverpool 1802-1835", *Transactions of the Historic Society of Lancashire and Cheshire*, 1972, 124, pp85-107

Pearson, JW, "The seed crushing industry", *Journal of the Royal Society of Arts*, 12th December 1919, pp50-62

Smith, Alan, "The Herculaneum china and earthenware manufactory, 1796-1840", *Industrial Archaeology*, 1969, 6, pp13-27

Tarn, JN, "Housing in Liverpool and Glasgow: The growth of civic responsibility", *Town Planning Review*, 1969, 39, pp319-334

Other

Economist 15th February 1908, p324

Feehan, Lawrence, 'Charitable Effort, Statutory Authorities and the Poor in Liverpool c1850-1914', Liverpool University PhD thesis, 1987

Hockenhull, N, 'Waterloo with Seaforth Local Board of Health: The Beginning', Paper read to Crosby and District History Society, March 1955

Kanya-Forstner, Martha, 'The Politics of Survival: Irish Women in Outcast Liverpool 1850-1890', Liverpool University PhD thesis, 1997

'Oxford Dictionary of National Biography', Oxford, Oxford Universty Press, 2004

'Statement on visit to the United Kingdom', United Nations Special Rapporteur on extreme poverty and human rights, November 2018

Websites

Boer War
https://www.zulu.org.za/destinations/battlefields/information/the-battle-of-spionkop-spioenkop-M57864

BBC
http://www.bbc.co.uk/news/uk-england-merseyside-33148863

Canadian Expeditionary Force, WWI
http://data2.archives.ca/e/e444/e011087783.pdf

Churches in Crosby and Vauxhall
https://www.genuki.org.uk/nearby-churches/53.484993%2C-3.038314%2C3
https://www.genuki.org.uk/nearby-churches/53.417984%2C-2.990035%2C3

Costain
http://www.costain.com/about-us/our-history/

Bibliography

Cunard Daily Bulletin
https://www.gjenvick.com/VintageMagazines/Maritime/CunardLine/CunardDailyBulletin/1905-06-28-CunardDailyBulletin-Ivernia.html

Gazette
https://www.thegazette.co.uk/London/issue/21484/page/2750/data.pdf
https://www.thegazette.co.uk/London/issue/25855/page/5121/data.pdf
https://www.thegazette.co.uk/London/issue/34286/page/3321/data.pdf

Gore's Directories of Liverpool and Birkenhead
http://specialcollections.le.ac.uk/cdm/compoundobject/collection/p16445coll4/id/112369/rec/34
http://specialcollections.le.ac.uk/cdm/compoundobject/collection/p16445coll4/id/278528/rec/9
http://specialcollections.le.ac.uk/cdm/compoundobject/collection/p16445coll4/id/278535/rec/7
http://specialcollections.le.ac.uk/cdm/compoundobject/collection/p16445coll4/id/278535/rec/18

Guide for Overseas Visitors
https://www.flickr.com/photos/internetarchivebookimages/14784009415/

Historic England
http://www.pastscape.org.uk

Liverpool Museums
http://www.liverpoolmuseums.org.uk/mol/visit/galleries/soldiers/research/kingsreg/index.aspx

Liverpool Well-Doers
http://www.welldoers.org/

Merseyside Roll of Honour
http://www.merseysiderollofhonour.co.uk/get2.php?cwgc=3038867

National archives
http://discovery.nationalarchives.gov.uk/details/r/a3a64b4f-403f-4f90-80ef-b541d43a66f7

Ordnance Survey maps
https://maps.nls.uk/view/114581398
https://maps.nls.uk/view/126437614
https://maps.nls.uk/view/126518927
https://maps.nls.uk/view/126521981
https://maps.nls.uk/view/126523106#zoom=5&lat=5032&lon=4527&layers=BT

https://maps.nls.uk/view/126523136

Peter Marsh Group
http://petermarsh.co.uk/timeline/

Population
https://www.british-history.ac.uk/vch/lancs/vol3/pp91-95

Porcupine
http://victorianpress.wixsite.com/liverpoolporcupine/single-post/2015/05/26/Independence-for-Lancashire

Pubs
http://breweryhistory.com/wiki/index.php?title=List_of_Robert_Cain_Pubs
www.merseypub.com/guide/pu101.htm

Robert Tressell
http://hastingschronicle.net/features/the-ragged-trousered-philanthropists-a-new-introduction/
http://www.unionhistory.info/ragged/tressell.php

St Saviour's Refuge, Paul Street
http://www.childrenshomes.org.uk/list/MH4.shtml
https://www.wearenugent.org/about/background/

Scotsman
https://www.scotsman.com/news/truth-behind-the-sinking-of-hms-hampshire-revealed-1-4146171

Scottish Highlands, Highland Clans and Highland Regiments (history of)
https://archive.org/stream/historyofscottis008kelt/historyofscottis008kelt_djvu.txt
http://www.electricscotland.com/history/genhist/historyofscottish08.pdf

Telephones
https://archiveshub.jisc.ac.uk/search/archives/50a5d416-8fc1-3a00-9345-9f16d7b07b73

Townshend family tree
https://gw.geneanet.org/newlandrichards?lang=en&p=william&n=townshend&oc=2

USA patents
https://patents.google.com/patent/US848704A/en

INDEX

Blackstock Street on pp171-173
Notes and some minor references not indexed.

Courtenay Road on pp174-175
People's names as in the text.

Abercromby see Liverpool areas/wards
accountant 4, 41, 43, 45, 119
  see Cariss, Pilling
Acme Engineering Co. 72-73
alcohol 12, 17, 63, 64
amalgamation see combination
Anglican see Church of England
Argentina 54
Armstrong, Richard Acland 2
Army see Regiments of the British Army
arsenic poisoning 76-77
- Royal Commission on 77
Aspinall, Clarke 29
Atkins, Susan and Atkinson, Susannah 125
Austin, Alfred 21

baker(s) 23, 25
Baptist 132
Battersby, Worsley 32
Belfast 27, 128
Berry, Albert 76
Birch, Ann, Louise & Mary 92-93
Birkdale, Lancashire 114, 124, 125
Birkenhead 19, 67, 119, 123
Birmingham 11, 70, 75, 125
Blackstock, Edward 5
Blackstock, Mr 5
Blackstock Street vii & passim
  (previously Canning Street)
- cornermen 34-35
- courts 5-8, 12, 32-34, 55, 58, 80, 82, 94, 95
- earnings 16-19, 23, 57, 90, 92, 100, 130
- factories 3, 5, 7, 13, 16, 35, 51, 55, 58, 64, 66-67
  candle factory 11

cattle cake: 75 &
  Liverpool Vesta Cake Company 75-76
glass bottle works 5, 6, 16, 25, 26, 27, 67
lime works 5, 8, 31, 39
paint factory 11
rice and flour mills: 3, 5, 98 &
  Irving, Son & Jones 7, 28, 30, 73-74, 98
saccharine works: 3 &
  Liverpool Saccharine Company 32, 76-77
saw mills/timber 3, 5
seed crushing (oil) mill: 5, 13
  & E&W Pearson 74-75, 81, 88, 95, 98, 100, 101
soap works: 3-4 &
  Tyson, Richmond and Jones 3, 7, 27-28, 67-70
  Wm Gossage & Sons 3, 4, 33, 67, 68, 69, 77
sugar refiner(y) 28, 30, 31
tannery: 3, 5, 7 &
  Smyth Bros (previously Nicholson's) 7, 26, 32, 77, 121
water meters & other engineering: Palatine Engineering 70-73
wood importer: RG Tickle & Son 77
- fire(s) 11, 12, 28, 30, 32, 35, 74, 76
- houses (other than courts) 23-24, 97-98, 100
- lodger(s)/boarder(s) 20, 23-24, 82, 85, 88, 91, 92, 98, 99, 130
- occupations 13-16, 22ff
- people 3, 8, 12-20, 79-103
  Caldwell family: 82, 85-86, 91
  daughter Alice 85

171

mother Harriet (née Oldham) 82, 83, 85-86, 130
sons Joseph, Peter & William 85, 86, 134
Carroll family: 83, 97-99, 102
daugher Mary 98
father James 82, 97-98
mother Mary Ann 82, 97-99, 130
sons James, Peter & William 98
Culshaw family: 83, 90-94
father Thomas 90-94
grandmother 91, 92
sister Ann 91
sons John, Robert, Thomas & William 80, 91, 93, 94, 134
Goulburn family: 83, 97, 99-100
father John 82, 99
mother Elizabeth 82, 99-100, 130
sons James, John & Robert 99-100
Hartley family: 82, 83, 94-97, 98, 102
daughters Hannah 94, Margaret E & Sarah 94, 96
father Samuel 80, 82, 94-96
mother Sarah 82, 94-96, 130
son Joseph 95, 96, 97, 134
sons Thomas & William 94
Kerr, Catherine: 65-66, 82, 83, 89-94, 97, 130
McDonald family: 82, 84, 100-103
aunt Edith F Fleming 101
daughters Dorothy Edbur & Edith R 101, 102
father Thomas 100, 101, 102
grandfather James Fleming 102-103
mother Emily/Emma/Louisa 102-103, 130

sons Frederick & Thomas 102
Oldham families (a) and (b): 79-81, 85, 91
husband (a) John 81, 83
wife (a) Martha 79-80, 81
daughters (b) Harriet & Mary 85-86 see Harriet Caldwell
father (b) William 80, 81, 83, 85
mother (b) Alice 85
sons (b) Thomas & William 80, 81, 85
Parkinson family: 84, 100-101
father John 100-101
mother Elizabeth 100, 101
Rusling family:
father Henry 81
son Albert 80, 81, 83
wife Sarah 81
True family: 82, 83
aunt Susannah 87
daughter Mary 88
father Ambrose 82, 86-89, 94
grandfather Edmund Bishop True 87, 88
grandmother Amelia 86-87
great-grandmother Marie Hunter 87
mother Mary 82, 87-89, 130
son Ambrose 89
son Edmund Bishop True 87-89, 134
son Thomas 89
Borrowman, David & Robert 61
Briggs, Thomas 67
carter Arthur Mayne 80, 81, 83
carter James Brannon 80, 83
carter Thomas Buckhurst 80, 83
coach-builder Joseph Wade 6, 7, 32-33

Index

coal carter Edward Knott 58, 80, 83
Cullen, Moses & Elizabeth 23, 25
Dell, Charles 82, 83
Fitzpatrick, James & Maria 23, 83
fowl-dealer Thomas Cafferdy 24
Glinn, William & Ann 85
Hamilton, John 12
Hogan, Mary 98
labourer Albert Wales 66
lime-burner Thomas Galley 24
Magee, John et al 25
master mariner David Martin 91
McQuade, John 98
Mills, John 61-62
Mulholland, James & Mary 99
oil manufacturer Mr Batty 28-29
Price, Joseph & May 90, 91
Quigley, Andrew & James 82, 83, 84
servant Ann Moore & Andrew Shacklady 91-92
Simpson, Mary 24, 25
Smith, Michael 29
Smith, Susan 88
starch-maker John Hubell 24
Tait, David 82, 83
tobacconist Hugh Clyde 24, 135
wheelwright/blacksmith William Gore 25
Young, John & Jane 85
- political representation 58-59
- pubs/public houses 2, 8, 60-62
    Eagle Vaults vii, 2, 6, 33, 60, 61-62, 67
    Grapes 60
    Green Flag Vaults 2, 60, 61
- school 3, 7, 19-20, 33, 35, 64

- smoke inspection/nuisance 26, 35, 76
- theatre 12
Blackstock Street Gardens 61-62
Blundellsands 5, 38, 44, 112-113, 116, 132
Blundellsands and Crosby railway station 1, 37
Board of Trade enquiry 58
boat-maker(s) 23-24, 25
Boer War incl. Kimberley, Ladysmith, Mafeking, Spion Kop 133-134
Bond, John 124
Bootle 58, 67, 73, 127
boot-maker(s) 8, 17
brewing 76-77 see Joplins Brewery, Liverpool Saccharine Company
Briggs, Ernest, Mary, Raymond & Wilfred 67
Briggs, James Burnett see Tyson, Richmond and Jones
Brighton-le-Sands 40
Briscoe, John George 118
British Oil and Cake Mills 75, 100
Bromfield, Mary 67
butcher(s) 8, 23, 25, 93
Byrne, Emily & Margaret 66

Calcutta, India 128
Camden, London 92
Canada 54
Cannington, John 25-27, 51, 67
Cape Town, South Africa 107
Cariss, Astrup 41-42, 126
carter(s) 3, 4, 8, 24, 25, 58, 80-81, 85, 87, 91, 93-94
cart-owner(s) 24, 25, 30
casual work see employment
Catholic see Roman Catholic
Catholic Benevolent Society 51
cellar housing 3, 17, 19, 56, 79
Census

- 1851 20, 22, 24, 116-117, 118, 124
- 1861 96, 116, 124
- 1871 91, 92, 95, 96, 125
- 1881 39, 47-48, 54, 92, 95, 96, 117, 125
- 1891 43, 44, 45, 47-48, 81, 82, 83-84, 90, 92, 94, 96, 107, 109, 119, 120, 125
- 1901 2, 47-48, 54, 58, 65, 80, 82, 83-84, 85, 90-91, 93, 94, 96, 102, 114, 119, 120
- 1911 47-48, 80, 82, 83-84, 88, 92-93, 94, 95, 96, 98, 102, 112, 115, 117, 120, 126

charity 2, 17, 18, 35, 50
Charity Organisation Society 49-50
Cheshire and Lancashire Moneylenders Assoc. 57
Chester 76
choice 63, 134-135
cholera 13, 21, 35, 64
Church of England 20, 50, 113, 132-133
Cobb, John 29-30
combination 68-70, 75, 100
commerce see trade
Congregational Church 132
conscription 134
Conservative 2, 3, 59-60, 106, 111, 134
Cook and Townshend, drapers 115-117
Cook, Henry James 115-117
cooper 24, 95
Costain (and Kneen) 38
cotton (incl. broker, dealer, porter, salesman, spinner, trader) viii, 4, 5, 8, 24, 29, 33, 39, 45, 49, 90, 93, 94, 96, 99, 107, 109, 114

Courtenay Road viii & passim
- houses viii, 4-5, 39-44, 105-106, 108
- people 4-5, 8, 105-128

Fay family: 45, 47, 105, 107, 119-113
  daughter Gladys 107
  father Charles 95, 106-113, 115
  grandfathers Charles Fay 37 & Richard Lawton 107
  mother Emily 106-112, 131
  son Charles Ryle 37, 96, 97, 107, 110-111, 112, 127
Hart family: 45, 48, 105, 120-123
  daughter Gladys & son Roderick 120, 121-122, 123
  father William 45, 120-121, 123
  mother Louisa 120-123, 131
Marsh family: 41, 45, 47, 99, 105, 126-128
  daughters Annie, Mildred & Salome 41, 127
  mother Ann 41, 131
  father Peter 41, 126-128, 131
  sons 127, 128
Pilling family: 45, 47, 105, 119-120, 121, 123, 124
  daughter Mary Alice 119-120
  father John 45, 119-120
  mother Eliza 119-120, 131
  son John Francis 119-120, 134
Pleydell-Bouverie family: 45, 47, 105, 113-115
  daughter Annie Marian 45, 114-115
  father Laurence 45, 113-115
  grandfather Laurence 113-114
  mother Annie 45, 114-115, 131
Rayner family: 45, 47, 105, 124-126

174

Index

daughters, incl. Ellen 124-126, 131
  father John 45, 124-125
  grandson Gerald Haigh 124, 125
  mother Ellen 124-125
  sons incl. Frank 45, 124-126
Townshend family: 41, 45, 48, 105, 115-118
  father William 117-118
  grandparents 115-117
  mother Fanny 45, 117-118, 131
  sons & daughters 118
Blackwood 39, 43, 47
D'Arcy, Theresa 39, 48
Goodbody, Edward & Eliza 38, 39
Hughes, Charles & Mrs Hughes 44, 47, 112
Jones, Robert F 4, 47, 77, 112 see Tyson, Richmond and Jones
Jones, William R & Mrs Jones 40, 48
Ladies' School Principal Miss Rollit 43-44
Lockie, Hortense 44
Master mariner Edward Drenning 40, 47
Miller, Charles 47, 112
Roberts, Mary 39, 47
Surveyor of shipping George Creighton 40, 48
Webster, J Stanley 48, 112
Wilson, James & Mrs Wilson 44-45, 47
Winshurst, Clarence & Maria 43, 47
- sewage 95
crime 11, 12, 17, 18, 24, 29, 30, 33-34, 49, 76
Crosby 3, 37-48 & passim
  see Merchant Taylors' School
- house-building 38-40
- streets/roads

Adelaide Terrace 117
Cambridge Road 27
Courtenay Road viii & passim
Mersey Road 27, 132
Norway Street 39
Oxford Road 38, 40, 41, 126, 127, 132
Sandheys Avenue 111
Sandheys Terrace 111-112
Crosfield, AH & Mr W 51, 68
Crosfield's soap company see Liverpool soap works
Cunard 126
Curzon, Lord 111

Dagenham, Essex 38, 67
Dawlish, Devon 102
Dawson, Elizabeth 119
Deacon, George 70, 71, 72
Derby 44
Derby, 15th Earl of 29, 35, 36, 71, 109
Derbyshire 116
diarrhoea 21, 56
docker(s) 3, 33
dock labourer/porter 25, 85, 93
domestic service 2, 23, 49, 65, 107, 119 see servant
draper(s) 45, 115-117, 124, 125, 127
dressmaker(s) 22, 24
Dublin 35, 68, 71
Duckworth, William 39
Dumfries, Scotland 44
Dundee, Scotland 128
dysentery 13

education 19-20, 33, 57, 135
Education Act 1870 20
Edwards, Edward 67
Egan, Tully 30
elections 59, 60, 106, 111, 127
employee/recruitment advertising 32, 33, 41, 43, 45-46

175

employment 3, 15, 18, 23, 49-50, 63, 66, 116, 117, 118, 129   see individual people, Finch 1842 survey
England (country) 18, 20, 28, 38, 44, 52, 68, 92
Epworth, Lincolnshire 80, 81
errand boy 101
Exchange constituency/ward see Liverpool areas/wards
Exchange railway station 86
exports see trade

fever 21
Finch 1842 survey 12-20, 64
fireman see ship's stoker
Firth of Clyde 24
fisherman 24
Flanders, Belgium 96
Forwood, AB 59
France 96

Gainsborough, Lincolnshire 74, 81
Garrett, Rev Charles 54
Garrett, George 55
George, David Lloyd 134
George Fraser, Son & Co. 107, 109-110
Germany 20, 25
Glasgow 20, 71, 128
Goole 66
Gossage, Mrs FD 51
Gossage's soap works see **Blackstock Street**
Gramsci, Antonio vii
Great Crosby 1, 117 see Crosby
Greenock 76
Grisewood, William 49-50

Halifax, Yorkshire 24
Hastings, Sussex 107
hawker 65, 99
Hawkins, Hannah 107

health 5, 9, 12, 17, 19, 21, 49, 56, 59, 95, 96, 100, 127, 128   see employment, housing, Liverpool Health Committee, Local Board of Health, Medical Officer of Health, overcrowding, sanitation, unemployment
Herculaneum pottery 5, 11
Hercules Permanent Benefit Society 42
HMS Hampshire 88
Heyworth, George & Harold 121
Heyworth, Hart & Co. 45, 121
Hooge, Belgium 96
Hope, William 72-73 see Palatine Engineering
Hornsea, Yorkshire 101, 102
housing 12, 19, 22, 54-58, 94, 135 see cellar housing, courts, slum housing
housing rent 4, 17, 40, 42, 43, 44, 58, 63, 90-91, 98, 100, 106, 119
Hoylake 52
Hughes, John 61
Hull, Yorkshire 45, 101, 130
Hydro Hotel see West Kirby

immigrant/immigration 3, 13, 20, 21, 45, 54
- Royal Commission on Alien Immigration 54
imports see trade
income 16, 23, 31, 57, 63, 85, 94, 95, 99, 101, 116
Indian Famine Fund 73
industrial
- acquisition / amalgamation / merger see British Oil and Cake Mills, combination, Lever Bros., E&W Pearson
- competition 68, 75, 76, 109
- injury/accident 76
- relations/disputes 1, 74
- revolution 16

Index

industry 3, 66
inequality 2, 3, 9, 13, 18, 57, 129, 135 see poverty, wealth/prosperity
International Seed Crushing Co. 76 see Liverpool Vesta Cake Company
Ireland 21, 22, 35, 65, 92, 133
- famine 13, 20, 21
Irish people/community 13, 20, 21, 28
Irish Relief Fund 35
Irving, Thomas Robinson 73, 74
Isle of Man 38, 65, 66

Jarrett, Frederick 121
Jones, William H, Arthur Percy & Frederick William 74
Joplin, Henry 61
Joplins Brewery 61
Juvenal Buildings 94
Jutland, Battle of 88

Keeling, Dorothy 57
Kelvin, Lord see William Thomson
Kerr, Annie 65
Kitchener, Lord 88
Knowsley, Lancashire 71

labour/labourer passim
Labour Corps 94, 96
Labour party 3
Lambeth, London 119
Lancashire viii, 4, 29, 30, 35, 36, 49, 63, 80, 91
Lancashire & Yorkshire Railway see railways
Lancashire Ladies Arts Society 42
Largs, Scotland 24, 135
Law Guarantee and Trust Society Ltd. 61
Leeds, Yorkshire 45, 101
Leith, Scotland 128
Leonard, Mary 107

Lever, William Hesketh 68-69, 70
Lever Bros. 67-70, 75
Liberal 3, 42, 59-60, 106, 111, 134
life expectancy 39, 135
Liverpool 58, 76, 92, 123
- Anti-Monopoly Association 12
- areas/wards
  Abercromby 21, 42, 55
  Everton 96, 101
  Exchange 8, 21, 55-56, 59
  Kirkdale 26, 60
  Litherland 120, 125
  Rodney 42
  Scotland 8, 13, 21, 55-56
  Toxteth Park 11, 98
  Vauxhall 1, 3, 8, 12-19, 21, 59-60, 133, 135
  Wavertree 116
  West Derby 96
- birth & death rates 56
- Central Relief 49
- city council/corporation (incl. departments, depots) 2, 3, 4, 7, 12, 20, 22, 42, 53-54, 59-60, 80, 85, 95, 118
- cornermen 8, 34-35
- coroner 29, 34, 76, 77
- Dispensary 19
- docks 1, 2, 11, 27, 66, 86, 89, 93, 109 (including Herculaneum and Prince's)
- dock labourer/porter 25, 85, 93
- dock strike(s) 73, 90
- Domestic Mission Society 5-6, 50
- Food Association 53-54
- Health Committee 27, 54
- Institute 41
- Land and House Owners Association 22
- Lord Mayor 54
- McGinn's lodgings 98
- Medical Officer of Health (MOH) 21, 54-56, 72

Duncan, William 21
Hope, William (EW) 54-56, 72
- Member of Parliament (MP) 3, 59-60
- North Corporation School 19
- North End Domestic Mission 50
- pawnbrokers 63-64
- Permanent Board of Reconciliation 74
- Personal Service Society 57
- police/policing 34-35, 49, 72, 96, 119
- port see docks
- Post Office 44
- prostitution 17, 18, 19, 49, 51, 64-66
- pubs 60-61
- railway development see railways
- Regiment see Regiments of the British Army
- Sanitary Act 1846 21
- school board(s) 20
- school(s) 19, 85
- ships/shipping 4, 9, 52
- Smoke Prevention Sub-Committee 26
- soap works: 3-4
    Crosfield's 4, 31, 68
    DC Keeling 68
    see **Blackstock Street** for Gossages & Tyson, Richmond and Jones
- St George's Hall ix, 53, 54, 73
- streets/roads
    Abbey Street 101
    Arley Street 8, 60
    Athol Street vii, 56, 133
    Bevington Bush Road 6, 7, 8, 51, 64
    Bevington Hill 133
    Bixteth Street 121
    Blackstock Street vii & passim
    Blackstone Street 27
    Bond Street 50, 60, 92

Brook Street 86-87
Burlington Street 6, 60
Byrom Street 115-117
Canning Street 5, 11
Chapel Street 121
Chisenhall Street 8
Clement Street 61
Courtenay Road viii & passim
Dale Street 29, 118
Dryden Street 79
Duke Street 11
Eldon Place 60
Eldon Street 28, 60, 133
Fenwick Street 31, 110
Ford Street 5, 21, 60
Gascoyne Street 80
Great Homer Street 79
Great Howard Street 4, 15, 22, 133
Iliad Street 79
Leeds Street 15
Limekiln Lane/Road 5, 51, 53
Lord Street 45, 126
Maguire Street 60
Naylor Street 8, 60, 99
Oriel Street 21, 60, 80
Paul Street 5, 21, 60, 64, 81, 85
Regent Road 126
Regent Street 45
Rumford Place 121
Sandhills Lane 27
Scotland Road 22, 35, 50, 66, 79, 133
Shaw's Brow 28
Silvester Street 133
Soho Street 98
Summer Seat 8
Tithebarn Street 8, 121
Vauxhall Road vii, 2, 6, 8, 12, 15, 16, 35, 56, 60-61, 66, 74, 76, 80, 81
Virgil Street 79
West Derby Street 92
William Brown Street ix, 28,

Index

- sugar 60, 76 see Liverpool Saccharine Company
- Tailoresses and Coatmakers' Union 89-90
- theatres 11-12
- Unemployed Association 53-54
- Vigilance Committee 65
- Well-Doers 51
- Window Garden Association 35, 79-80
- winter 1894/95 51-54
- Women's Citizen Association 57
- workhouse 85, 96

living conditions 1, 34-35 see housing, slum housing
Local Board of Health
- Waterloo-with-Seaforth 1, 27, 37, 38-39, 105
Local Government Board   109
London   126
Londonderry   72
Lucknow, Siege of   113

Machine Gun Corps   96, 134
Magdalen Home   51, 64-66
Magdalen House   115
Maghull, Lancashire   43
Malta   20, 25
Manbré, Alexander & Alfred   76 see Liverpool Saccharine Company
Manbré and Garton Ltd   76
Manbré Sugar and Malt Ltd.   76
Manchester   11, 37, 76, 107, 109, 110, 123, 124, 125, 128
- Brewers' Central Association 77
- Ship Canal 109
Manhu Food Company   74
Mansfield, Archibald & Ralph   11
Mansion House Relief Fund 35
McArthur, Charles   59-60
McDonald, Ellen   65, 66
Meadows, Christopher   61-62

merchant   4, 16, 32, 40, 59, 77, 117, 118, 123, 125
merchant marine   93, 134
Merchant Taylors' School, Crosby   67, 110
Mersey Oakum Works   8
Mersey Oil and Cake Mills   100
Mersey (river)   8-9, 11, 28-29, 43, 52, 54, 67, 89, 109, 112, 119, 120, 123
Merseyside   38, 123, 129
message boy   91, 94
Methodist (Wesleyan)   26-27, 67, 132
Miller, Rayner & Hansom   126
Millers National Union   73-74
mobility   9, 24
Moneylenders Bill Select Committee   57
moneylending   57, 63
Morris, Richard R   40, 41
mortality   21

National Telephone Company 99, 100
needs (physical/material) see housing, living conditions, poverty, religion, slum housing
New York, USA   126
Nicholson, John & William   7, 32
Norfolk, Duke of   45
Northcliffe & *Daily Mail*   69
Northern Soapmakers Association   68
Norway (country)   42
Nugent, Father James   49, 50-51, 64

office boy   33, 87
Ogglet (now Oglet)   28
old age pension   102
Oldham, Lancashire   37
Ordnance Survey maps   2, 5, 16, 105, 112
Orkney, Scotland   88

out-workers 90
overcrowding 13, 23, 24, 35, 54-55, 98, 101

pawn shop(s)/pawn broker(s)/pawning 17, 18, 19, 57, 61, 63-64, 73
Pearson Brothers, Edward & William 74, 75, 81, 100 see E&W Pearson, British Oil and Cake Mills
Périn, Charles 50
Peter Marsh and Sons 127
piecework(ers) 89-90
politics see Conservative, Liberal, Liverpool city council/corporation
Poor Law Commissioners 21
poor relief 17, 18, 21-22, 35, 49, 50, 51, 54, 81
Poor Servants of the Mother of God 49, 51
population 2, 54, 56, 132, 133
Port Sunlight see Lever Bros.
Post Office 99
Potter, Thomas 94-95, 96
pottery 16 see Herculaneum pottery, Mansfield
Poulton-le-Fylde, Lancashire 124
poverty 2, 51, 57, 63, 129
Presbyterian 132
Preston 29, 44
Price, Elizabeth 107
Priest, Thomas Ellis 42-43
Primrose League 106
prostitution see Liverpool
Protestant 19, 43, 45, 50
public health see health
Public Health Act 1848 37
pubs see **Blackstock Street** & Liverpool
Public Trustee 123

Radcliffe, Reginald 39
Radnor, Earls of 45, 113

railways 106, 109
- development 13, 27, 37
- Lancashire & Yorkshire 27, 37
- London & North-Western 93
- overhead 86
- station(s) 66 see Blundellsands and Crosby, Liverpool (Exchange, Great Howard Street, Sandhills, Waterloo), Waterloo (nr Crosby)
Rawtenstall, Lancashire 114, 115
Rayner, JJ & Co
Rayner, William 45 see Rayner family
Redistribution of Seats Act 1885 8, 59
Reform Act 1884 3, 59
refuse (collection) 95
Regiments of the British Army
- East Kent 134
- East Lancashire 96
- King's Liverpool 120, 133
- Liverpool 94, 96
- Seaforth Highlanders 96, 113
- 72nd Foot 113
- 78th Foot 113
register of electors
- 1889-90 90
- 1894-95 90
- 1899-1900 80, 82, 83-84, 90-91, 94, 97
relief see poor relief
religion 45, 46, 131-133
Richards, Margaret 120
riot(s) 29
Rock Ferry, Cheshire 43
Roman Catholic Church/religion 19, 28, 45, 50-51, 80, 131-133
- Liber Status Animarum (Lenten returns) 80
- papal encyclical *Rerum Novarum* 1891 50
- parish ix, 80

Index

- Pope Leo XII 50
Rothwell, Yorkshire 101
Royal Insurance 121
Royal Naval Volunteer Reserve (RNVR) 134
Runcorn, Cheshire 30
Rusholme, Lancashire (Manchester) 107
Russia 88

sailor 3, 24, 25, 33, 86, 87, 89
Sailortown 64
Sale of Beer Act 1830 60
Salisbury Cathedral 113
Salford, Lancashire 76
Samuelson, James 19, 51, 79
Sandhills railway station 37
sanitation 22, 35, 37, 54-55, 95
Scotland (country) 20, 52, 65, 92, 102
Scotland (road, ward) see Liverpool areas/wards, roads/streets
seaman see sailor
Sefton, 2nd Earl of 11
servant 23, 24, 25, 33, 39, 43, 45, 49, 86, 91, 92, 96, 107, 114, 115, 116, 117, 119, 120, 124, 125, 131
Seward, Richard 43
sewerage/sewer(s) 21, 38, 95, 105
Sheffield 65-66, 70
Shimmin, Hugh 2, 12
ship-owner(s) 4, 45, 110, 117, 118
shipping agent 4, 109-110
shipping clerk(s) 40, 118
shoe-maker(s) 15, 20, 24, 25
Shrewsbury, Earl of 32
Shropshire (county) 116
Sills, Mary 65
Simcock, William 38
slum housing 3, 22, 79 see housing
Smyth, John Tapp 32, 39

Smyth, WS 121
socialism 50, 107
Somerset (county) 65
soup (kitchen) 21, 53-54
South Africa 133
Southampton, Hampshire 70, 114, 126
Southport, Lancashire 37, 106, 111, 126
- Member of Parliament (MP) 106, 111
spiritual needs see religion
St Helens 26
St Saviour's see Magdalen Home
St Vincent de Paul Society 50
stability 87, 94, 134-135
Stevenson, Elizabeth 120
stoker (ship's) 3, 86, 88, 91, 93-94, 99
stoker (stationary) 98
strawboard lining 101
Suffolk (county) 116

Taggart, JG 60
tailor(s)/tailoress(es) 15, 17, 20, 22, 24, 25, 65, 89-90, 124, 126, 130
Taporley, Cheshire 123
Tate, Henry 54
Taylor, Mother Magdalen 51
teacher 118
telephone linesman/service 99-100
Thomson, William (Lord Kelvin) 71, 73, 77
Torrens Act 1968 55
Townshend, John 115-117
trade 2, 3, 4, 16, 45, 66, 109-110
trade unions 51, 90 see Liverpool Tailoresses and Coatmakers' Union, Mersey Quay and Railway Carters & Millers National Union

Tressell, Robert (aka Noonan) 106-107, 109
tripe dresser 99
typhoid 35, 56

unemployment 1, 29, 49-50, 53-54, 129 see Finch 1842 survey
Unilever see Lever Bros.
United States of America (USA) 54
Urban District Council (UDC)
- Waterloo 1, 95, 110-111, 127

Vauxhall see Liverpool areas/wards, roads/streets
Voluntary Service Company (in Boer War) 133

Wales (country) 18
Wales, Susan 66
Waterloo see Local Board of Health, UDC
- and Crosby 1, 106, 118
- hare-coursing 61-62
- railway station (Crosby) 1, 97
- railway station (Liverpool) 4, 66
- train crash 1903 97
water supply 20, 70-73
Watson, Joseph 68, 69
wealth/prosperity 2, 3, 9, 13, 21, 28, 50, 57, 68, 119
West Kirby, Cheshire 120, 121-122, 123
Wigan, Lancashire 93
Wilson, Frances 106-107
Windermere, Cumbria 112
women 6, 15, 18, 23, 54, 55, 61, 82, 106, 116, 124-125, 129, 130-131 see individual people, domestic service
- charwomen 85, 86, 87, 88, 92
- clothing industry 89-90, 117
- heads of household 15, 39-40, 82
- householders 4, 106

- jobs/occupations 13, 14, 15, 54-55, 70
- moneylenders 57
- politics 106
- support networks 6, 64
- survival strategies 57
Women's Liberal Association 106
wool 4, 114, 115, 124
World War I 38, 62, 67, 86, 93, 94, 96, 119, 120, 126, 129, 134

yacht club(s) 32
Ypres, Belgium 96